D0508346

Women in Pacific Northwest History
An Anthology

Women in Pacific Northwest History

An Anthology

Edited by
KAREN J. BLAIR

University of Washington Press
Seattle and London

Copyright © 1988 by the University of Washington Press
Second printing, 1990
Printed in the United States of America

All rights reserved. No part of this publication may be reproduced or transmitted in any form or by any means, electronic or mechanical, including photocopy, recording, or any information storage or retrieval system, without permission in writing from the publisher.

Library of Congress Cataloging-in-Publication Data

Women in Pacific Northwest History : an anthology / edited by Karen J.
    Blair.
        p.   cm.
    Bibliography: p.
    Includes index.
    ISBN 0-295-96705-6.   ISBN 0-295-96689-0 (pbk.)
    1. Women—Northwest, Pacific—History—19th century.   2. Women—
Northwest, Pacific—History—20th century.   I. Blair, Karen J.
HQ1438.A19W65   1988
305.4'09795—dc 19   87-22867 CIP

The paper used in this publication meets the minimum requirements of the American National Standard for Information Sciences—Permanence of Paper for Printed Library Materials, ANSI Z39.48-1984. ⊚

To my grandmothers,
Margaret Stilson LeVanda and Hedwig Harevich Bunoski

CONCORDIA UNIVERSITY LIBRARY
PORTLAND, OR 97211

Contents

Illustrations

Preface

When we visualize the history of the Pacific Northwest, we can quickly reconstruct the roles that men played. Early explorers, trappers, missionaries, traders, the Indian chiefs, loggers, sailors, pioneer farmers, miners, businessmen, and aeronautical engineers—all these leap easily to mind. Women are conspicuously absent from the colorful pictures that rise before us. Yet how considerably this omission distorts the truth. The bias that has dismissed women's varied and critical contributions to Washington and Oregon history begs for correction.

In this volume, we begin to set the record straight. Twelve articles by as many scholars—historians, anthropologists, a sociologist, and one professor of journalism and communications—bring to light the active roles women have played in the history of the Pacific Northwest from 1850 to the present. To argue their case the researchers have used a wide and ingenious array of tools—biography, oral history, newspaper files, minutes of meetings, diaries, letters, poetry, speeches, census records, photographs and paintings, court records, police reports, demographic studies, and quantification.

The collection that results is the first attempt to document and interpret a broad range of experiences of women in Northwest history. The essays portray women of many ages, races, ethnicities, classes, educational backgrounds, talents, and achievements. They were rural and urban, pioneers and contemporaries, who led public as well as private lives. In total, their stories accomplish the task of challenging the mistaken notion that only men have participated in important ways in the development of the Pacific Northwest.

Although individuals and groups of women described here experienced serious inequities, they managed to enrich the region through their thought and work. In fact, they left their mark everywhere—in the parks, libraries, and hospitals they founded, in the public drinking fountains and street lights for which they lobbied, in the schools and clubs at which they labored, and in the homes, gardens, and businesses they managed. If the fruits of their efforts were to be erased from our landscape, the results would be bleak indeed, leaving this region far less hospitable for habitation.

I have divided the articles in this volume into five general sections: woman suffrage, work, race and ethnicity, arts, and new directions for research. In the brief introduction to each section, my purpose is to alert readers to some of the broad questions that the articles raise, from the special perspective of women's history.

The completion of this collection, as well as my own development as a historian of Pacific Northwest women's history, owes much to the members of Seattle's Women's History Discussion Group. I wish to thank Audra Adelberger, Jean Coberly, Margaret Hall, Nan Hughes, Kathy Friedman Kasaba, Doris Pieroth, Laura Shapiro, Paula Shields, Nancy Slote, Susan Strasser, Antoinette Wills, and, most especially, Susan Starbuck, for their scholarly companionship, rigorous criticism, unfailing inquisitiveness, seriousness of purpose, and unflagging good humor. I would also like to express my appreciation to Judy Hodgson, who, as Director of the University of Washington Women's Information Center, sponsored the conference that inspired the anthology; to Bev Wessel and Cynthia Blair for their typing; to Sue Davidson, Julidta Tarver, Carol Zabilski, Kathie George, and Leila Charbonneau for their assistance in editing the collection; to Mark Benson for his help with proofreading.

KAREN J. BLAIR

Women in Pacific Northwest History
An Anthology

Part 1

WOMAN SUFFRAGE

The age-old maxim that "woman's place is in the home" came under increasing attack by suffragists in the mid-nineteenth century. Arguing that women were fully capable of making intelligent election-day decisions, the suffragists agitated from 1848 to 1920 to win female representation in the most nondomestic or public of locations, at the polling place. The Northwest produced a good share of strong-minded American reformers who worked to overcome popular resistance to woman's full rights to citizenship. Abigail Scott Duniway and May Arkwright Hutton were among those who devoted themselves to correcting the injustices and inequities that impeded women.

Rabble-rouser Abigail Scott Duniway (1834–1915), as Ruth Barnes Moynihan informs us in her article, lived a life typical of mid-nineteenth-century rural women before her family made the two-thousand-mile overland journey from Illinois to Oregon. Eventually Duniway was able to draw on her early experiences when she became a spokesperson for the need to redress the inequities and hardships in all women's lives. She had assisted her mother at a multitude of tedious household routines—cleaning, sewing, weaving, churning butter, tending chickens, rearing children, preparing fruit for winter drying, chopping wood, and planting. She was, however, prepared to assume similar responsibilities when she married a farmer at the age of eighteen and bore him six children. She stored her recollections of women's hardships not only on the farm but on her 1852 migration on the Oregon Trail, an experience that brought danger, sickness and death, shortages of necessities, and remoteness from friends and culture rather than the glory, adventure, and fortune celebrated in popular legend. She collected further experiences as a teacher and a writer. With the foreclosure of the family farm and a wagon accident that disabled her husband, the role of family breadwinner fell totally to Duniway. She gained further insights into the difficulties women faced in making a living, as she tried her hand at supporting her loved ones as a millinery shopkeeper and a journalist.

Keenly aware of the special hardships and injustices she suffered as a woman, Duniway generalized her difficulties to those faced by all women. Thus inspired, she applied her considerable talents to seeking full citizenship rights for women. She toured the region widely, lecturing, debating, reporting, and involving herself in the suffrage campaigns of several states. She wrote seventeen novels on women's issues, and edited and published a weekly women's rights newspaper, the *New Northwest*. Having apprenticed herself to Susan B. Anthony, on the latter's 1871 tour of the Pacific states, Duniway made herself a presence throughout the West by rallying women to organize as clubwomen and suffragists. True to her own principles, she not only defied conventions of society by devoting herself to the suffrage cause but she ensured the ire of her sister suffragists by refusing to endorse prohibition. The movement to outlaw the production and sale of alcoholic beverages raised no less controversy in the late nineteenth century than does the contemporary effort to balance the dangers of narcotics against the preservation of the individual's freedom of choice. Duniway remained adamant in her support of wide freedoms, and practical in her refusal to alienate the antiprohibition forces from the campaign for woman's rights. Probably no figure better exemplifies the most venerated qualities of western womanhood—hard-working, strong, and unshakably determined in the face of adversity.

Like Duniway, Washington State activist May Arkwright Hutton was a suffragist who attracted notoriety. Duniway and Hutton shared flamboyance, tirelessness, intelligence uninhibited by formal education, a wide interest in public issues of all kinds, and a controversial place among the general populace as well as women's rights advocates. Born in Ohio in 1860—twenty-six years later than her Oregon counterpart—Hutton was handed responsibilities early. Motherless at a young age, she took on the care of her aging grandfather. Like Duniway, she married at eighteen, and did not find wedlock a protective haven. In fact, she married twice more, moving west to Idaho with the third spouse, working hard to make ends meet by running a boardinghouse, and cooking in a mining town.

A miners' strike in which her husband was involved pushed Hutton into public life. Her book, *The Coeur d'Alenes, or a Tale of the Modern Inquisition in Idaho,* (Denver: By the author, 1900), a story sympathetic to the workers, was a best-seller among mine workers. Later, a silver mine claim made her hugely wealthy, but money never eradicated her sympathy for working people, unions, and women without privilege. In fact, these loyalties distanced her from acceptance by people of means in Spokane, her home after 1906. Her working-class loyalties probably also contributed to the ugly split between her and the middle-class, proper suffragists of western Washington—most notably, state suffrage president Emma Smith DeVoe of Tacoma.

Hutton's bold personality, the bright red automobile in

which she campaigned for suffrage, her massive size, and her open, humorous, and unladylike style were threatening to the somberly conventional suffragists on the Washington coast. Her attempts to pack the 1909 state suffrage convention with her eastern Washington supporters resulted in a nasty breach, an exclusion of Hutton's friends from the state meeting, and a banishment of both the Hutton and DeVoe camps from the national meeting.

Despite these divisions, Washington women succeeded in securing the vote in 1910. Hutton was still young and vigorous in 1910, and she began to climb in Democratic politics. Illness and premature death, however, prevented her from making contributions to political life beyond the suffrage fight. DeVoe, her Tacoma rival, rose in the Republican party and was rumored to be in the running for senatorial candidacy in the 1920s. But DeVoe's career was also halted by death, from cancer. Thus the political skills of these two leaders served to advance the position of women, but were not tested very far beyond the suffrage struggle. It was another suffragist—also a westerner—Jeannette Rankin, who became the first woman to attain national elective office, to the House of Representatives, in 1917.

Hutton, Duniway, and other women's rights activists throughout Washington and Oregon tapped a wide range of techniques to persuade the public of the need for woman suffrage. How to win access to the public ear was a crucial question to the advocates of reform. Some subscribed to the "still hunt" or quiet, ladylike approach, such as formation of women's discussion groups to support change. Others endorsed more boisterous "hurrah campaigns" with fanfare, parades, and "Votes for Women" banners flying atop the mountains of the region. Regardless of style, however, coverage by major newspapers was unarguably an expeditious way to call attention to the cause. Lauren Kessler's piece, "The Fight for Woman Suffrage and the Oregon Press," demonstrates the difficulties the suffrage movement faced in its attempts to get fair—or any—press coverage. Kessler examines thirteen major Oregon newspapers in twelve cities, in the months just prior to the 1884, 1900, 1906, 1908, 1910, and 1912 statewide voting on woman suffrage. She finds an unfailing dearth of news stories, feature stories, editorials, and letters to the editor in most of them. A few noteworthy exceptions emerged in 1906. At that time, the National American Woman Suffrage Association bigwigs brought much ballyhoo to the campaign, and won Northwest as well as national headlines. Simultaneously, the established *Oregonian* found itself competing with the upstart *Oregon Journal,* and felt obliged to cover local issues more fully than it had previously done. Again, in 1912, the year Oregon voters finally endorsed woman suffrage, the drama of whether the elderly fighter Abigail Scott Duniway would live to vote captured some headlines. On balance, coverage was remarkably poor.

Ultimately, Kessler blames the sexism of members of the press—particularly the powerful *Oregonian* editor Harvey Scott (brother of Abigail Scott Duniway)—for the failure to give exposure to women's arguments for the vote. If informal networks of debate—for instance around the stove of the Oregon general stores—had arisen, these might have satisfied the deficiency of coverage among the male votership. Kessler found that no such systems did emerge. Consequently, press neglect was especially serious and hurtful to the women's cause.

Virtually ignored by the press, turn-of-the-century women developed an array of alternate techniques to ensure that the suffrage question remained before Northwest citizens.

Conferences, rallies, speeches, debates, club meetings, guest sermons, their own publications, broadsides on fences, buttons, and banners flying from mountaintops—these were among the tactics the suffragists used. Their resourcefulness, the courage and resilience of their leaders, as seen in Duniway and Hutton, may well be admired by feminists of today.

Of Women's Rights and Freedom: Abigail Scott Duniway

Ruth Barnes Moynihan

"When women go for their own rights they generally get them," said Abigail Scott Duniway of Oregon in January 1871. She was announcing the establishment of her weekly *New Northwest* "upon the rock of Eternal Liberty, Universal Emancipation and Untrammeled Progression."[1] Such was the enthusiasm, determination, and optimism with which thirty-six-year-old Mrs. Duniway joined thousands of other post–Civil War Americans in the demand for woman suffrage. The nation had finally achieved universal suffrage for men— both white and black. Those voters included newly freed slaves, recent immigrants, illiterates, and criminals, as well as gentlemen of property and educated scholars. Could women be far behind?

Almost forty-two years later, in 1912 when she was seventy-eight, Abigail Scott Duniway finally became the first woman voter in Oregon. In Idaho and Washington, where she had also campaigned, women had become voters in 1896 and 1910 respectively, but most American women could not vote until the ratification of the Nineteenth Amendment in 1920.[2]

Abigail Scott Duniway spent almost half a lifetime writing, lecturing, traveling, and debating—throughout the Pacific Northwest and often elsewhere. She was an indomitable publicist for women's rights on the frontier and the foremost representative of western women in the national movement. For sixteen years she published her widely read weekly *New Northwest*, founded state and local suffrage societies in Oregon, Washington, and Idaho, and lobbied almost every session of the legislatures of those states. She held a vice-presidency in the National Woman Suffrage Association, founded and presided over the Oregon Federation of Women's Clubs, and was even nominated for governor of Washington Territory in 1884. By personal example and determined leadership, she inspired thousands of women to seek the autonomy she claimed for herself.

Despite enthusiastic support and widespread admiration among many men and women, Abigail Duniway also experienced personal loss, hatred, and slander. She lived in a time when American society

Some portions of this chapter have previously appeared in another version as part of "Abigail Scott Duniway: Pioneer Suffragist of the Pacific Northwest," Linfield College *Casements* 4, no. 1 (Spring 1984).

Abigail Scott Duniway, editor of *New Northwest*, 1871
(courtesy David C. Duniway)

was changing profoundly, and so was the woman's movement. The hegemony of pioneer free-thinking egalitarianism among first-generation suffragists, like herself and Elizabeth Cady Stanton and others, had virtually ended when Abigail Duniway died in 1915. As she wrote her autobiography at the age of eighty, Duniway reveled in the pathbreaking heritage of her log-cabin pioneer progenitors, and in her pathbreaking career on behalf of women, but she also attacked what she saw as dangerous fanaticism and religiosity among some new-generation suffragists who opposed her leadership. Her significance obscured by that controversy and acrimony, she has had to be rediscovered as a courageous pioneer feminist and as a worthy representative of frontier womanhood.

Born in 1834 in a log cabin in Tazewell County, Illinois, not far from Fort Peoria, on the northern edge of the sparsely settled frontier, young Jenny Scott (as she was called by her family), was the third child and second daughter among the twelve children born to her Kentucky-born parents. Five living sisters provided a supportive peer group of equally strong-minded future suffragists, while three younger brothers (the firstborn had died as a baby) completed the household.

Two of those brothers died young, but Harvey Scott, just three years younger than Abigail, became her lifelong rival in brilliance and influence. Harvey spent more than forty years as powerful editor of the *Oregonian*—and powerful opponent of woman suffrage. Although he appeared to condone and encourage his sister's editorship of the *New Northwest,* he may also have encouraged the demise of the paper when its political influence began to seem too dangerous. Certainly his paper's editorials against women voters were major causes of suffrage defeats in Oregon in 1884, 1900, 1906, 1908, and 1910. Only after Harvey Scott's death did Abigail Scott Duniway finally share the forbidden fruit of political equality in Oregon.[3]

Life was not easy for little girls, or their mothers, on frontier farms in the early nineteenth century. No one worried about requiring young Jenny Scott to work with her brother on such "unfeminine" chores as planting ten-acre cornfields or hoeing potatoes or chopping wood, in addition to the "abominable," "feminine" tasks of picking wool to prepare it for yarn-making, peeling bushels of apples to dry for winter eating, or caring for all the younger children while her mother spent hours at the weaving loom. The physical labor of milking cows and churning butter and tending chickens was also assigned to farmers' wives and daughters, while almost all frontier women deplored the debilitating job of carrying water and washing heavy dirty clothes by hand. Relieving women of such work—by means of hired labor or new technology—later became one of Abigail Scott Duniway's primary concerns.

Although she learned to read by the age of three or four, Abigail Jane Scott had only a few months of formal education. She suffered from frequent illnesses, developed an intense dislike for domestic drudgery, and delighted in all available books and newspapers. These included Horace Greeley's *New York Tribune,* filled with information about the reform issues of the era, and Amelia Bloomer's *Lily,* a temperance paper that printed frequent essays by one of the nineteenth century's most eloquent women activists, Elizabeth Cady Stanton. Charles Dicken's polemical novels became Duniway's model of literary excellence, and righting the world's wrongs her life's major goal. Her younger sister later called Abigail Scott Duniway "the burden-bearer of our childhood."[4]

In 1852, when Abigail Jane was seventeen, the Scott family took the overland trail to Oregon. Following the large Neill Johnson family, relatives who had left the previous year, the Scotts joined thousands of other ox-drawn covered wagons on the six-month, two-thousand-mile search for the so-called Eden of the West, where the climate was bountiful and the land was free. Jenny Scott had orders from her father to keep the family's daily journal of the trip. That duty became the foundation of her future journalistic career.

Unfortunately, cholera and other unforeseen troubles stalked everyone on the trail that year. Not far from Fort Laramie, Wyoming, three months after leaving home, Mrs. Scott—who had been an "invalid" ever since the stillbirth of her twelfth child in September—came down with cholera one night and was dead a few hours later. Jenny Scott never forgot that her overworked mother had always feared and suffered through her many pregnancies and had only reluctantly obeyed her husband's traveling orders. For the rest of her life Abigail Duniway argued against involuntary motherhood and religious prescriptions for wifely obedience.

There were more deaths in the Scott party before they arrived in Oregon, including three-year-old brother Willie, a recently married cousin, a "worthy young man" who was Jenny's "sweetheart," and several others. The rest of the Scotts barely survived. With their property destroyed, their hearts broken, and their father quickly remarried, the Scott children found that self-sufficiency had become a necessity. Toughness and resilience learned from such overland trail experiences shaped the lives of most mid-nineteenth-century western pioneers before the amenities of railroad and commercial development. Abigail Duniway was one of the most vocal of those "unrefined" pathbreakers. She believed that one should "Trust in God and keep your powder dry" and that "self-preservation" was the "primary law" of existence—as applicable to women as to men. "Ladies" were likely to be parasites on society; it was working women who constituted true womanhood, and who deserved legal rights with which to protect themselves.

Abigail Jane Scott left her family to become a schoolteacher soon after they arrived in Oregon. A few months later, while she was still eighteen, she became Mrs. Benjamin Duniway, a frontier farmer's wife. Within a few years she had survived a destructive tornado, a disastrous fire, and near-fatal hemorrhaging during her second child's birth. Then, at twenty-five, she published a novel, *Captain Gray's Company, or Crossing the Plains and Living in Oregon.*[5] It was full of arguments about the necessity of improvements in women's health and personal autonomy, though Duniway did not yet advocate political equality. Critics objected to its "fool love stories," and even claimed her husband must be henpecked. She was devastated, but not for long.

Abigail Scott Duniway became a regular contributor to the radical new Republican *Oregon City Argus* and the *Oregon Farmer,* along with her farm work and child rearing duties. Then another tragedy struck. Her husband, having mortgaged their farm without her permission in order to help out a friend, suddenly faced foreclosure because of financial depression and disastrous floods in 1861. No laws protected a wife's right to the value of her contribution in the property, an inequity which became one of Duniway's major public concerns. Then in 1862, Ben Duniway was run over by a heavily loaded teamster's wagon. His injury left him with lifelong pain, too disabled to return to farming.

The Duniways lost their farm and Abigail Scott Duniway had to become the family breadwinner, first as a schoolteacher, then as a millinery shopkeeper—virtually the only kinds of work a respectable nineteenth-century woman could undertake. She also had two more children (six altogether). The last childbirth, when she was thirty-five, left her forever "crippled," she later said, with chronic pain and bladder problems and justifiable fear of further involuntary motherhood. Such a condition was not unusual, but many other women of Duniway's era became semi-invalids because of it. Abigail Duniway, however, certainly did not.

For one thing, Abigail Scott Duniway's business activities had ended her domestic isolation. She met other women and learned about their troubles. Her shopping expeditions to San Francisco introduced her to other suffragists and activists, while the money she made gave her self-confidence. She had long dreamed of editing a newspaper. Now she saw its necessity for publicizing injustices and arguing the cause of women's rights. Abigail Scott Duniway moved her family to Portland in May 1871, bought type and a printing press, set up an office in the upstairs bedroom, and began publishing her *New Northwest*.

Even if she had done little else, Duniway's weekly newspaper would have been a major accomplishment. Packed with information about national or international events and attitudes related to women in her era, the paper also printed sixteen of Mrs. Duniway's own serial novels and the detailed descriptions of her extensive travels. From the columns of *New Northwest* one may derive an extraordinarily rich picture of frontier women and of the passions involved for and against the voting rights we now take for granted. We can also learn a great deal about Mrs. Duniway herself.

Abigail Scott Duniway combined zeal for the feminist cause with keen powers of observation and prodigious physical energy. Despite the terrible transportation facilities of her time, especially in the sparsely settled Pacific Northwest, she made frequent lecture tours throughout the Willamette Valley, among the Northwest's coastal villages, and to central and eastern Oregon, Washington, and Idaho. In regular newspaper columns, she reported details about her trips and the people she met, building up a wide-ranging network of concern about women's rights among both men and women. She also represented western women at several national suffrage conventions, traveling in 1872 by train from San Francisco, in 1876 and 1880 by stagecoach from Walla Walla eastward, and in both 1884 and 1885 by Pullman car on the newly completed railroad from Portland. Although her editor brother, Harvey Scott of the *Oregonian,* often provided her with free passes, she managed most of the costs by giving lectures wherever she could along the way, averaging more than two hundred every year. She also canvassed for *New Northwest* subscribers and organized suffrage associations wherever possible. Hers was a full-time commitment—and a grueling schedule.

Abigail Duniway argued that giving women social, financial, and political autonomy would benefit intellectual and economic development in the region as well as among individuals. She was an unabashed "booster" of the whole Pacific Northwest, promoting new settlements and new business possibilities just as enthusiastically as she promoted improved conditions for women. In fact, she was the one who constantly assured her listeners, and perhaps created the myth, that western women already had more freedom than eastern women because enlightened western men would *surely* grant woman suffrage very soon.

The rhetoric of Abigail Scott Duniway's suffrage campaign derived from the same Jeffersonian tradition as that of Elizabeth Cady Stanton and other first-generation suffragists. Her pioneer farmer heritage gave her an admiration for entrepreneurial pragmatism, and a firm disdain for aristocracy and inequality. Like Stanton, she proclaimed the injustice of an "aristocracy of sex" or the denial of equal political and economic opportunity to the wives, mothers, and sisters of enfranchised men. The "radicalism" of her feminist goals did not preclude a defense of property rights, small-scale land speculation, and railroad building, along with support for Knights of Labor union organization and various joint-stock cooperatives. Duniway's politics were evolutionary rather than revolutionary. Her attitudes were shared by many who were to become the Populists of the 1890s.

Mrs. Duniway was, in fact, a member in the 1890s of a small populist study group made up of prominent Oregonians. The group developed and promoted the so-called Oregon system of reforms—legislation by initiative and referendum, provisions for public petitions, and the secret ballot. She also became a founder of the Oregon woman's club movement, hoping that it would be a means of educating women in parliamentary procedures and the necessity of women's rights.

Abigail Duniway made her first connection to the National Woman Suffrage Association as manager of an extensive two-month lecture tour by the famous and controversial Susan B. Anthony. In the fall of 1871 Duniway invited Anthony to the Pacific Northwest, much to the horror of some post–Civil War conservatives, especially those of southern background like Seattle's editor Beriah Brown. After Anthony's Seattle speech, Brown denounced both women as dangerous revolutionaries, "aiming at nothing less than the breaking up of the very foundations of society, and the overthrow of every social institution." Their "licentious social theories," he said, would destroy home, marriage, and nation, for the female character was much too delicate to be exposed to politics and public issues. A contemporary Phyllis Schafly by the name of Mrs. J. Blakesley Frost followed Anthony and Duniway throughout their tour, giving antisuffrage lectures. (The *New Northwest* reported that Frost's audiences were much smaller.)[6]

There are many stories from the columns of the *New Northwest* that illustrate the vicissitudes of Abigail Duniway's career. One of her favorites was about "old footsie toaster." She was traveling by stagecoach to Yakima in eastern Washington when an inebriated fellow traveler remarked belligerently: "Madam! you ought to be at home, enjoying yourself, like my wife is doing. I want to bear all the hardship of life myself, and let her sit by the fire, toasting her footsies." When the stage finally reached his house, however, they saw "his protected wife, busy with an ax, chopping away at a pile of snow-covered cord wood." Abigail Duniway had the last laugh. "I see, my friend, that your wife is toasting her footsies!" she said. The man's new nickname stuck with him for life.[7]

On another occasion, "Mother" Duniway went to newly settled eastern Oregon and northern Idaho in late November, traveling for hours in an open carriage in bitter cold and rain. In the tiny hamlet of Moscow, Idaho, now the thriving location of the University of Idaho, she encountered the reality of frontier housewifery which she and her mother and relatives had once experienced. It was a scene like many in Duniway's novels:

> We had had a tedious way. The roads were bad in places, worse in some, and worst in others, and we were not sorry when a blacksmith shop, a post office, and two or three single-roomed box-houses greeted our longing eyes. . . . The woman of the house where we halted was in bed with a new baby, a bouncing boy of a dozen pounds. There were other children running about, and a young girl was busy at the house-work. The one room was at once parlor, bed-room, kitchen, store-room, dining-room, and pantry. The invalid mother felt the privations of her pioneer life most keenly, and expressed her opinion freely. God bless her.[8]

One can imagine what that woman's comments must have been with a distinguished guest from Portland under such circumstances. Mrs. Duniway's account continued with one of her many eloquent polemics about the virtues and unjust hardships of frontier women and their right to voluntary motherhood and equal opportunity.

During this same trip, Duniway also lectured in Palouse, Washington, where her bed was located in a roofless unfinished hotel "upstairs among the stars." She spoke to a large crowd in the hotel's dining room:

> and the speech was fairly begun when *crack* went the floor, and *smash* went the benches, and *down* went the people into the cellar below, leaving the undersigned well-braced against a tottering partition to prevent it knocking her on the head. Luckily nobody was hurt, but the confusion was indescribable. The fallen and frightened crowd after a while emerged from the cellar through the *debris,* somebody lifted the partition from the burdened shoulders of the speaker, and we all repaired to another room, where the lecture was resumed amid a general feeling of thankfulness that nobody had been injured. By morning the break was repaired and everybody was happy.[9]

Other Duniway adventures did not always conclude so pleasantly. Opponents sometimes accused her of practicing free love and holding "bacchanalian revelries" in her rooms as she traveled. Rumors circulated that her husband and children were neglected. (They were actually hard at work printing, managing, and selling her newspaper.) Political "dirty tricks" plagued her publishing company and her travel itinerary. In Jacksonville, in the southern part of Oregon in 1879, she even achieved a minor martyrdom. "The 'militia's' been out and egged us!" she reported. "And they've burnt us in effigy, the image being a fair likeness of George Washington, so we're told, though we didn't see it. . . . Only one egg hit us, and that was fresh and sweet, and it took us square on the scalp and saved a shampooing bill."[10]

Nevertheless, Abigail Scott Duniway had an enthusiastic constituency of farmers' wives and other pioneers. Among her supporters were many men as well as women, like such city founders as the Sylvesters of Olympia and the Yeslers of Seattle. Leading Portland businessmen and politicians—Mayer, Reed, Ainsworth, Denny, Hirsch, Mitchell, and others—all Republicans, helped her cause with interest-free loans. She was regularly invited to speak at legislative assemblies where suffrage bills received significant support. Despite the harsh opposition she encountered, there seemed to be good reasons for Duniway's confidence that her cause would soon succeed.

In 1872, for example, Oregon's legislature voted twenty-one for suffrage and twenty-two opposed, almost making it the first state in the union to have women voters. (Wyoming and Utah, which had approved woman suffrage in 1869 and 1870, were still territories at that time.) Washington Territory legislators, who had first acted on a suffrage bill as early as 1854, defeated suffrage by only eighteen to twelve in 1873 and fifteen to eleven in 1875. Washington's Constitutional Convention of 1878 came within one vote of approval. Duniway claimed a great victory when the Territory's women did become voters in 1883. No one yet knew (as we shall see below) that their victory was only temporary, that they would be cheated out of the privilege for another generation.

A younger generation of women, many of them inspired by the Washington Territory victory, became newly active suffragists around this time. National Woman's Christian Temperance Union leader Frances Willard lectured in Portland that winter, sharing a platform with Abigail Scott Duniway. To the latter's delight, Willard urged WCTU members to change their antisuffrage stance. The woman's vote, she said, was essential in order to achieve the Union's goal of liquor prohibition throughout the country.[11]

Both Washington and Oregon already had long-active state woman suffrage associations, both founded in 1871, and usually opposed by more conservative WCTU women. Mrs. Duniway considered herself leader of both Oregon's and Washington's fight for suffrage legislation, hoping and expecting any new suffragists to follow her lead in regard to tactics and arguments. She did not approve of making prohibition "the tail to the suffrage kite," but she hoped to persuade new suffragists of the wisdom of her view.

The campaigns of 1883 and 1884 in Washington and Oregon respectively, proved her hopes mistaken. Prohibitionists, both men and women, now convinced of the value of political power for their cause, rallied behind the issue of woman suffrage and then insisted that Abigail Scott Duniway was a *hindrance.* That fall, as the Washington legislature prepared to consider an act removing the word *male* from the Territory's suffrage law, Mrs. Duniway arrived in Olympia as usual to lobby for women. But several Washington women were in a "panic," she was told. Certain prosuffrage legislators, who were also Democrats and prohibitionists (Duniway was always a Republican), warned them to keep Mrs. Duniway away. "It makes the members mad to see you on the streets! . . . Your very presence will kill the bill!" they claimed.[12]

Reluctantly, she returned to Portland. Other longtime Washington suffragists begged her to return. A week before the November fifteenth vote she did. After detailing the whole legislative battle to *New Northwest* readers, foretelling the exact vote and designating beforehand which two Council members were secretly "pledged to whiskey," Duniway presided joyfully at the ratification banquet to celebrate the victory. Washington women were *voters.* Oregon was sure to follow.[13]

Oregon's state constitutional amendment on woman suffrage was to come before the voters in June 1884. The Republican-controlled legislature had approved it twice as required, in 1880 and 1882. Promises of support were widespread, even from Editor Harvey Scott. Abigail Scott Duniway was even nominated for governor of Washington Territory, which she immediately declined.[14] And she was named one of five vice-presidents of the National Woman Suffrage Association. When Mrs. Duniway crossed the country to attend the April 1884 convention, she was jubilant with expectation.

Unfortunately, she was wrong. While she was gone, the prohibitionist women of Washington launched an ambitious local option campaign. In places like Seattle, newly elected Democrats toppled the ruling Republicans. In Oregon the WCTU suddenly organized its own suffrage campaign, with prohibitionist Mary Clement Leavitt hired from the East to lecture throughout the state, and white-ribboned women urging woman suffrage as a means of fighting whiskey. Thousands of new male voters, unemployed since the completion of the transcontinental railroad the previous fall, thronged into Portland. Harvey Scott's *Oregonian,* while he as "out of town," launched a three-month antisuffrage editorial campaign. Faulty ballots were printed, and ward bosses recruited unemployed voters at $2.50 a vote. Abigail Scott Duniway returned from the East to unforeseen disaster.[15]

Mrs. Duniway immediately blamed the WCTU women. She also blamed her brother's *Oregonian,* and other betrayers, but she felt that they had been influenced by the apparent strength of prohibitionists who should have followed her advice to keep quiet. Duniway's WCTU opponents obviously did not agree, and were furious at her criticism. They were ideologists; Abigail Duniway was always a pragmatist.

The situation deteriorated as Duniway campaigned vigorously against the local option movement in Washington, finally rejoicing in its defeat in 1886. She knew that hop growing and breweries were major industries in both the Willamette and Puyallup valleys of the Pacific Northwest in the mid-1880s. Profits were huge, and some farms were hiring more than twelve hundred workers in their hop fields each year.[16] Duniway was convinced that Washington women might lose their voting rights if they were not careful how they used those rights.

WCTU women were rightly afraid of the political power of whiskey, as well as of its often devastating effects in individual households. But Abigail Duniway was also rightly afraid of the political power that could prevent woman suffrage everywhere. There was "but one cure for intemperance," she said, "and that was not the ballot *per se,* but the independence, liberty, and financial and political standing that the ballot represents.[17] The *New Northwest* reported that women laborers were being employed at the new Oregon City textile mills at half the pay of men. It documented the way current laws of marriage and divorce prevented women's financial freedom. And it deplored the lack of education or opportunity that restricted women's personal autonomy. Drunkenness, said Duniway, was a disease that required personal moral reform and medical cures, not legal measures that would stir up opposition to all other necessary reforms. If women had political and economic rights, they would not marry drunken husbands or tolerate abusive behavior, she explained. For Abigail Duniway the right to vote was the key to all other issues.

In January 1886, Abigail Scott Duniway's daughter died of consumption. She herself was exhausted and depressed. Friends suggested she step aside for a while to "let the prohibition fever quiet down." Her husband and sons urged her to give up her newspaper and buy a ranch in Idaho. The "boys" were eager to move on to new fields and did not want to continue their work for the *New Northwest*. They claimed the paper was not sufficiently profitable, although the record books show that it was doing better than in 1880.[18] Since they were equal partners in the Duniway Publishing Company, Abigail Duniway had to accede to their opinions.

Accusations that Mrs. Duniway had "sold out to whiskey" were widely circulated, and even published in WCTU papers. As far away as Boston the women of the Massachusetts Woman's Christian Prohibitory League accused her of bringing "disgrace on the Woman Suffrage cause." Abigail Duniway never quite recovered from her hurt and anger. Reflecting their totally different approach to the entire woman's rights campaign, they censured her for "attempting to conciliate the liquor power" and continued, "we feel that we voice the sentiment of every true woman in America when we say: God grant that the ballot may never be given to women if, in order to obtain it, we must conciliate men."[19]

That fall of 1886, Abigail Scott Duniway reluctantly sold her beloved *New Northwest* "at a good profit" to a close friend of Harvey Scott's. She agreed that others should take over the suffrage organization leadership if they would. All her own funds were now tied up in the Idaho land. The new publisher promised to print all her contributions, but—oddly enough—the newspaper went out of business within two months.

Shortly afterward Washington women lost their right to vote. Duniway's worst fears had proved accurate. Washington's Territorial Supreme Court in Feburary 1887 set free a convicted murderer because he had been tried by a jury that included women. The judges were all Democrats named by President Grover Cleveland after he came to office in 1885. (Most first-generation Washington pioneers and women voters were Republicans.) They claimed that a technical error in the 1883 woman suffrage law effectively nullified the legality of mixed juries. Washington's 1888 legislature passed a corrected suffrage law. Then a saloonkeeper's wife, Mrs. Nevada Bloomer, brought a damage suit about being refused the right to vote. She lost the suit and did not appeal, thus negating the suffrage law once again. Her status and failure to appeal clearly suggest that hers was a test case engineered by the opponents of suffrage. With Duniway's *New*

Abigail Scott Duniway
(courtesy Oregon Historical Society)

Northwest silenced, there was no way to publicize the details or mo-
bilize reaction in the Territory's scattered frontier communities.
Washington became a state in 1889, but its women had to wait another generation before they could vote for prohibition—or anything
else.[20]

Abigail Scott Duniway never stopped her work for woman suffrage. She continued to lecture and write and to organize women's
clubs and suffrage campaigns for the rest of her life. Always she argued that women must work *with* men, rather than as antagonists,
in order to achieve their equal rights goal. Even after Oregon's victory in 1912, when she herself was badly crippled from arthritis and
approaching eighty, she insisted that she had not "retired." She wanted
the vote for *all* American women. Having been bitterly slandered by
President Anna Howard Shaw and others in the National American
Woman Suffrage Association, Duniway allied herself with women like
Laura Clay, Jane Addams, and Alice Paul.[21] The latter eventually
started the campaign for an Equal Rights Amendment.

As Abigail Scott Duniway suspected, the men who threw eggs at
her in Jacksonville, Oregon, in 1879, or who refused to allow their
wives to speak to her or read her newspaper, or who wrote slander-
ous editorials against her on numerous occasions, saw much more at
stake than the ballot's supposed danger to female virtue. For example, it was an expensive and complicated enterprise for enemies
to establish in 1882 a *pro*whiskey newspaper misleadingly entitled
Northwest News. It was mailed to all of Duniway's *New Northwest*
subscribers, undermining her credibility and causing endless legal and
financial complications for the Duniway Publishing Company. Then,
just after winning a court suit to keep its name, the rogue newspaper
went out of business—two weeks after the 1884 Oregon suffrage
amendment was defeated.[22]

Why did it take so long to get votes for women in Washington and
Oregon, not to speak of the rest of the country? Clearly, the answer
is complicated. Powerful political and financial interests were threatened by the potential of women voters. It was the status quo of "po-
lite" society, the financial prerogatives of those already in power, the
hegemony of corrupt politicians that was threatened by doubling the
voting populace. People opposed a woman's right to vote, as they
still do her equal rights, for many reasons that have nothing to do
with sex.

Abigail Scott Duniway told young women of her time that new
freedoms had been "bought for them at a great price." She knew
what kind of a price it was. But she believed "the debt that each

generation owes to the past it must pay to the future." And she did her best to prove that "when women go for their own rights, they generally get them," sooner or later.[23]

Notes

1. *New Northwest*, May 5, 1871. Further biographical information and documentation appear in Ruth Barnes Moynihan, *Rebel for Rights: Abigail Scott Duniway* (New Haven: Yale University Press, 1983). See also Duniway's *Path Breaking: An Autobiographical History of the Equal Suffrage Movement in Pacific Coast States* (Portland, Ore.: James, Kerns and Abbott, 1914; reprint, New York: Schocken Books, 1971). Her papers are in the David Duniway Collection, Salem, Oregon.

2. A basic history of America's woman suffrage movement is contained in Eleanor Flexner, *Century of Struggle: The Woman's Rights Movement in the United States* (Cambridge, Mass.: Harvard University Press, 1959).

3. See an excellent discussion of this relationship in Lee Nash, "*Harvey v. Abigail*: Sibling Rivalry in the Oregon Campaign for Woman Suffrage," unpublished forthcoming essay.

4. Catherine Scott Coburn to Duniway, Oct. 12, 1912, in ASD Scrapbook II, Duniway Papers, Salem, Oregon.

5. Portland: S. J. McCormick, 1859.

6. "Editorial Correspondence," *New Northwest*, September–November 1871.

7. Duniway, *Path Breaking*, pp. 89–90.

8. "Editorial Correspondence," *New Northwest*, Dec. 7, 1877.

9. "Editorial Correspondence," *New Northwest*, Nov. 30, 1877.

10. "Editorial Corespondence," *New Northwest*, July 17, 1879.

11. "Frances Willard's Visit to Portland," *New Northwest*, Jan. 21, 1883.

12. *New Northwest*, Nov. 1, 1883.

13. *New Northwest*, Nov. 15, 1883.

14. *Washington* [D.C.] *Post*, Jan. 24, 1884. Clipping in ASD Scrapbook, Duniway Papers.

15. Joseph Gaston, *Portland, Oregon: Its History and Builders*, vol. 1 (Chicago and Portland: S. J. Clarke Publishing Co., 1911), p. 562.

16. *New Northwest*, Mar. 22, 1883; Gaston, *Portland, Oregon*, 1:334–35; Ezra Meeker, *The Busy Life of Eighty-five Years* (Seattle: The author, 1916), pp. 225–29; John E. Caswell, "The Prohibition Movement in Oregon," *Oregon Historical Quarterly* 40 (1939): 79.

17. "Editorial," *New Northwest*, June 10, 1886.

18. The Duniway Publishing Co. Ledgers are at the Oregon Historical Society, Portland.

19. Reprinted in "Editorial Correspondence," *New Northwest*, Sept. 30, 1886.

20. See T. A. Larson, "The Woman Suffrage Movement in Washington," *Pacific Northwest Quarterly* 67 (April 1976):54; Norman H. Clark, *The Dry Years: Prohibition and Social Change in Washington* (Seattle: University of Washington Press, 1965), p. 37.

21. Letters from these women, and others, are in the Duniway Papers; also extensive correspondence with Anna Howard Shaw.

22. See *Rebel for Rights,* pp. 179–80, notes 30–33, p. 250; details of the Duniway court case against the *Northwest News* were reported in *New Northwest,* Oct. 5, 1882 to June 26, 1884.

23. Duniway, *Path Breaking,* p. 297.

May Arkwright Hutton:
Suffragist and Politician

Patricia Voeller Horner

May Arkwright Hutton has been described as a large, homely woman with a "heart of gold." Flamboyant descriptions of her abound and are interesting for what they omit.[1] She was the leader of the eastern Washington suffrage movement and was actively involved in Democratic politics. In 1912 she was elected the first woman delegate to attend the Democratic National Convention in Baltimore. This paper will examine an aspect of May Hutton heretofore ignored: her ideas and how they manifested themselves in her activities, primarily in the Washington State suffrage movement and Democratic politics.

May Hutton lived at a time when woman's role was severely circumscribed. Woman was viewed as pure, pious, domestic, and delicate. Home and family were considered her areas of influence, while economics, politics, and the working world were considered man's domain.[2] May Hutton appears not to have been influenced by these ideas about "woman's place." She lived according to her own value system, one developed through an unusual childhood and her working-class background. She involved herself passionately in social issues, was active politically on the local and state levels, and was a strong advocate of suffrage for women.

May Arkwright was born in a coal mining community in Washingtonville, Ohio, July 21, 1860.[3] Her mother died when she was very young and her father took her out of school two terms before her tenth birthday to care for her blind grandfather.[4] She took her grandfather from meeting place to public square to hear speakers expounding on the issues of the day. One of these speakers was a young lawyer named William McKinley. May's grandfather invited him to spend the night with them, and after guiding the two men to the Arkwright home, May served them cider and her homemade doughnuts. She recalled that they discussed the war, reconstruction, and women's rights. This discussion of women's rights was the first May had heard and made her aware that women did not enjoy the same political and economic rights as men. According to May, McKinley deplored this fact and stated that woman was the "intellectual equal of man and should be his political equal."[5]

May regarded her grandfather highly, and he seems to have exercised a positive influence on her life. In a letter to William E. Borah,

May Arkwright Hutton
(courtesy Eastern Washington Historical Society)

This picture from May's personal album is labeled, "All dressed up and no place to go." *(Courtesy Eastern Washington Historical Society)*

later a U.S. senator from Idaho, she gave her grandfather credit for her aggressive stance: "When I was a child my grandfather used to say, 'Hitch your wagon to a star, girlie. You may never reach the eminence to which you aspire, but place no limit on your aspirations.'"[6]

When she was eighteen, May Arkwright married Frank Day in Mahoning County, Ohio. She left no recollections of this marriage, nor of her second marriage at twenty-two to a coal miner named Gilbert Munn. May's marriage to Munn was short-lived. In 1883, less than one year after her marriage, she joined forty miners and their families from Youngstown, Ohio, and migrated to Idaho, 2,500 miles away, to take part in the gold rush.[7]

May settled in Wardner Junction, Idaho, and worked as a cook in the back of a saloon. This job appears to have lasted only a short time before she opened her own boardinghouse in Wardner Junction. By September 1887, four years after arriving in Idaho, May had met Levi (Al) Hutton, a train engineer who ate regularly at her boardinghouse. On November 17, 1887, she and Al were married and moved into an inexpensive two-room flat in Wallace, Idaho, above the railroad tracks.[8]

Ten years after their marriage, in 1897, May and Al bought a one thirty-fourths interest in the Hercules mine and were part of the fortunate few whose mining shares paid off. In 1901 the Hercules began producing silver, and in 1902 May and Al received their first dividend check of $750. Within ten years they would become millionaires.[9]

After the silver strike, the Huttons moved from their hillside home in Wallace, where they had lived for twelve years, to a more comfortable house on a corner lot. May was not accepted in the Wallace social circle of mine owners' wives, a problem that would follow her throughout her life. She did not fit the guidelines for a "proper" Victorian lady. Her size (about 225 pounds), her tendency to dress with a flair, her lack of formal education, and her past occupation as a boardinghouse keeper did not qualify her to associate with the more cultured, pious, and delicate Victorian women, regardless of her newly acquired wealth. Nevertheless, May joined the Wallace Shakespeare Club, and she and Al were visited by Clarence Darrow and his family and also entertained Carrie Chapman Catt, an Eastern suffragist, and Ella Wheeler Wilcox, a nationally known poet.[10]

In 1904, benefiting from her newly acquired wealth and leisure time, May ran for the Idaho state legislature on the Democratic ticket. She didn't feel she had a very good chance of winning, but thought that if she talked with all of the delegates personally, she might succeed in being nominated. She is reported to have told the delegates that since there was so much publicity about her running for the legislature, it would be nice if she could at least make a respectable showing. Wouldn't they, therefore, vote for her on the first ballot? Then on the second ballot they could vote for whomever they pleased. Evidentally May convinced them. She won the nomination on the first ballot and began a hard campaign to defeat her Republican opponent. The outcome was close: May came within eighty votes of victory. She is quoted as saying that she was defeated by the mine owners, who contributed $20,000 to ensure her defeat. In an article entitled "Woman Politician Tells of Struggle," in the Portland *Oregon Journal,* May was asked if men took kindly to her candidacy for the legislature. She replied, "I can't say that they did, . . . but I got the vote of the women; that's one thing I would like to have understood."[11]

In 1906 May and Al moved from Wallace to Spokane, where they had a four-story office building constructed, making their home on the top floor. By this time May's political philosophy was quite clear. She was first and foremost a Democrat, and like the majority of people associated with mining, felt that William Jennings Bryan, who advocated the free and unlimited coinage of silver, was the best choice to lead the nation.[12]

May appears to have given socialism some thought and announced at one point that she was a Socialist, "or nearly one," adding for the press her thoughts on the subject: "One of these days this country is going to wake up and find that more than half the people are socialists. . . . Socialism is coming and it may be coming faster than many suppose." In 1912 May again spoke on the subject: "As sure as the world, unless progressive ideas prevail and progressive laws are enforced we'll have socialism in this country. It's evolute [*sic*] or revolute." Socialism was for May an idea whose time was coming, but one that could be staved off if social reforms were instituted to meet societal needs.[13]

One of the most important social reforms for May was woman suffrage. Women in Idaho had been enfranchised since 1896, but upon moving to Spokane May lost her right to vote.[14] She joined the National American Woman Suffrage Association in 1905 and attended its thirty-fifth convention in Portland that same year. While living in Idaho she met Abigail Scott Duniway, Oregon's suffrage leader, and Emma Smith DeVoe, a suffrage organizer from Illinois who had been sent to the Northwest to help organize Idaho and later Washington. After moving to Spokane, May began actively working with the Seattle-based Mrs. DeVoe for the enfranchisement of Washington women and held the position of first vice-president of the Washington Equal Suffrage Association, with Mrs. DeVoe as president.[15]

There is little record of May's suffrage activities during 1906 and 1907, except that she attended the National Suffrage Convention again in 1906 and spoke on women's suffrage and its effect on Idaho politics. Correspondence indicates that May became more active in 1908 and worked closely with Mrs. DeVoe in what appears to have been a somewhat subservient relationship. On one occasion May asked Mrs. DeVoe to provide her with an outline from which she would prepare a speech, and on another flattered her with the statement, "we need you and cannot win without you." This feeling was reiterated in a later letter when May told Mrs. DeVoe that she was needed in Spokane to "rouse us up again."[16]

May took the initiative in late June 1908 when she suggested to Mrs. DeVoe that a suffrage plank be presented at the upcoming Democratic convention in Denver. She thought that the plank should read: "We declare for a educational qualification for *all* voters, regardless of sex, race, color or previous condition of servatude [*sic*]." This suggestion was not well received. Penciled at the bottom of May's letter was a note to Mrs. DeVoe from her husband, Henry: "Emma dear, this plank *won't do*. The Southern delegates would fight it to the death. 'Educational qualification without regard to sex' is all right, but let it stand there. . . ."[17]

May attended the convention and reported to Mrs. DeVoe that the plank was not included in the Democratic platform. She also noted that she had talked with Samuel Gompers, "the great labor leader," and reported that he was "indignant" that the plank had been rejected, but assured May that "if none of the advocates of the cause never raise their voices in its behalf, it will nevertheless prevail universally in another decade or two."[18]

May advised Mrs. DeVoe that she fully agreed with Mr. Gompers and would be busy until after the election organizing Democratic women to elect William Jennings Bryan, and would therefore not be spending much time on suffrage. Nevertheless, May agreed to write a speech for the upcoming state convention, and, responding to an inquiry from Mrs. DeVoe, stated that she could not possibly take the presidency of the state suffrage organization: "No woman that I know of can fill that position but Emma Smith DeVoe." May's humor and good feelings toward Mrs. DeVoe are evident in the conclusion of her letter: "In the cool October days, Mrs. DeVoe will come to Spokane, and she and Mrs. Hutton will take the big red automobile and get converts for the suffrage cause, primarily, and have a good time generally."[19]

May's enthusiasm waned somewhat as the year progressed, and she informed Mrs. DeVoe that she was having some difficulty with her convention paper because of a houseful of relatives from Ohio. May was also expected to respond to the governor's address of welcome, and asked Mrs. DeVoe if she would write this response for her to memorize. It appears that May was both physically and emotionally spent: "I do not know what is the matter with me lately, but I cannot concentrate on anything. . . . My state of mind and health is such that I cannot accomplish much."[20]

A November 1908 letter from May to Dr. Cora Smith Eaton, treasurer of the Equal Suffrage Association, gives the first hint of organizational independence on May's part, as well as hostility toward the west-side suffragists: "[I] have decided that we will conduct our campaign on the east side along entirely different lines than the Seattle women are persuing. I have been in politics a great many years and *know* that the *still* hunt is the winning hunt. . . . You say you are weary distributing posters, 'Votes for Women.' We are not, because we didn't post any in Spokane. I have however, something less than a ton in cold storage, and will use them when we are ready for the men to vote on the question. In my opinioin, these posters in the face of the people at this time only arouses antagonism which we particularly desire to avoid."[21]

May's suffrage activities increased in 1909, and she reported to a friend that she and Mrs. LaReine Baker had been working quite alone on the eastern side of the mountains. May traveled to Walla Walla to speak at the American Federation of Labor convention, organized debates on women's suffrage in the Spokane area, and offered prizes to high school students for the best essay on "Why Women Should Be Given the Ballot." By March 1909 she was working furiously to prepare for the upcoming suffrage convention in Seattle. Parlor meetings were held nightly to enlist members in the Equal Suffrage Association, and May reported to LaReine Baker that "membership is rolling up to beat the band."[22]

As membership increased, so did the conflict between the eastern and western factions of the Equal Suffrage Association. In correspondence with LaReine Baker, May enclosed a letter she received from Cora Eaton, stating that this had been her only communication from Dr. Eaton "since she informed me that if I did not do as Mrs. DeVoe dictated I would be eliminated from the work in Washington." May also communicated with Abigail Scott Duniway during this period, telling her of the increased Spokane membership and her hope that this would "make the 'Big Noise' sit up and take notice." In other correspondence May made it clear that she no longer favored Emma Smith DeVoe for president of the Equal Suffrage Association. She stated that Spokane area suffragists would be willing to join with discontented suffragists on the other side of the mountains to amend the constitution and change the management: "I do not consider those who make a profession of and earn a livelihood in, any reform, are the best elements for success."[23]

May was fighting back, evidentally reacting to an attempt by DeVoe forces to change her tactics or purge her from the Washington suffrage movement entirely. She stepped up her campaign for members in the Equal Suffrage Assocation by offering to give any young lady a round-trip ticket to Seattle to attend the convention if she would bring in fifty paid memberships to the organization. May told Mrs. Baker she was certain the eastern suffragists and the "rebels of Seattle" would have enough delegates at the convention "to elect Mrs. Homer Hill president . . ." and thereby displace Mrs. DeVoe.[24]

Mrs. DeVoe and her allies by this time realized that they had an angry and vigorous force to contend with on the eastern side of the mountains. Mrs. DeVoe's husband asked Dr. Eaton to comment on May's integrity, and she responded with undisguised hostility: "As to the rich woman's [Mrs. Hutton, of Spokane] paying fake dues for fake members to fake clubs, I think there is little fear of it. Her devotion to the cause knows no bounds but money, but when it comes to spending money even for vengeance, I think she would be very economical. I never knew anyone in my life who hung on to money the way she does. She is reported in the Spokane Spokesman Review as having offered a ticket to Seattle to the convention to every high school girl who gets 50 members to the local club, but it is not likely that even one girl will be able to fulfill the requirements. This lady likes the notoriety of offering money prizes, but she makes the conditions so hard that her purse is not endangered."[25]

A later letter from Dr. Eaton to Mrs. DeVoe discussed the organization of new suffrage clubs and the reading of the Equal Suffrage Association constitution on this issue. She was disappointed to find that the constitution allowed any four members to form a club and thereby be entitled to one delegate. Dr. Eaton and Mrs. DeVoe would not be able, then, to control the number of delegates May brought to the convention, and Mrs. DeVoe's presidency appeared in jeopardy. But Mrs. DeVoe and Dr. Eaton were not to be so easily defeated. On June 17, 1909, Dr. Eaton wrote May telling her that she was returning her yearly dues to the Equal Suffrage Association: "The return is made for the reason that I believe you are ineligible to membership in the Washington Equal Suffrage Association because of your habitual use of profane and obscene language and of your record in

Idaho as shown by pictures and other evidence placed in my hands by persons who are familiar with your former life and reputation."[26]

May responded to this letter angrily, telling Dr. Eaton that as an elected officer she would be at the state convention and would have with her as many delegates as their membership entitled. She ended the letter: "Perhaps, Doctor, you thought to frighten me with this array of accusations. You have made them and it is up to you to prove them, which you will be given ample opportunity to do." May passed the letter from Dr. Eaton freely among her friends and co-workers, but did not press the issue beyond her reply to Dr. Eaton.[27] The letter to May from Dr. Eaton appears to have been an undisguised threat, warning May that if she persisted in threatening Mrs. DeVoe's leadership, her reputation would be badly tarnished.

May continued her membership drive, and the Spokane branch of the Washington Equal Suffrage Association became the largest in the state. But when the state association met in Seattle, the Spokane delegates were challenged for withholding the names of their members until two days before the meeting. The Spokane women and their Seattle supporters were not allowed in the general meeting, and Mrs. DeVoe was again elected president. Later, at the national suffrage association meeting and in response to the conflict, both the eastern and western factions were denied the right to vote, though both groups were seated.[28]

In a letter to Mrs. Carrie Chapman Catt, Dr. Eaton elaborated on the Seattle debacle and attempted to justify it with an exposé of May's alleged bad character. She stated that May was known as Bootleg Mary in the mining camps, that she ran a "bad house, kept for immoral purposes," that her language was "profane and insulting," and that she was generally more of a hindrance than a help in the suffrage campaign. Her removal from the state organization, according to Dr. Eaton, was a "surgical operation—an amputation, following the opening of a very foul abscess."[29]

Harriet Taylor Upton, another Seattle suffragist, had a somewhat different view of what happened at the Seattle convention: "Dr. Cora as treasurer and later as Chairman of the committee turned down 23 different clubs. All were in favor of an anti-DeVoe candidate. . . . Now the truth of the matter is that Mrs. DeVoe wanted to be President and Dr. Eaton espoused her cause. If she had stepped aside and not resorted to these unprincipled things, the convention would not have had [to put up with] Mrs. Hutton. . . . but it would even have been better to have had her than to have resorted to the means which Dr. Eaton and Mrs. DeVoe resorted to. They simply lost their heads and were badly advised by their attorneys. . . . The Spokane people were not given a hearing at all before the credentials committee. . . ."[30]

The social differences between May Arkwright Hutton and Emma Smith DeVoe were extreme and may have contributed to their counterproductive power struggle. May was not cultured, ladylike, or sophisticated, whereas DeVoe was a "lady," variously described as sweet, womanly, and tactful. May had little formal education and saw suffrage as a hobby, wheareas DeVoe was an educated, professional organizer who must have felt politically and organizationally superior to May. In addition, May was a staunch and committed Democrat who believed in political involvement, while DeVoe was a conservative Republican who felt that politics should take a back seat to suffrage. The Cora Smith Eaton correspondence also suggests that there was some antagonism toward May because of her newly acquired wealth, while May felt a class division between herself and most upper-class women because they had not had to work the way she had.[31]

Although May was no longer an official member of the Washington Suffrage Assocation, she was not to be removed from the struggle, and on October 7, 1909, she organized the Washington Political Equality League with an office in the Hutton Building in Spokane. There were now three organizations working for woman suffrage in Washington State, with Mrs. Hill of Seattle in charge of one, Mrs. DeVoe in charge of another, and May Hutton responsible for the third. May wrote Mrs. Hill that she was more than willing to meet with any of the leaders so their work would not overlap, and stated that she could "well affort to let bygones be bygones, having been completely vindicated by home women who know us best."[32]

With the assistance of a publicity person, May kept the issue of suffrage before the eastern Washington public throughout 1909. In July 1909 she wrote Mrs. Hill that the *Spokesman-Review* was not very favorable to the cause of suffrage, "but I intend to whip them into line in the next ten days."[33] How she succeeded in this task is not clear, but newspaper interviews and articles on suffrage and the role of women proliferate throughout this period.

As if to assure Washington voters of her moderate position on suffrage, May actively assaulted the image of militant suffragists, taking to task specifically the English suffragist Emmeline Pankhurst for advocating violence to aid women's rights: "Men will grant favors to their own mothers and wives that they will not concede so readily to strangers. . . . Our campaign in Washington is an appeal, not a fight. We never allow our workers to be abusive to men."[34] May's primary appeal was to common sense, guided by her feeling that if the justice of the suffrage cause was presented to male voters by their mothers, daughters, sisters, and wives, it would be successful. May also expressed faith in the fairness of western men; this faith appeared to be genuine and can probably be traced to her years of close association with men, both in her boardinghouse-cook days and in her early years in Idaho politics.[35]

May's suffrage speeches and interviews stand out because of her sensitivity to working women and her hostility to wealthy, upper-class women. In a short speech written in 1909, she stated that college educated women were not interested in women's political emancipation, though one would think that their education would broaden their outlook and make them more sensitive to their less fortunate sisters. According to May, education had had an opposite effect: "As a rule they are self-centered, exclusive, ultra-conventional, and content to rest upon their college-earned laurels. . . ." and "as a class they have not suffered enough." May stated that her work for the attainment of suffrage was not for these women, but for the "laundry worker, the shop girl, the stenographer, the teacher, the working woman of every type, whose home and fireside and bread are earned by their own efforts."[36]

In a letter to the editor responding to Mrs. Stuyvesant Fish, a wealthy eastern woman who did not feel that women needed the vote, May carried her argument one step further. She stated that even if Mrs. Fish didn't feel that she needed the vote, she had a responsibility to achieve it for less fortunate women for whose poor living conditions "Mrs. Fish and people of her class are in a great measure responsible."[37]

May did not see a contradiction between women having the vote and the fulfillment by them of their traditional roles as wives and mothers, though she felt that suffrage would have an educating and therefore broadening effect on women, and would thus help both women and men better understand one another. For May, the enfranchisement of women would also ensure their equality before the law, especially in wages and work. In short, suffrage for women would mean "a square deal for all." May also felt that women had a right to participate in making the laws under which they were forced to live, stating that "man is not woman's keeper, and has no more inherent right to think and vote for her then he has to suffer punishment for her crimes."[38]

On a personal level, May saw suffrage as giving women the chance to be men's helpmates and companions rather than their toys. But being a helpmate and companion did not, for May, negate what she felt were women's natural functions as mothers. Indeed, May saw suffrage as potentially improving the conditions under which husbands and wives labored and lived, and thereby improving the lives of their children and contributing to a healthier society.[39]

May also felt that in the long run women would make better citizens than men, "for man's sensibilities have naturally become dulled by his contact with the world, while woman's sensibilities are more keen from her more secluded environments." In short, May was subscribing to the prevalent idea of the day that women would bring a different sensibility to politics—what she called, in one interview, the "mothering" of politics. At the same time, May was careful to note in her interviews that women "will never become so obsessed with zeal for the suffrage cause or politics as to forget their womanhood, or what is due true manhood."[40]

The constitutional amendment granting women the vote in Washington State was passed by the voters November 11, 1910, with 52,299 in favor and 29,676 opposed. According to Lucile Fargo, even May's severest critics acknowledged that she "was a born leader, and above all, that she got things done," and in a telegram May was praised for the "quiet, ladylike manner in which the campaign was conducted." Abigail Scott Duniway in her autobiography said that May "managed her part of the [suffrage] program with ability and tact," and Spokane area newspapers were unanimous in their praise of May's organizational abilities as well as her political influence, "which is excelled by the influence of no man nor woman in the state. . . . she is a woman of high ideals and her influence must not be underestimated nor ignored."[41]

May remained active in Democratic party politics after the passage of the Washington Suffrage Amendment in 1910 and was named, along with Mrs. A. P. Fassett, the first woman juror in Spokane County. May wrote in a December 1910 letter that she was the first woman to register to vote in Spokane and had spent thirty days in Olympia working successfully for the passage of a bill advocating an eight-hour workday for women.[42]

May's status in Democratic party politics was acknowledged when she and three other women were named delegates to the State Democratic Convention of May 1912 in Walla Walla. Champ Clark received the Washington nomination, much to May's chagrin, and May was elected to be the first woman delegate ever to attend the Democratic National Convention, to be held in Baltimore. A newspaper article gave one man's view of May's election: "I'll tell you boys, she's the girl to tie to." The reporter than applauded May's restraint in going along with the delegation for Clark, though she was "wild to vote for Bryan." May received the largest number of votes of any

Washington delegate, and when asked to respond to her election, after receiving an ovation, she said: "I would not have the nerve to come before this body and ask to be sent to Baltimore if I did not think I had earned that distinction."[43]

May arrived in Baltimore on a hot, muggy June day in 1912 and became instant copy for the eastern newspapermen. She instructed them to omit the Mrs. from her name and was described as a "big, motherly looking woman. . . . with a round, rosy face, and expressive blue eyes that flash when she discusses the rights of women." She is reported to have endeared herself to reporters by calling them "dearie" and by having a good deal to say in a humorous fashion. The reporters seemed most taken by the fact that May was from the West, and attributed to the West her "masculine directness of purpose and a masculine capacity for giving and receiving blows."[44]

Although May received an amazing amount of press coverage, the experience was unusual for her because she did not give a formal speech. She was one of many delegates, and she is reported to have been a conscientious one, staying in her chair throughout the lengthy sessions. Again, her personal choice, Bryan, was not nominated and neither was the Washington delegation's choice, Champ Clark. Instead, the nominee was Woodrow Wilson, who according to May, "like all college professors, is not altogether practical."[45]

Throughout 1911, May had mentioned in letters to friends that she hadn't been feeling well, and the convention seemed to aggravate her poor health. Nonetheless, she stopped in Ohio on her way back from Baltimore and made thirteen speeches for suffrage and was invited to California to "work among 'laboring men'" to assist in the suffrage campaign in that state. She also gave suffrage talks in Oregon and addressed women's clubs in the state of Washington, and in a March 1912 letter to a friend stated that she was "better, but far from well."[46]

In July 1914 May and Al moved from their residence on the fourth floor of the Hutton Building in downtown Spokane to a new home on Seventeenth Avenue, and during that same year May suffered an attack of Bright's disease. A January 1914 article in the *Daily Chronicle* stated that May had been seriously ill for several months: "Formerly tipping the scales at 240, she weighs just 147 today." But May told the reporter she was "feeling fine," though she did wonder how she was going to be able to walk around "on these pipestems."[47]

On October 6, 1915, May Arkwright Hutton died in her home at the age of fifty-five. The coroner listed the official cause of her death as "degeneration of the heart." May was eulogized in newspapers across the United States as an "author, suffragist, philosopher, hu-

May and Al Hutton mowing their lawn in Wallace
(courtesy Eastern Washington Historical Society)

Al, May, and Al's brother Stephen after a successful day of fishing
(courtesy Eastern Washington Historical Society)

manitarian and probably one of the best known women in the great Northwest. . . . [who] always fought on the moral side of all questions, [and] never forgot the poor and unfortunate.[48]

May Arkwright Hutton cannot be easily categorized. She was a suffragist, but she did not fit the mold of the refined, educated eastern suffragist. She was a homespun variety who, like the majority of eastern suffragists, disparaged radical tactics in the suffrage movement but, unlike them, appealed to the goodness and fairness she felt was native to western men, while identifying primarily with working-class men and women.[49]

May was also a politician who believed in and enjoyed being part of the democratic process and was comfortable working in this distinctly male system. Indeed, May is said to have "learned to get what she wanted in a man's way, by working and fighting for it."[50]

In addition to her work as suffragist and politician, May Hutton was also a wife, and from all accounts, a devoted one. During the Democratic National Convention in Baltimore, she told a reporter that Al was the boss in the family, that he was "the grandest man in the world," and that she would not have made progress in the suffrage movement "if he had not permitted me to become identified with it." It is possible that May was attempting to fit into the mold of what she felt was a typical married woman, but it is equally possible that she was being candid. She did, however, look at being a wife and mother with an eye to life's harsh realities for the working person: "motherhood in all its beauty, and home where love and contentment reigns supreme, are luxuries denied the average woman today. Economic conditions of today have forced the woman out of the home, away from the cradles into the world to earn her bread."[51]

One aspect of May that seems particularly unique for a woman of her social class and time is her desire to be remembered as an important and effective person: "What a beautiful thing it is to have lived so that when one passes to the Great Beyond, all with one accord will join in praises for one's good works."[52] In a 1908 letter to her brother Lyman in Youngstown, Ohio, May told him how proud her grandfather would have been of her suffrage work and concluded: "Now Lyman, you just watch my smoke, because I am going to *do things!*"[53] In a letter to Senator Borah, May said she was nearly as busy as a U.S. senator addressing numerous suffrage meetings, but that she considered this good practice," for you know my ambition is to be a United States Senator."[54] At the time of her death May was climbing politically, and it is conceivable that she could have achieved her dream had she lived.

May Arkwright Hutton was a strong woman with a dominating and arresting personality who went about her activities with aggressiveness, humor, and a distinct flair for the dramatic. Striking silver freed her from a life of toil to pursue with zeal the things she was interested in; being childless freed her from woman's traditional role of mothering. Coupled with these personal characteristics, May Hutton had unique and progressive ideas and was not afraid to put them before the public, and, when possible, act on them. She also believed passionately in the democratic process and truly felt she could make a difference. Integrally linked to May Hutton's belief in herself was her belief in the common people and their inherent fairness and goodness. She leaves for women of the twentieth century a proud heritage, not because she achieved greatness in a traditional sense but because she dared to be herself at a time and in a place where this was a difficult thing to do. May Hutton was an agent for change who improved the lives of those around her and set a worthy example for those who have followed.

Notes

1. Charles Gonser, interview, Spokane, Nov. 2, 1977. See also Benjamin H. Kizer, "May Arkwright Hutton," *Pacific Northwest Quarterly* 57, no. 2 (April 1966): 19; T. A. Larson, "The Woman Suffrage Movement in Washington," *Pacific Northwest Quarterly* 67, no. 2 (April 1976): 57; Lucile F. Fargo, *Spokane Story* (New York: Columbia University Press, 1950), p. 225; James W. Montgomery, *Liberated Woman: A Life of May Arkwright Hutton* (Spokane: Gingko Publishers, 1974), p. 105; and Margaret Bean, "She Was a Woman Who Spoke Her Mind," *Spokesman-Review Magazine* (July 12, 1936).

2. See Barbara Welter, "The Cult of True Womanhood, 1820–1860," in Ronald W. Hogeland, ed., *Woman and Womanhood in America* (Lexington: D. C. Heath and Company, 1973), for an elaboration of this idea.

3. Lucile Fargo, "Mrs. Hercules: The Story of May Arkwright Hutton," no date, unpublished manuscript, Spokane Public Library, p. 68, states that May was actually born Mary Arkwright, but took the name May after marrying Al Hutton.

4. Memorial Scrapbook 2, Hutton Family Scrapbooks, Eastern Washington Historical Society, Spokane. These scrapbooks do not have page numbers, nor are some of the newspaper clippings within the scrapbooks dated. Unless otherwise stated, all references to Scrapbooks 1 to 6 will refer to undated newspaper clippings.

5. Ida Husted Harper, ed., *The History of Woman Suffrage,* 6 vols. (Na-

tional American Woman Suffrage Association, 1922), vol. 5, 1900–1920, pp. 133 and 134. See also Scrapbook 2.

6. Hutton to Borah, Sept. 28, 1909, Charles Gonser private papers.

7. Fargo, "Mrs. Hercules," p. 18 (Frank Day); Montgomery, *Liberated Woman,* p. 9 (Gilbert Munn); Scrapbook 2 (move to Idaho).

8. Fargo, "Mrs. Hercules," pp. 45 and 54, and Montgomery, *Liberated Woman,* p. 33. See also Ivan Pearson, *Voices of the Pioneers,* cassette 30, Spokane Public Library, June 4, 1970.

9. Ivan Pearson, "The Hutton Settlement," *Pacific Northwesterner* 11 (Summer 1967): 33 and 34. The *Wallace Free Press,* Aug. 17, 1901, states that the discovery was "what is believed to be the richest ore ever taken out of the Coeur d'Alenes."

10. Pearson, *Voices of the Pioneers;* Charles Gonser, *Voices of the Pioneers,* cassette 12, Spokane Public Library, May 10, 1960; Grace Roffey Pratt, "The Great-Hearted Huttons of the Coeur d'Alenes," *Montana: The Magazine of Western History* 17 (April 1967): 25; and Fargo, "Mrs. Hercules," pp. 156 and 160.

11. Gonser, *Voices of the Pioneers,* and Montgomery, *Liberated Woman,* pp. 91 and 92 (campaign); Scrapbook 3 (mine owners); *Journal,* Scrapbook 3 (quotation).

12. Hutton to Mrs. Ella Green, Nov. 10, 1908, Charles Gonser private papers.

13. Scrapbooks 2 and 5 (quotations).

14. Suffrage bills had been introduced in the Washington Territorial Legislature in 1854, 1869, 1871, 1873, 1875, and 1881. Finally, in 1883 a woman suffrage bill was passed, only to be voided later the same year by the Territorial Supreme Court on a technicality.

15. Harper, *History of Woman Suffrage,* pp. 133 and 135; Fargo, "Mrs. Hercules," pp. 161 and 188; and Scrapbook 1.

16. Harper, *History of Woman Suffrage,* p. 176 (convention speech); Hutton to DeVoe, March 20 and June 15, 1908, Emma Smith DeVoe Collection, box 2, Washington/Northwest Room, Washington State Library, Olympia.

17. Hutton to DeVoe, June 25, 1908, DeVoe Collection, box 2. It is not clear whether the plank was modified for the convention.

18. Hutton to DeVoe, Jan. 9, 1909, Charles Gonser private papers.

19. Hutton to DeVoe, July 17, 1908, and July 29, 1908 (Bryan), and Aug. 21, 1908 (presidency), DeVoe Collection, box 2.

20. Hutton to DeVoe, Sept. 7, 1908, DeVoe Collection, box 2.

21. Hutton to Eaton, Nov. 5, 1908, Charles Gonser private papers.

22. Hutton to Mrs. Edith De L. Jarmuth, Jan. 11, 1909, Charles Gonser private papers (eastern side); Hutton to Mrs. Homer Hill, March 26, 1909, Charles Gonser private papers, and Scrapbook 2 (activites); Hutton to Baker, April 7, 1909 and May 3, 1909, Charles Gonser private papers (membership).

23. Hutton to Baker, May 3, 1909, Hutton to Duniway, May 22, 1909, and Hutton to Mrs. Leona W. Brown, May 28, 1909, all in Charles Gonser

private papers. See also Hutton to Mrs. Homer Hill, June 4, 1909, Charles Gonser private papers.

24. Hutton to Baker, May 31, 1909, Charles Gonser private papers.

25. Eaton to J. H. DeVoe, June 4, 1909, DeVoe Collection, box 2.

26. Eaton to DeVoe, June 4, 1909, and Eaton to Hutton, June 17, 1909, DeVoe Collection, box 2.

27. Hutton to Eaton, June 19, 1909 (quotation), and Eaton to DeVoe, June 24, 1909, DeVoe Collection, box 2.

28. Montgomery, *Liberated Woman,* pp. 110 and 111.

29. Eaton to Catt, Oct. 24, 1909, DeVoe Collection, box 2.

30. Upton to Catt, Nov. 17, 1909, DeVoe Collection, box 2.

31. Eaton to J. H. DeVoe, June 4, 1909, DeVoe Collection, box 2. See also, Fargo, "Mrs. Hercules," pp. 190–192, for support of this position. A letter from May to a woman who had made a negative comment about her wealth also exemplifies this point: ". . . if I happen to have money, I got it honestly and I will spend it as I please, without the suggestions of yourself or any of the class of women with which you drill. My only crime in the eyes of you and your ilk is the fact that I had brains enough to make money and brains enough not to allow a set of grafters to boodle me out of it under the guise of working for womans [*sic*] suffrage." See Hutton to Miss. B. A. Sapp, December 10, 1911, DeVoe Collection, box 3.

32. Fargo, "Mrs. Hercules," p. 202; Hutton to Hill, Oct. 21, 1909, Charles Gonser private papers.

33. Hutton to Hill, July 13, 1909, Charles Gonser private papers.

34. Hutton to Mrs. Leonia Brown, Sept. 23, 1909, Charles Gonser private papers. See also an article in a Portland paper by Mary Corner, Scrapbook 2, and the rough draft of a speech entitled "Washington Trust Your Women As Idaho Has Done," Oct. 1, 1908, Charles Gonser private papers.

35. Hutton to Mrs. Homer Hill, Oct. 21, 1909, Charles Gonser private papers.

36. Rough draft of a speech, untitled, June 4, 1909, Charles Gonser private papers (educated women); letter to the editor, *Spokesman-Review,* March 30, 1909, Scrapbook 3 (working women).

37. Scrapbook 2.

38. Hutton to Myrtle Weldon, no date, Charles Gonser private papers, and rough draft of "Washington Trust Your Women As Idaho Has Done," Oct. 1, 1908, Charles Gonser private papers. Although May did not think much of Theodore Roosevelt, she did enjoy using one of his favorite phrases (square deal). Letter to the editor, Sunday *Spokesman-Review,* no date, Charles Gonser private papers.

39. Letter to the editor, *Spokesman-Review,* Oct. 25, 1909, Charles Gonser private papers. See also Scrapbook 1, and rough draft of "Washington Trust Your Women As Idaho Has Done," Oct. 1, 1908.

40. Letter to the editor, Sunday *Spokesman-Review,* no date, Charles Gonser private papers. In a letter to the editor of the *Boston Post* in Washington, dated April 8, 1915, Scrapbook 5, May changed her position somewhat. Responding to the editor's comment that women would "purify pol-

itics," she stated: "Women as a class are no better than men and no one is more thoroughly acquainted with this fact than women." See also "Politics Need Mothering" from an Ohio paper, Scrapbook 1, and Aileen S. Kraditor, "Ideology of the Suffrage Movement," in Barbara Welter, ed., *The Woman Question in American History* (Hinsdale, Ill.: Dryden Press, 1973), pp. 83–92, for an elaboration of this idea.

41. Fargo, "Mrs. Hercules," p. 222; Abigail Scott Duniway, *Path Breaking: An Autobiographical History of the Equal Suffrage Movement in Pacific Coast States* (Portland: James, Kerns and Abbot Co., 1914), p. 243; Scrapbook 2 (May's influence). T. A. Larson, "Idaho's Role in America's Woman Suffrage Crusade," *Idaho Yesterdays* 18 (Spring 1975): 6, would disagree with these conclusions. He has stated: "Whether she did more harm than good in the Washington campaign is debatable."

42. Scrapbook 5. See also Hutton to Mrs. Minnie J. Reynolds, Dec. 15, 1910, and Hutton to Rev. Anna Shaw, Feb. 10, 1911, Charles Gonser private papers.

43. *Telegram,* May 7, 1912, Scrapbook 5.

44. Newspaper articles, May 20 and June 23, 1912, Scrapbook 5.

45. Scrapbook 5.

46. Hutton to Rev. Anna Shaw, Sept. 21, 1911, Charles Gonser private papers (California); Hutton to Mrs. M. M. Ross, March 14, 1912, Charles Gonser private papers, and Fargo, "Mrs. Hercules," p. 248.

47. *Spokane Daily Chronicle,* January 1914, Scrapbook, Hutton Settlement Management Collection, Spokane.

48. Spokane *Daily Chronicle,* Oct. 6 and Oct. 9, 1915, Scrapbook 6, and Montgomery, *Liberated Woman,* p. 128.

49. See Aileen S. Kraditor, *The Ideas of the Woman Suffrage Movement, 1890–1920* (Garden City, N.Y.: Doubleday, 1971) for a discussion of the tactics and ideology of twentieth-century suffragists.

50. *Town Crier,* Seattle, Oct. 9, 1915, Scrapbook 6.

51. Baltimore, June 23, 1912, Scrapbook 5 (Al); Scrapbook 1 (economic conditions).

52. Hutton to Al Hutton, Aug. 18, 1909, Charles Gonser private papers.

53. Hutton to L. B. Arkwright, Nov. 16, 1908, Charles Gonser private papers.

54. Hutton to Borah, Nov. 22, 1909, Charles Gonser private papers.

The Fight for Woman Suffrage and the Oregon Press

Lauren Kessler

"The press," said Rabbi Stephen Wise of Portland, "is a people's university that never shuts its doors." But the Oregon press of the late nineteenth and early twentieth centuries did not function as a university—a purveyor of ideas, a forum for serious discussion—and did indeed shut its doors to one of the most significant political questions of the day: the enfranchisement of women. The ideas, arguments, and goals of Oregon woman suffragists were consistently excluded from the mainstream press.

To determine if Oregon suffragists were able to gain access for their ideas in the pages of the state's newspapers,[1] this study looked for the presence of specific suffrage ideas in news stories, feature stories, editorials, and letters to the editor in thirteen Oregon newspapers[2] during the two months prior to each of the six votes on the amendment.[3] The six suffrage ideas were: (1) men and women were created equal; therefore, if suffrage is the natural right of men, it is also the natural right of women; (2) women's lack of the franchise subverts the equalitarian principles on which the United States was founded; (3) granting suffrage would correct the inequities (in occupational opportunities, education, and wages, for example) between the sexes; (4) women need the ballot for their own economic protection; (5) enfranchised women will benefit society; (6) the ballot will enhance the traditional values of women.[4]

Out of all the newspapers reviewed for each of the six time periods, only two granted all six suffrage ideas access. Both papers—the *Oregonian* and the *Oregon Journal*—served the state's most populous city, Portland, and both papers granted access only once, during the same period—the two months prior to the 1906 election.

It is essential to note that the campaign of 1906 presented a special case.[5] Twice before, in 1884 and 1900, suffrage advocates had succeeded in placing their amendment on the ballot. But in these days before the initiative and referendum, this was a lengthy and enervating process. It was necessary for both houses of the legislature to approve a ballot measure in two successive sessions (the legislature met every other year) before the measure could be put to a general

This chapter was published under the title "The Ideas of Woman Suffrage and the Mainstream Press" in the *Oregon Historical Quarterly* 84, no. 3 (1983): 257–75.

vote. Thus suffragists expended enormous amounts of time and energy persuading legislators merely to allow the amendment to reach the voters. By 1906 this had changed. The initiative and referendum permitted suffragists to place their amendment on the ballot after simply securing the required number of signatures. It could be argued that the suffragists had more energy to devote to the actual campaign now that they did not have to spend years lobbying in Salem. But speculation such as this is unnecessary, for the very nature of the 1906 campaign was different from the two that preceded it.

Under Abigail Scott Duniway's leadership, Oregon suffragists had worked quietly and, for the most part, out of the public eye. Duniway called her campaign style the "still hunt" because it shunned demonstrations, mass rallies, and other public displays, which she felt would serve only to "rouse the rabble" and motivate the opposition.[6] But the 1906 campaign was, in the parlance of the day, a "hurrah campaign." This public style of campaigning, the antithesis of Duniway's "still hunt," was the method used by the National American Woman Suffrage Association (NAWSA), and the Nationals were in charge of Oregon's 1906 campaign. In the summer of 1905, NAWSA held its annual convention in Portland, the first time in thirty-seven years that the organization had met west of the Mississippi. When the convention ended, many of the Nationals stayed in Oregon to organize the next year's campaign. They were hungry for a state victory and were convinced that Oregon would be next.[7] During the two months prior to the June 1906 election, the Nationals organized numerous meetings, rallies, conferences, and conventions, many of them held in Portland. Never before had the movement been so visible. Never before—and not again until 1912—had suffragists given journalists so much to report on.

In Portland, the 1906 campaign was unique in another way which deserves at least passing mention. Harvey Scott's *Oregonian*, long the undisputed leader of Oregon journalism, was then being seriously challenged by C. S. "Sam" Jackson's *Oregon Journal*. The *Oregonian* was almost a half-century old when the *Journal* began publishing in 1902. At first, the *Journal* posed no real threat to the venerable, politically omnipotent *Oregonian*, but by 1906 Jackson's upstart publication boasted a circulation in excess of 25,000 and was rivaling the *Oregonian* for advertising linage.[8] The two papers thus competed to outdo each other in covering the local political scene.

The access of woman suffrage ideas to these two newspapers must be seen in light of the special circumstances of the 1906 campaign and within the context of two competitors battling each other for readers in the state's most populous city. Although both newspapers did grant access to all six suffrage ideas, the *Oregonian* was, in fact, far less open to these ideas than the *Journal*. Not only did the *Oregonian* print less than one-third the total number of ideas the *Journal* did, but the *Oregonian*'s suffrage stories were shorter, more uniform (primarily news briefs and announcements compared with the *Journal*'s lengthy news and feature stories), and less prominently placed.

Two other papers took advantage of the high visibility campaign of 1906, although neither granted full access. Both the *Eugene Guard* and the *Pendleton East Oregonian* carried stories that included five of the six suffrage ideas during the campaign coverage. But none of the remaining nine discussed the issue of woman suffrage in any depth. Even during this most highly visible campaign run by experienced professionals who traveled throughout the state giving public lectures and organizing local groups, full access was denied suffrage ideas by all but the two Portland papers (see Table 1).

In only one other election campaign did suffrage ideas fare relatively well in terms of their access to the press—the final and victorious campaign of 1912. The coverage by both the *Oregon Journal* and the *Salem Statesman* during the two-month period made mention of all six suffrage ideas. In fact, the *Journal* gave the suffrage movement its most extensive coverage during the 1912 campaign. The *Oregonian,* the *Medford Mail-Tribune,* and the *Eugene Guard* all granted access to five of the six suffrage ideas, while the *Pendleton East Oregonian*—the only newspaper to consistently support suffrage since 1906—included at least a moderate number of suffrage stories and ideas. Access to the remaining newspapers was poor. The *Coos Bay Times* and the *Daily Astorian,* for example, published no suffrage stories during the two months. The *Albany Democrat* and the *Corvallis Gazette-Times* published one story apiece.

Although press coverage of the 1912 campaign did contain some bright spots, the majority of newspapers refrained from publishing or discussing the ideas of woman suffrage. This is not surprising in light of the press's history of excluding suffrage ideas, but it is surprising when one considers that the 1912 campaign presented, once again, a special case. The campaign was not as energetic or quite as public as that of 1906, but national leaders did tour Oregon and mass rallies were held in Portland and other cities. Suffrage clubs were in abundance, with most areas boasting at least one organized and active group. There were, in other words, "news pegs" on which reporters could hang their suffrage stories. Aside from such obvious pegs as a speaking tour made by automobile through downtown Portland by national suffrage leader Dr. Anna Howard Shaw, the 1912 campaign presented reporters and editors with at least two ad-

TABLE 1
Selected Oregon Newspapers[a] and Access of Suffrage Ideas,
1906 Campaign

Newspaper	Suffrage Stories	Suffrage Ideas	Diversity of Ideas[b]	Diversity of Sources[c]
Albany Democrat	7	0	0	0
Daily Astorian	1	2	1	2
Corvallis Gazette	0	0	0	0
Coos Bay News	4	3	3	2
Eugene Guard	10	9	5	4
Medford Mail	4	0	0	0
Oregon City Enterprise	3	2	2	1
Pendleton East Oregonian	18	14	5	3
Portland Oregon Journal	67	62	6	5
Portland Oregonian	37	21	6	5
Roseburg Review	5	3	1	1
Salem Statesman	9	4	3	3

[a]Microfilm for the *Baker Democrat* was unavailable for this period.

[b]Diversity of ideas is the measurement of the variety of ideas mentioned in newspaper coverage of the campaign. The highest possible score would be six, indicating that all six suffrage ideas were mentioned at least once during the two-month period.

[c]Diversity of sources is the measurement of the variety of sources linked to the suffrage ideas stated in the stories. Source categories were (1) Oregon State Equal Suffrage Association spokeswomen and members and suffrage "insiders" (those formally allied with the suffrage movement both in and outside the state) (2) government and public officials (including, but not limited to, mayors, governors, legislators, and other elected and appointed officials) (3) newspapers (any of the thirteen newspapers or any of their editors, reporters, or representatives) (4) nonsuffrage groups (organized local, state, and national groups not allied with the suffrage movement), and (5) individual commentators. The highest possible score would be five, indicating a diversity of sources.

ditional reasons—unique to this campaign—to cover the suffrage issue in some depth.

First, Oregon's two neighbors, Washington (1910) and California (1911), had each recently enfranchised their women. This gave the issue regional importance. Oregon, the state that had taken pride in championing such democratic measures as the initiative and referendum and the direct election of U.S. senators, was not lagging behind its western neighbors. Second, Abigail Scott Duniway, grande dame of the Oregon suffrage movement, was seventy-eight years old in 1912. Her enthusiasm remained, but her health was failing.[9] As a symbol, if not as an active leader, Duniway was a potent factor in 1912. She was an Oregon pioneer and a member of one of the first families of the state. She had almost singlehandedly organized the state suffrage movement in 1870. She had traveled by horseback, stagecoach, and riverboat throughout the Northwest, delivering speeches and organizing local clubs. Now she was old and ill. She might die, after forty-two years of tireless work, an unenfranchised woman. Surely this is the stuff of journalism. But even with a reasonably public campaign to report on, a salient regional issue to discuss, and a powerful symbol to evoke, the Oregon press denied access to the ideas of woman suffrage during the 1912 campaign (see Table 2).

If the Oregon press, by and large, granted little access to woman suffrage ideas during the "special case" campaigns of 1906 and 1912 when journalists had unusually good opportunities to deal with the issue in a substantive manner, how then did suffrage fare in the less than spectacular campaigns of 1884, 1900, 1908, and 1910? The picture here is bleak. Even in the absence of "reportable" events, the press should have felt the responsibility to discuss the suffrage issue in some depth. The equal suffrage amendment was on the ballot and of some concern to every Oregon voter. Certainly there is evidence to suggest that the press discussed other ballot issues during these election years (see discussion at end of chapter). Woman suffrage, however, was almost universally ignored (see Table 3).

A reader of the *Albany Democrat,* for example, who had read every issue of that newspaper in the two months prior to the 1884, 1900, 1908, and 1910 elections would have been exposed to a total of four suffrage stories and three suffrage ideas. A *Coos Bay Times* reader

TABLE 2
Oregon Newspapers and Access of Suffrage Ideas, 1912 Campaign

Newspaper	Total Suffrage Stories	Total Suffrage Ideas	Diversity of Ideas	Diversity of Sources
Albany Democrat	1	1	1	1
Daily Astorian	0	0	0	0
Baker Democrat	7	1	1	1
Corvallis Gazette-Times	1	0	0	0
Coos Bay Times	0	0	0	0
Eugene Guard	13	8	5	3
Medford Mail-Tribune	15	13	5	5
Oregon City Enterprise	10	7	3	3
Pendleton East Oregonian	18	12	4	3
Portland Oregon Journal	33	28	6	4
Portland Oregonian	27	27	5	5
Roseburg News	11	12	4	3
Salem Statesman	21	10	6	3

TABLE 3
Oregon Newspapers and Total Suffrage Ideas Gaining Access,
1884, 1900, 1908, and 1910 Campaigns

Newspaper	Total Suffrage Ideas Mentioned			
	1884	1900	1908	1910
Albany Democrat	0	0	3	0
Daily Astorian	3	1	0	0
Baker Democrat	*	0	1	0
Corvallis Gazette (*Gazette-Times*)	*	0	2	0
Coos Bay Times (*News*)	3	0	0	0
Eugene Guard	0	0	8	0
Medford Mail (*Mail-Tribune*)	a	0	0	1
Oregon City Enterprise	a	0	6	0
Pendleton East Oregonian	a	0	11	1
Portland Oregon Journal	b	b	9	3
Portland Oregonian	9	20	3	1
Roseburg Review (*News*)	0	0	9	0
Salem Statesman	9	7	0	4

ªMicrofilm unavailable for issues during these periods.
ᵇ*Oregon Journal* began publication in 1902.

would have had the same experience. The *Corvallis Gazette* (*Gazette-Times*) published a total of two stories containing two ideas during all four election campaigns. *Baker Democrat* readers would have found only one story with one idea. In Oregon City, readers of the *Enterprise* fared slightly better: their paper published four stories with six ideas. Readers in Medford, Roseburg, and Astoria would also have had a difficult time learning about woman suffrage through the pages of their newspapers.

It cannot be argued that Oregon voters were ignorant of the ideas of woman suffrage because their newspapers failed to discuss the issue. Certainly discussion could have taken place through less formal channels of communication. But regardless of the existence of other channels, it can be argued that it is the responsibility of a constitutionally protected press in a democratic society to inform voters of the issues they must vote on and to offer substantive discussion of these issues. On the issue of the enfranchisement of women, the Oregon press neglected this duty.

The question is why. The answers are complex and, in certain cases, speculative. They range from specific characteristics of the Oregon press to the general status of women in late nineteenth-century America.

Certain characteristics of the Oregon press during this period appear to have had a direct bearing on the lack of access afforded the ideas of woman suffrage. First, most of the newspapers were published in and designed to serve small communities. For the most part, small population correlated with limited access. Except for Salem and Portland, all cities of publication during the twenty-eight years studied had populations under ten thousand, with the bulk under five thousand. Newspapers serving the smaller cities gave far less access to the ideas of woman suffrage than those few serving larger audiences. It may have been that in the small towns of Oregon the lack of a rigid social structure allowed for informal discussion and debate among groups. That is, the issue of woman suffrage may have been discussed at the local dry goods store or at private social gatherings. Perhaps because an interpersonal, nonstructured forum for the exchange of ideas existed in small communities, the local newspaper did not feel compelled to offer itself as a public forum. In larger communities where the population was both diffused and segmented into distinct neighborhoods, informal discussion may have been more difficult and the press may have taken on the responsibility of presenting issues of importance to the community. While this explanation has some validity, it is probably more likely that the opposite situation existed: small towns, attracting and reinforcing a relatively homogeneous population, may have functioned as closed enclaves resistant to change and to nonconforming ideas. It is possible that discussion of woman suffrage ideas did not take place either formally or informally in these small communities. The cities of Portland and Salem, with their rapidly increasing populations, their cultural and economic diversity, and their regular exposure to new ideas via itinerant lecturers and visiting politicians, were necessarily less resistant to change. It is logical that the ideas of woman suffrage received their fullest discussion in the few newspapers that served the most diverse urban audiences.

A second characteristic of the Oregon press linked to access was the taking of an editorial stand either for or against woman suffrage. By endorsing or opposing the suffrage amendment, a paper at the very least signaled its recognition of the issue. This editorial recognition often meant that the paper included woman suffrage in its agenda of issues to be covered. In addition, editorials frequently stimulated letters to the editor, which in turn stimulated more letters to the editor, thus opening the way for a discussion of enfranchisement. The nine newspapers that editorially endorsed the suffrage amendment during one or more campaigns published an average of 9.81 ideas within any two-month period. The three papers editorially opposing suffrage published an average of 8.83 ideas. But the majority of newspapers took no editorial stand. In fact, every one of the papers studied failed to mention the suffrage amendment in the editorial columns during at least one, and as many as all six, campaigns. Those papers taking no editorial stand on the suffrage issue published an average of 3.04 ideas during any two-month period. Clearly, access would have been enhanced had the newspapers broached the issue in their editorial columns.

A third characteristic of the Oregon press of the late nineteenth century was the power of Harvey Whitefield Scott. Scott was more than just the editor of the state's largest and most influential newspaper. He was a molder of public opinion and a model for small town editors. And he was a staunch and vocal opponent of woman suffrage. Suffrage leader Abigail Scott Duniway called him "the meanest enemy of woman suffrage that the state possesses today."[10] Her vision was probably clouded by the fact that Scott was not only a virulent opponent but also her brother. Scott's opposition was not "mean"; in fact, within the intellectual context of the late nineteenth-century West, his arguments were well reasoned. Although he may not have been the meanest enemy of woman suffrage, he was almost certainly its most powerful opponent. As editor of the *Oregonian,* Scott communicated with the largest newspaper audience in the state. His editorials were almost certainly read by hinterland editors. Small town editors of Republican newspapers looked to the *Oregonian* for guidance on political issues of the day and often modeled their thinking after Scott's. He was, in press historian George Turnbull's words, "the schoolmaster of the Oregon press."[11] He not only educated his readers, he helped educate an entire generation of Oregon editors.

It is clear that Scott had power beyond his editorship of the *Oregonian.* The *Corvallis Times,* a Democratic newspaper, grudgingly credited him with transforming Oregon from a Democratic to a Republican state in twenty-five years.[12] He has been credited with delivering Oregon to McKinley in 1896, a year when Bryanism was a powerful force in the West.[13] The *Providence Journal* (Rhode Island) called him "the leading figure of the Pacific Coast." The *New York Tribune* said he was "a force to be reckoned with in Oregon life." The *Salt Lake Telegram* commented that "his voice has been the most potent ever raised within [Oregon's] borders."[14] "Oregonians," wrote one historian, "drank deeply of Mr. Scott's intelligence."[15] Scott himself was well aware of his position of influence. As one of his *Oregonian* colleagues wrote: "Mr. Scott often remarked, when efforts were made to stimulate in him the spirit of political ambition, that he would not 'step down' from the editorship of the Oregonian into the United States Senate. And this was no boast; for the editorship of the Oregonian, as carried by Mr. Scott, was truly a higher place, a place of wider responsibilities and of larger powers than any official place possibly attainable by a man geographically placed as Mr. Scott was."[16]

Scott's journalistic and political influence in Oregon is a fact. The extent to which this man may have hindered the access of woman suffrage ideas not only to his own newspaper but to other Oregon journals as well is not and can never be known. It is, however, reasonable to assume that Scott played an important role in the denial of access.

The more general explanations for lack of access have to do with definitions of news. It is, for example, possible that newspapers are— and have always been—event oriented rather than issue oriented. It would follow that, because Oregon suffragists did not organize a sufficient number of reportable events, they and their ideas were denied access to the press. It is true that during the 1906 campaign, which abounded with demonstrations and public lectures, more attention was paid to woman suffrage and more suffrage ideas were communicated in the press than during any other campaign. But even during this most highly visible statewide campaign, only two of the thirteen newspapers granted complete access. During the energetic, event-filled campaign of 1912, the Oregon press did no better. Although the other four campaigns were reasonably quiet, following Duniway's "still hunt" strategy, it is clear that suffragists planned and executed a wide variety of public events, including lecture tours, conventions, and banquets. But even in the absence of *any* planned suffrage activities, each newspaper was presented with six events of irrefutable statewide importance: the six votes on the suffrage amendment.

Another possibility is that, in the words of one historian of the Oregon movement, "woman suffrage arguments, either for or against, had after a while ceased to be news."[17] In other words, news is what is new. Certainly one can see how reporters, readers, and even the suffragists themselves would have tired of presenting the same ideas and arguments for forty-two years. But, if ideas were excluded because they became old and shopworn, one might reasonably expect access for the ideas when they were new or at least relatively "young"— that is, during the first campaign of 1884. But in fact far more ideas can be found in the press coverage of the last campaign of 1912— when the ideas were four decades old—than in coverage of the first.

If suffrage ideas were excluded from the press even when these ideas could have reasonably been considered newsworthy and even when suffragists presented the press with a variety of reportable events, perhaps a more satisfactory explanation for lack of access lies with who was making the news rather than with what was considered newsworthy. One contemporary critic of the mass media suggests that "what is or is not news on any occasion depends on who is talking to whom."[18] When those with power and influence talk, the press listens. The activities and ideas of those with power are news. The activities and the ideas of nineteenth-century women—as a group denied political power, economic influence, and legitimate status outside the home—are not news. This may be particularly true when the powerless address their remarks to the powerless (when women talk to women). Two specific observations lend credence to this explanation.

First, the state press, even when it did report on suffrage activities, did not listen to what Oregon suffragists were saying. The "enfranchised women will benefit society" idea, which dominated the coverage of all six campaigns, was precisely the argument Oregon suffragists avoided mentioning in their speeches and campaign literature. The link between enfranchisement and prohibition had hurt the Oregon movement in its early years and had caused trouble in Washington as well. Duniway's battle with the WCTU wing of the state suffrage association in the late 1880s and her run-in with the anti-suffrage liquor lobby prior to the 1906 election made her wary of using an argument that linked woman's enfranchisement to a particular reform. In fact, Oregon suffragists were not the source for most of the mentions of this "expediency" idea. State suffragists were talking about natural rights and the equality of the sexes while the press was talking about woman's role as a purifier of society. The image of the enfranchised woman as the nation's housekeeper may have been in keeping with some conception of "true womanhood," but it was decidely not what Oregon suffragists were trying to communicate.

Second, the access afforded suffrage ideas during the campaigns of 1906 and 1912, when the largest number of ideas were included, can be attributed not to the activities of Oregon woman suffragists but rather to influential outsiders. In 1906 it was the presence of the eastern NAWSA workers that stimulated newspaper coverage of the movement. Although female, NAWSA members like Dr. Anna Howard Shaw had both national reputations and male friends in high places. In 1912, suffrage ideas were catapulted into view when politicians, businessman, and clergy finally allied themselves with the movement and began mouthing the arguments woman suffragists had been expounding upon for four decades. It took outsiders to make the woman suffrage movement worthy of substantial coverage by the press. For the most part, the activities of insiders—Oregon women suffragists—were perceived by the press as less newsworthy.

Although both specific characteristics of the Oregon press and operational definitions of news played a part in the denial of access, another larger concern must be examined: the role of the newspaper in late nineteenth-century Oregon. One cannot criticize the press for failing to present "a representative picture of the constituent groups in society"[19] if editors did not see this as their function. If newspapers of the time were not concerned with monitoring their respective environments and reporting on the activities and issues within their readership areas, then to fault them for failing to do so would be an error of "presentism."[20] Running what were essentially one-man operations, most small town editors did not have the time, or perhaps lacked the perspective, to comment on what they saw as the responsibilities of a newspaper. But *Oregonian* editor Harvey Scott, *Oregon Journal* editor Sam Jackson, and *East Oregonian* editor Bert Huffman did leave behind statements, and it appears from this limited evidence that they saw the press as having wide responsibilities.

"A great journal," wrote Harvey Scott, "is a universal newsgatherer and a universal truth-teller. It cannot afford to have any aims which are inconsistent with its telling the truth."[21] Scott further defined the responsibility of a newspaper by saying that its excellence "depends on it being an expert, efficient purveyor of each day's occurrences."[22] Clearly, Scott defined a "free and responsible press" in terms consistent with the Hutchins Commission guidelines proposed almost one hundred years later (see note 19). Sam Jackson, editor of the *Pendleton East Oregonian* and later of the *Oregon Journal*, wrote: "A newspaper must be public spirited . . . it must ever diffuse knowledge."[23] Jackson, then, was not only concerned with "show[ing] all the life and activity possible,"[24] but with what Harold Lasswell called "equivalent enlightenment"—passing on knowledge to the reading public. Bert Huffman, Jackson's handpicked successor at the *East Oregonian*, went a step further when he wrote: "The newspaper, like the torchbearer exploring the cave, should walk a step in advance of the crowd following."[25] While it is true that the remarks of three editors cannot be generalized into a statement of how all Oregon editors perceived the role of their newspapers, there is other evidence suggesting that editors were concerned with monitoring their environments. For example, all the newspapers studied reported on a variety of issues of statewide and local concern: government corruption, the initiative and referendum, the direct election of senators, local option, civic improvements, education, and sanitation, to name a few. In addition, most newspapers granted access to a variety of local groups involved in the political, cultural, and social life of their communities. But these same newspapers excluded suffragists and suffrage ideas from their pages. It appears that most editors were interested in discussing signficiant issues and reporting on the activities and concerns of local groups, and their denial of access to the suffragists must be seen in this light.

Although the Oregon press can be faulted for shirking its responsibility regarding a full and substantive treatment of the issue of woman suffrage, the denial of access can also be evaluated in terms of the larger societal context. If the press is a mirror of society, then perhaps the exclusion of woman suffrage ideas reflected the norms and values of the society. On the most fundamental level, political scientist John Roche argues persuasively that the concepts of individual liberty and the marketplace of ideas are and have always been myths.[26] American society and the American press have never been open to a diversity of ideas. Ideas and beliefs inconsistent with those held by community leaders have rarely been tolerated. If, as Roche believes, American society operated as a series of closed enclaves from which divergent ideas and nonconformists were routinely excluded, then perhaps Oregon society of the late nineteenth and early twentieth centuries can be seen as a closed enclave and the exclusion of woman suffrage ideas as merely part of a larger intolerance. While this explanation is enticing, it ignores the fact that a number of status quo threatening ideas were tolerated, as least to the extent that they were included in the press, during this time. Both the direct election of senators and the initiative and referendum amendments to the Oregon constitution were direct threats to the dominance of political party "regulars"— men who were often powerful community leaders and even newspaper editors—yet these ideas were discussed fully in the Oregon press. Local option, a threat not only to the powerful state liquor wholesalers association but also to the hundreds of hop growers in Marion, Polk, Linn, and Benton counties, was discussed fully in the press. Seen in this context, the exclusion of woman suffrage ideas becomes, if not unique, at least unusual, forcing one to look beyond Roche's "myth of libertarianism" explanation.

For it was this most vital of women's issues, enfranchisement, that was excluded from the press, not just any divergent idea. It was not merely antilibertarianism at work, but sexism. Lasswell writes that "the most serious threat to effective communication stems from community values like power, wealth and respect."[27] Those with power and wealth, those who commanded respect, were men.[28] Men controlled the government and men controlled the newspapers. Woman suffrage posed a powerful and immediate threat to one overwhelming community value: male dominance. It is entirely possible that male editors purposefully excluded substantive discussion of woman suffrage—that is, stood in the way of effective communication—simply because they were men threatened by the idea of female equality.[29] If representation in the media signifies social existence, then exclusion signifies nonexistence or, as one contemporary critic put it, "symbolic annihilation."[30] Although Oregon women were, in a political sense, "nonpersons," they did exist and they did fight long and hard for their rights. By trivializing their concerns, by excluding their ideas, male editors denied the social existence of woman suffragists just as the Oregon constitution denied their political existence.

But denial of access is not only "symbolic annihilation," it is an ultimate form of social control. Those who have the power to define reality and set the social agenda—those in control of the media of communication—hold the key to social control. One critic has argued that the media purposefully promote passivity, which precludes widespread participation and ensures maintenance of the status quo.[31] But it is more subtle than that. The media need not promote passivity; they need only exclude certain ideas—ideas which threaten to change the status quo. If "equivalent enlightenment"—the sharing of knowledge between expert and layman—is the key to informed participation as Lasswell believes, then denial of access, a barrier to equivalent enlightenment, may result in uninformed participation or no participation at all. More simply put, the Wobblies believed that "the power to transmit ideas is the power to change the world." Is not, then, the power to *omit* ideas the power to keep the world the same? In the interests of preserving male hegemony and maintaining the status quo, Oregon editors symbolically annihilated woman suffragists by denying their ideas access to the press. Whether this denial was purposeful and vindictive or merely an unconscious reflection of the way men perceived women, the result was the same: the Oregon press created a barrier to social change by restricting the flow of ideas.

Notes

1. For a full discussion of the concept of access—the openness of the press to the ideas of constituent groups—see Lauren Kessler, "A Siege of the Citadels: Access of Woman Suffrage Ideas to the Oregon Press, 1884–1912," Ph.D. diss., University of Washington, 1980, chap. 1. For the purpose of this study, access was operationally defined as the simultaneous achievement

of three conditions: (1) the mentioning of woman suffrage ideas with relative frequency within any two-month period, (2) the presence of all six suffrage ideas in press coverage within any two-month period, and (3) the linking of suffrage ideas to a variety of sources outside the suffrage movement, suggesting that woman suffrage had become an acceptable and legitimate topic for debate and discussion.

2. The thirteen Oregon newspapers selected were the largest circulation newspapers that existed in the most populous Oregon towns of the time. All parts of the state were represented: the north and south coasts, mid and lower Willamette Valley, southern Oregon, and eastern Oregon. The selected papers were the *Albany Democrat,* the *Daily Astorian,* the *Baker Democrat,* the *Corvallis Gazette* (after 1909, the *Gazette-Times*), the *Eugene Guard,* the *Coos Bay Times* (when unavailable, the *Coos Bay News*), the *Medford Mail* (after 1909, the *Mail-Tribune*), the *Oregon City Enterprise,* the *Pendleton East Oregonian,* the Portland *Oregonian* and *Oregon Journal,* the *Roseburg Review* (when unavailable, the *Roseburg Evening News*), and the *Salem Statesman.* The University of Oregon library has the most complete microfilm collection of state newspapers and most of those listed above can be found there. The Oregon Historical Society, Portland, and the State Library, Salem, both have scattered holdings.

3. From Abigail Scott Duniway's correspondence to her son Clyde and to national suffrage leaders and from the details concerning the suffrage campaigns found in her *Path Breaking* (Portland: James, Kerns and Abbot Company, 1914), it was clear that Oregon suffragists began their campaigns in earnest from six to eight weeks prior to each election. Duniway, when she had control of the campaigns, attempted to keep them quiet until the last possible moment in order not to arouse and antagonize antisuffragists and other special interest groups opposing woman's enfranchisement. For this reason, the selected newspapers were analyzed for a period of eight weeks prior to each election.

4. The ideas were culled from manuscript sources including the Abigail Scott Duniway papers, held by David C. Duniway, Salem, Oregon; the Eva Emery Dye papers, the Bethenia Owens-Adair papers, and the Oregon State Equal Suffrage Association records, all at the Oregon Historical Society, Portland, Oregon; editorials in Duniway's prosuffrage weekly *New Northwest* and two other Portland-based prosuffrage newspapers, *Pacific Empire* and *Woman's Tribune* (microfilm and scattered hard copies available at Oregon Historical Society, Portland); and suffrage campaign literature and several general histories of the movement.

5. For a discussion of the 1906 campaign and its coverage by the *Oregonian* and *Oregon Journal,* see Lauren Kessler, "Sam Jackson, Harvey Scott and the 1906 Campaign for Woman Suffrage in Oregon: A Study of Newspaper Bias," paper presented to the West Coast Journalism Historians Conference, Berkeley, California, March 1980.

6. Duniway, *Path Breaking,* p. 106.

7. National American Woman Suffrage Association, *Proceedings of the*

37th Annual Convention of NAWSA (Warren, Ohio: The Tribune Co., 1905), pp. 89–90.

8. *American Newspaper Annual Directory* (Philadelphia: N. W. Ayer and Son, 1907), p. 727.

9. According to her own account in *Path Breaking,* Duniway was bedridden during most of the 1912 campaign work.

10. *New Northwest,* June 12, 1874.

11. George Turnbull, *History of Oregon Newspapers* (Portland: Binfords and Mort, 1939), p. 133.

12. *Corvallis Times,* Mar. 9, 1903, quoted in *Portrait and Bibliographic Record of the Willamette Valley, Oregon* (Chicago: Chapman Publishing Co., 1903), p. 72.

13. One of Scott's major editorial battles was against the free coinage of silver. It began in 1877 and culminated in 1896 when it was "universally admitted that Republicans then carried the gold standard issue in Oregon through the efforts of Mr. Scott." See Alfred Holman, "Harvey Scott, Editor," *Oregon Historical Quarterly* 14, no. 2 (1913): 111–13.

14. All are excerpts from obituaries quoted in Leslie M. Scott, "Tributes to Mr. Scott's Achievements in Journalism," in Harvey W. Scott, *History of the Oregon Country* (Cambridge, Mass.: Riverside Press, 1924), 1: 110–12.

15. Lee M. Nash, "Scott of the Oregonian: The Editor as Historian," *Oregon Historical Quarterly* 70, no. 3 (1969): 202.

16. Holman, "Scott, Editor," p. 130.

17. Martha Francis Montague, "The Woman Suffrage Movement in Oregon," (M.A. thesis, University of Oregon, 1930), p. 97.

18. Harvey L. Molotch, "The News of Women and the Work of Men," in Gaye Tuchman, Arlene Kaplan Daniels, and James Benet, eds., *Hearth and Home: Images of Women in the Mass Media* (New York: Oxford University Press, 1978), p. 178.

19. This is one of several guidelines for press responsibility proposed by the Commission on Freedom of the Press, *A Free and Responsible Press* (Chicago: University of Chicago Press, 1947), pp. 21–28.

20. David Hackett Fischer, *Historian's Fallacies* (New York: Harper and Row, 1970), pp. 135–40.

21. From a March 15, 1879, editorial by Scott quoted in Leslie M. Scott, "Review of the Writings of Mr. Scott," introduction in vol. 1 of Scott, *History,* p. 107.

22. From one of Scott's editorials quoted in William Swing, "Combative Oregonian Editor Harvey Scott," *Sunday Oregonian,* Dec. 4, 1960, p. 44.

23. From a Nov. 23, 1897 editorial by Jackson quoted by Gordon Macnab, *A Century of News and People in the East Oregonian* (Pendleton: East Oregonian Publishing Co., 1975), p. 92.

24. C. S. Jackson to Fred Lockley, July 31, 1902, C. S. Jackson correspondence, Special Collections, University of Oregon. Lockley, a young reporter at the *East Oregonian,* took over some editorial responsibilities at the paper when Jackson became editor of the *Oregon Journal.* Lockley later

moved to Portland and wrote a regular column for the *Journal* for many years.

25. Macnab, *Century of News,* p. 120.

26. John P. Roche, "American Liberty: An Examination of the Tradition of Freedom," in *Shadow and Substance* (New York: Macmillan, 1964).

27. Harold D. Lasswell, "The Structure and Function of Communications in Society," in Wilbur Schramm and Donald Roberts, eds., *The Process and Effects of Mass Communication* (Urbana: University of Illinois Press, 1972), p. 95.

28. Women were respected for their piety, purity, and domesticity and not as citizens of and contributors to public life according to Barbara Welter, "The Cult of True Womanhood: 1820–1860," in Thomas R. Frazier, ed., *The Underside of American History* (New York: Harcourt Brace Jovanovich, 1971), pp. 206–28. Julie Roy Jeffrey makes essentially the same point in *Frontier Women: The Trans-Mississippi West, 1840–1880* (New York: Hill and Wang, 1979).

29. One thoughtful historian has speculated that turn-of-the-century men were threatened by female equality because men's own roles were uncertain and they "depended on women to mask the ambiguities in their definitions of manliness" at a time when the "strenuous life" was disappearing and cooperation, not individualism, was being stressed. See Peter G. Filene, *Him/Her/Self* (New York: Harcourt Brace Jovanovich, 1974), p. 123.

30. Media critic Gaye Tuchman contends that the media's condemnation, trivialization, or lack of attention to a certain group means the symbolic annihilation of that group; that is, the group ceases to exist (or never exists at all) in the minds of the audience. See Gaye Tuchman, "The Symbolic Annihilation of Women by the Mass Media," in Tuchman et al., eds., *Hearth and Home,* p. 3–38.

31. Herbert I. Schiller, *The Mind Managers* (Boston: Beacon Press, 1973), p. 29.

Part 2

WORK

Women have always worked in their own homes, at cleaning and child raising, sewing and entertaining, nursing, supervising and organizing. These responsibilities did not disappear when, in addition, by need or by choice, women took on occupations outside the domestic realm. In this collection, we look at some examples of Northwest women engaged in paid work. Among these are an in-depth examination of the work in political office and a study of the defense work done by women during World War II. Like farming and journalism—other occupations we encounter in this book—political office holding and heavy industry have been dominated by males. Such woman-dominated fields as nursing, teaching, clerical work, prostitution, hairdressing, cannery work, and domestic work would reveal different patterns. To study these patterns in the Northwest, we must await further scholarship. Research has been done, however, on women's work of another sort: volunteer work. Pervasive among women nationally, volunteer work offered them a unique opportunity to make their influence felt in the public realm.

Volunteer work was performed by countless Northwest women, but it is seldom accorded distinction, because—like private housekeeping—it brings no monetary reward. But women who were unwelcome in business and professions often spent their ingenuity on benevolent, temperance, and Grange associations. Karen J. Blair's article, "The Limits of Sisterhood: The Woman's Building in Seattle,

1908–1921," enumerates many of the organizations that turn-of-the-century women founded throughout the state of Washington, from study clubs to nursing associations. Through groups such as these, women initiated a staggering range of projects—public libraries, parks, vocational education, and street lights, to name a few. Their effectiveness refuted the popular myth that women could not cooperate. In fact, their many programs necessitated that they teach each other to research problems, raise funds, make reports, write speeches and deliver them forcefully in public, petition and lobby legislators in Salem and Olympia, and shape public opinion, in order to bring about the changes they desired.

The story of women's clubs also documents members' success at strengthening a woman's sphere with its own values, skills, and rewards. The pride of women in their unique culture is reflected in Blair's account of the efforts of the Washington State Federation of Women's Clubs to showcase women's accomplishments in a Woman's Building at the Alaska-Yukon-Pacific Exposition of 1909. Clubwomen planned the building to display female cultural achievements—songs, watercolors, needlework, and poetry—while providing hospitality for the women's groups that convened in Seattle. They made available nutritious meals in an attractive place for a modest price; they also offered child care by trained nurses, so that mothers could enjoy the exhibits unencumbered while their children played in comfort. To do all this, clubwomen tapped their new-found organizing talents—coercing the legislators to fund the structure, collaborating with University of Washington women to sponsor the building's maintenance after the fair for use by campus women, and uniting women on campus to raise money for the furnishings.

Their success had two important results for women of

Seattle. For young women on campus, the building provided a place to practice the cooperation and sisterhood
their elders had already experienced. Here they met, debated, socialized, and initiated and carried out projects.
For the clubwomen, however, a different purpose was
achieved: the recruitment of young members for their
causes, who would perpetuate their public reform efforts.

All goals were squelched after 1916, when the university assigned the building for other purposes and refused
to offer women another in its place, despite many efforts
by campus and community women to plead its usefulness.
Although women had originally formed female alliances
in response to their exclusion from the male-dominated
public world, they had come to value the political and
emotional advantages of a sisterly support system. Thus
these Northwest women now suffered deep disappointment, feeling that the foundation for their personal and
public advancement was undermined by the loss of the
building.

The administrators who turned a deaf ear to arguments
in favor of a meeting space were aided by a new popular
belief: the concept of the "new woman." Among women
activists themselves, this new belief overrode the presumably outmoded concept of networking strategies among
women for their progress. In an enlightened era, the new
woman was to find easy entry to the previously all-male
worlds of politics, business, and the professions. It was
assumed that she no longer required the friendships, the
schooling in techniques provided by her peers, in order to
use ballot box, educational institutions, or other avenues
to her own advancement. In fact, the absence of the "old-
fashioned" alliances hampered women's ability to challenge remaining inequities, and contributed to the fifty-
year silence of the women's movement. Not until the

building was restored in 1983, as the Women's Information Center, did the campus see a physical space devoted to facilitation of women's strength through cooperation. The restored building is a symbol of the contemporary revival of "women helping women."

Let us turn to the Northwest women who have worked outside the home for a paycheck. In addition to a plenitude of women who have worked as waitresses, salespersons, educators, and social workers, the region has not been wanting in examples of successful woman lawyers, judges, and physicians. Mayor Bertha Knight Landes's career, however, was the culmination of generations of women's dreams. Seattle led the nation, in 1926, as the first large American city to elect a woman as mayor. Doris H. Pieroth's portrait of Mayor Landes reveals that the first generation of women officeholders relied on skills, experiences and beliefs acquired in the woman's sphere. While Landes benefited from a college education and a spouse supportive of her public life, her life pattern resembled that of most middle-class women. That is, of primary importance were husband, children, and church. An interest in and a talent for volunteer work led her gradually to climb within women's organizations, taking higher and higher office in larger and grander organizations, until she presided over the entire Seattle Federation of Women's Clubs. There, like most clubwomen of her day, she defended woman's involvement in civic reform as "municipal housekeeping," or the proper and logical extension of her role in the domestic sphere. For almost a century, multitudes of feminists had asserted that the differences between men and women should serve as the basis for woman's involvement in public life, not her banishment from it. Domestically cultivated talent, perceptions, and knowledge could lend special, valuable insights to public issues and problems. That her peers catapulted Landes to the Seattle City Council and mayoralty was unusual for its time, but her belief in a woman's special viewpoint was not.

Mayor Landes promised to represent women's values in government, and to transform government by women's presence. This made it inevitable that she stand for decency, enforcement of prohibition, regulation of cabarets and dance halls, civic service, improved recreation, municipal ownership of utilities, city council government, and opposition to corruption. Pieroth suggests that Landes's very firmness on these issues, and her refusal to compromise for political gains, ensured her failure to win reelection. Women's vision of an honest operation of a real democracy ultimately could not undermine the entrenched system. Landes's failure to implement and protect her positions brought grave disappointment to newly enfranchised women.

The Great Depression of the 1930s inhibited many of women's hopes for full participation and wide influence, but World War II opened doors to new opportunities in the marketplace. Now all hands were needed to produce for the defense industry, and Northwest women were suddenly encouraged to relegate family responsibilities to second place and take up war-related tasks. Where they had previously been concentrated in low-paying, low-status occupations, now they were invited to work in more lucrative fields, heretofore almost exclusively the province of men. Karen Beck Skold addresses this phenomenon in the Portland area, where three Kaiser Corporation shipyards hired women in great numbers. Skold raises questions about their training, duties, motivations, obstacles, satisfactions, and drawbacks, and explores their wages, hours, and the conditions under which they worked in

wartime. How did their experience compare with that of
men in the workplace? Did they enjoy cooperation, or did
they suffer harassment by male colleagues? How did they
balance wage-earning with responsibilities at home?

Skold describes the widespread participation by women
who came to represent, during 1942–45, a significant
portion of the overall labor force in the shipyards. Attracted by high wages, better jobs than had been available
before, a chance to provide patriotic service to their country and to try new opportunities, they equaled men in productivity and hoped to continue their work after the war
emergency was over. Skold praises the high quality daycare centers available in Portland, Vanport, and Vancouver, which suggested a new social willingness to provide
facilities for women who had responsibility for children.

For all the positive experiences of this wartime period,
however, sexism by no means disappeared at the workplace. Women were overrepresented in unskilled positions, as laborers, helpers, and welders, and women over
thirty-five had to resign themselves to sweeping and other
menial jobs. Women were underrepresented as journeymen in most crafts, and Oregon saw only one loftlady,
three woman riggers, and one woman wiring on the 50
foot masts of Liberty ships. Ultimately, the aberrant nature of women's swift career and wage advancement became apparent, at the war's end. Women were rapidly dismissed and sent back to the home or to traditionally female
wage-earning occupations, as men returned from the military to reclaim "male" jobs.

The Limits of Sisterhood:
The Woman's Building in Seattle, 1908–1921

Karen J. Blair

A modest, two-story wooden structure has stood on the University of Washington campus in Seattle since 1909. Known as the Woman's Building, it served to nurture cooperation among all women at the Alaska-Yukon-Pacific Exposition and then, more important, between female students at the school and the community's clubwomen. In 1916, however, female separatism and the sisterhood that it cultivated lost the battle to a new ideology—women's equality with men in the larger society. Only seven years after its inception, the space was assigned for other purposes and no facility was substituted by the institution to serve such an outmoded goal. The history of the emergence and downfall of the Woman's Building serves to illustrate a national phenomenon of the era, that of women's efforts to halt, in colleges and all society, the demise of respect for women's collaborative efforts. Here is simply one example of the broad and unsuccessful effort to stay the erosion of sisterhood.

Mature women, since the late nineteenth century, had formed their own clubs and societies in reaction to their exclusion from the male-dominated public sphere.[1] They worked together, despite male criticism that club projects caused members to neglect their domestic responsibilities;[2] and they learned the significance of sisterly cooperation in effecting change. Club members consciously courted college women by establishing women's centers where the upcoming generation could practice cooperation, learning early to value it and carry it into adulthood. The perpetuation of the multitudinous successes of clubwomen depended on their recruitment of the younger "new woman" of the day, but these youth were attracted instead to broader changes that seemed to herald an end to women's enforced isolation. New permission to bicycle and dance, attend coeducational universities, and embark on a wide range of careers surely signaled an end to barriers and forecast true equality between the sexes. Underestimating the importance of sisterhood in preparing them for life, the "new women" no longer embraced the values and beliefs of their mothers. This article chronicles the failure of the associated womanhood to combat, in the emerging generations, the supremacy of the newer ideology of integration.

This chapter has been published in *Frontiers* 8 (Spring 1985): 45–52.

Seattle women at the turn of the century were not unlike their counterparts all over America in seeking to wrest some social, political, and economic power from the men who dominated public life. Despite creative and extensive efforts, however, they were frustrated in their attempts to win the vote and were held back from achieving high positions within influential institutions. Instead, they found their greatest success in creating a separate women's sphere from which they built a collective pride in women's special strengths. It was also in this "women only" environment that they addressed problems affecting themselves and their loved ones, and brought pressure for change.

Women implemented this strategy in a great variety of women's clubs. While they seemed to endorse the popular feeling that women and men possessed more differences than similarities, club members nevertheless challenged the widely held Victorian notion that woman's place was in the home. They insisted that women's moral, domestic, nurturing, and sensitive qualities should also be exercised outside the home. They called this activity "municipal housekeeping" to suggest it was not so far from their usual role; historians have labeled similar efforts at public improvement "progressive reform" when it was men who were seeking civic change. To become reformers, clubwomen nurtured a pride in the moral superiority and sensitivity that women were said to possess. Clubs served as the locus and the vehicle for sisterly cooperation in accomplishing their goals. They also succeeded in developing new skills in their members, such as researching and writing papers, delivering them publicly, running meetings, and organizing committees. More than a few members gained experience in securing speakers, writing publicity, raising money, lobbying legislators, and circulating petitions. All of these were abilities that had lain underdeveloped in women who had been isolated at home, running households and raising families.[3]

In turn-of-the-century Seattle, great numbers of mature women were already comfortable and experienced in women's club strategies for broadening women's influence in society. Some of them rallied to initiate a special woman's building at the upcoming international fair of 1909. Their plan introduced three significant concepts to the region's associated womanhood. First, it emphasized the importance of a physical structure where interaction between women could take place. Such a structure would legitimate sisterhood by enabling it to occur in a formal setting. Second, it initiated a partnership between young women and their older sisters as a means both to a broader base for older women and to provide new guidance, almost an apprenticeship, for the younger women who would one day become leaders of this women's movement. Finally, the plan legitimated women's efforts to collaborate in order to attain influence despite their exclusion from official channels of power in society.

Speaking for her organization of ninety clubs representing 2,800 members, the president of the Washington State Federation of Women's Clubs, Lena Erwin Allen of Spokane, presented the proposal for the Woman's Building to the State Fair Commissioners in the spring of 1908. She asked that the legislature fund a woman's reception and display center for the 1909 summer exposition. Like other structures planned for the fair, it would be permanent. It was "the wish of Washington women that the building at the close of the fair be donated to the University of Washington for the exclusive use of the young women of that institution."[4] The fair could leave a legacy to the university women of the state, a place as well as a purpose for future leaders who would struggle to expand women's role in society.

Allen's position in Washington was a powerful one. She represented a strong network of white, middle-class, and upper-class mature women—mothers as well as career women—who had formed a network of voluntary associations. More important, she headed a federation that was already known for achieving considerable success in its work. Since its founding in 1896, the federation had used its collective strength to convince the governor to appoint a woman physician to the State Hospital for the Insane. In collaboration with the Spokane County Association of Nurses, it had successfully lobbied for state registration of nurses.[5] It had also worked for an eight-hour labor law for women, permission for salesgirls to sit while working in stores, the appointment of one grade-school teacher to the commission to select textbooks, and the selection of two women on the school boards of every large city in the state. No aspect of women's rights escaped the attention of federation members. Better conditions for female prisoners, scholarships for girls, and a woman on the Board of Regents at the University of Washington were other issues for which the federation agitated. Certainly men also benefited from the reforms that Allen's organization deemed essential. Public libraries, conservation, and pure food laws brightened the world for both sexes of all ages.[6] In the absence of overt political rights, such as voting, holding office, or serving on juries, such actions demonstrated women's commitment to the creation of effective alternatives that would have an impact on society and their own roles within it. In short, limited access to official channels of power bred ingenious new routes to change for women.

Clubwomen were beginning to see that they could ensure continued success for their efforts by cultivating public enthusiasm for their projects. Thus the Washington State Federation of Women's Clubs thought that the Woman's Building at the 1909 fair on the University of Washington's new campus should be erected to assist in furthering their beliefs. For the duration of the fair, it could publicize the special talents of women by displaying women's work, lauding women's achievements, providing services for female fair-goers, housing receptions for women's organizations, and exposing city residents and tourists to the work of the national sisterhood. It would stand as a living monument to achievements in women's sphere. Afterward, the building could be turned over to the women students. Here, club members knew, female college students could learn a lesson untaught in the official university curriculum. Here would be a designated place for instilling in youth the beliefs that clubwomen possessed. Girls could associate to develop confidence in their special abilities and perpetuate change within a male-dominated society through collaboration with others of their sex. Thus federation officers contacted their legislators in Olympia and lobbied for funding to erect the Woman's Building.

Many university women rallied around the club members' plan. Students were as interested in promoting sisterhood within a woman's sphere on campus as the older women were in perpetuating it in their clubs. Certainly their dean of women was willing to embrace the idea. After all, her very job description verified her responsibility "to help in the women's work for Washington, to put students in touch with the big women's movements going on throughout the state."[7] Dean Annie Howard realized that in all likelihood this building would stimulate the prescribed interaction between women students and women's organizations outside academia.

Dean Howard had cause for alarm regarding women's loss of status on campus. Recent expansion, in an effort to modernize the institution, had attracted more male instructors and students than female. The 1878 peak in women faculty (80 percent) was reversed by 1910, when only 7 of 115 teachers were women. A rapid decline in women graduate students had begun after 1896, when they had filled 90 percent of the places. After that, the remaining women teachers and students were channeled into three fields—home economics, nursing, and physical education; 37 percent of the women faculty taught in these areas by 1910.[8] Although a great many women regarded these programs as crucial in establishing dignified professions, a woman's center would be welcome as a gathering place to recoup and increase women's lost status.

Howard promoted the Woman's Building by sponsoring a tea in the women's dormitory for alumnae and women students, and securing a pledge from each group that it would raise five hundred dollars to furnish the building, after the fair, for campus and community women's use.[9]

It is significant that this alliance of alumnae, students, and the dean of women sought to furnish the building themselves, in the style of autonomous women's clubs, rather than request university assistance. Expecting little from the institution itself, they had grown accustomed to functioning on their own without calling for university aid. They might have begun to create a legitimacy for their beliefs inside the university bureaucracy by justifying their needs to the administration and trying to win official support, as the male students would later do. But they rejected that possibility, feeling that it would be easier to seek the aid of other women, tapping their self-reliance to strengthen their autonomy. Ultimately, this segregation would fail to protect them as a closer institutional alliance might have.

The fund-raising tea became an important step, marking a renewed effort for cooperation among university women. The event initiated the University of Washington's Alumnae Association.[10] It also provided the new (1906) Women's League of faculty, students, and alumnae with its first major project. The alumnae began regular social and fund-raising meetings in each other's homes, and the women students held two "county fairs" at the gymnasium to gather funds for postexposition furnishings for the Woman's Building. From the first, the structure created "one means to the great end of cementing the bond of university sisterhood."[11] Together, campus and community women could accomplish much that otherwise would have remained undone.

Dean Howard had no trouble convincing a variety of women to contribute to the fund. She emphasized the importance of a center for their mutual advantage—to build skills in coeds so they could cooperate with citywide women's organizations, to provide space for cultural programs, and to foster social interaction between the campus and "cultured women of the city"—all essential if students were to graduate with a proper foundation in women's work.[12] Her dreams of improved facilities for women students grew beyond the Woman's Building. Citing the threefold increase in the number of women undergraduate students at the University of Washington in recent years (two hundred to six hundred), she envisioned more housing, a women's gymnasium, a swimming pool, a home economics building, and rooms for the campus YWCA. She noted that because the single dormitory and six sororities were full, three-quarters of the female students had to board in town with no place on campus to eat lunch, rest, study, or socialize.

In the fall of 1908, Dean Howard was replaced. For reasons not clearly stated in the Board of Regents' Minutes, Iris Weed became the new dean of women. It is conceivable that Howard's bold public insistence on greater and greater resources for women students was unwelcome to the administration. Nevertheless, the State Fair Commissioners voted to erect the Woman's Building at the fair, and the regents agreed that it would be used by the university women after the fair closed in the fall of 1909.[13]

Every great American fair had erected a Woman's Building. Philadelphia in 1876, Chicago in 1893, Atlanta in 1895, and St. Louis in 1903 provided a showplace for women's achievements, a celebration of women's cooperative sisterhood. The Woman's Building at the Alaska-Yukon-Pacific Exposition also became an important social center, providing services for women, display space for their achievements, and a place in which to receive both local and national celebrities during the conventions of regional and national women's organizations. These receptions were vital to the strengthening of cooperative sisterhood in Seattle: they provided proof that a wide variety of women's associations were strong and successful.

Every inch of the building's structure was designed to highlight women's achievements and to provide them with services. The stucco building itself was two stories high. Dominating the main floor was a large 80 by 30 foot reception room with a fireplace, chandeliers, a piano, a library, hardwood floors, fresh flowers, and walls covered with artwork by Washington women. Readings by women writers were held there as well as lectures on a wide variety of topics of interest to women, from art to sewing. A good many gatherings attracted such large numbers that the functions had to be moved to auditoriums at the fair, city churches, or the grand Seattle Women's Clubhouse on Capitol Hill. The YWCA sponsored a restaurant that served meals to fair-goers of both sexes, with profits earmarked for a much-needed "Y" building in downtown Seattle. The second floor of the fair building contained a large hall with display cases for Washington women's needlework, artwork, sheet music, novels, poetry, and short stories—an impressive range of accomplishments. In addition, there were three rest rooms upstairs, with couches for tired mothers, a large crib for infants, and a nursery, supervised by two nurses, containing toys for thirty children. The nursery was widely used, often caring for as many as three hundred children in a single day.

Seattle women enthusiastically participated in the events at the Woman's Building. They were no less persuaded than other American women of the wisdom of association for mutual benefit. In this

Exterior (*top*) and interior (*bottom*) of the Women's Building, Alaska-Yukon-Pacific Exposition, 1909 (*photos by F. H. Howell, courtesy Special Collections, University of Washington Libraries*)

region, nurses, school teachers, music teachers, and women physicians formed special professional associations. Seattle waitresses and garment workers had founded their own unions. Local women created religious and benevolent groups, secret societies like Eastern Star, auxiliaries to men's clubs, and city improvement associations. Politically minded women established suffrage clubs and Peace Mothers. White, middle- and upper-class women, who had leisure time to devote to extradomestic activities, once their children entered school, joined the WCTU, DAR, Ladies' Musical Club, and Woman's Century Club. Northwest women excluded from these groups developed associations of their own: Colored Ladies Society, Japanese Methodist Girls' School clubs, the Fidelia Club for Italian girls, and the Seattle Council of Jewish Women's Settlement House. A large number of local associations held gatherings at the Woman's Building during the course of the fair, as did larger networks of women, like the Washington State Federation of Women's Clubs, the National Council of Women, and the National American Woman Suffrage Association.

It is fitting, of course, that in the summer of 1909 the Washington State Federation of Women's Clubs held its thirteenth annual conference in the Woman's Building at the fair, for it was here that they hoped to teach University of Washington students to work for women's causes. The breadth of those causes was evident in the issues discussed at the conference. To some extent, the women reinforced traditional images of themselves by endorsing the celebration of Mother's Day and the teaching of home economics and child care to high school girls while bemoaning the decay of the family. Simultaneously, however, they sought broader opportunities for young women. For example, they reported on their efforts to establish a trade school for girls, to install sex education lecturers in the schools, to promote children's playgrounds throughout the state, and to encourage simpler garments for school girls. Finally, members took active steps to ensure their own influence over society. The meetings reported on their progress in establishing public baths, shaping conservation legislation, discouraging the spread of billboards and cigarette smoking, and eliminating the forced labor of convicts on chain gangs. The women took pride in their responsibility for the passage of pure food laws and the building of public libraries throughout the state,[14] all accomplished without the aid of sanctioned political tools, such as suffrage or positions in government.

The National Council of Women, an alliance of organizations whose membership totaled two million, also made a showing at the Seattle fair. Fresh from an international conference in Toronto, fifty participants arrived, including Pauline Steinem of the Toledo School Board (grandmother of Gloria Steinem) and Florence Kelley, general secretary of the National Consumers' League. In their speeches and meetings with the mayor and the governor, they publicized the need for woman suffrage and the dangers of sexism in religion, education, and the workplace. The *Seattle Post-Intelligencer* gushed: "Some of the most useful social and civic energies of the time owe their origins to women and to the civic and social organizations women have called into being."[15]

Far more controversial than the conventions of the Washington State Federation of Women's Clubs and the National Council of Women was that of the National American Woman Suffrage Association, which held its forty-first conference at Seattle's exposition. The conference, which lasted eight days, brought to the city six hundred delegates, including a "who's who" of American feminists. Most significant, it paved the way for a suffrage victory in Washington State the following year, an event that was felt far beyond the state borders. This Washington victory in fact ended the era of the "doldrums" that had frozen national suffrage successes since 1896 and ushered in a wave of state-by-state triumphs that culminated in the passage of the federal amendment in 1920.

By no means did the suffrage leadership assume that their cause was widely embraced by the populace in 1909. They sent their celebrities, including the organization's president, the Reverend Anna Howard Shaw, M.D., to dazzle Seattle. In addition, speeches were given by Lucy Anthony, a niece of Susan B. Anthony; Oregon activist Abigail Scott Duniway; octogenarian and editor of Boston's *Woman's Journal,* Henry B. Blackwell; his daughter Alice Stone Blackwell; and Charlotte Perkins Gilman, who pointed out that women could make the entire world as humane as they had made the family, if only they were permitted to try.[16] In the event that the two thousand conventioneers were not persuaded, suffragists took to the pulpits in Seattle's churches on Sunday, July 4, conveying their message to a number of Protestant congregations.[17]

The prominent Washington State suffragists were also visible, using this opportunity to develop all the local support they could muster, pressing prosuffrage badges and balloons on fair-goers, and displaying "Votes for Women" banners at the exposition and on top of Mount Rainier. They used the exposition to advantage, generating substantial enthusiasm for the most controversial women's rights issue of the day.

In general, newspaper coverage was extensive and favorable for all the women's activities at the fair. Portrayed in a serious light, women's concerns and strategies for change won increased popular respect. The *Seattle Times* editorialized about the suffrage fight, both nationally and statewide, as "being conducted with vigor and intelligence, . . . by some of the most remarkable women in the country at the present day, and their coming cannot help doing us all a great deal of good. . . . If these women of national reputation cannot convince the male Washingtonian, he cannot be convinced by anything short of a flat iron or a rolling pin."[18]

Although it is impossible to measure the impact on Seattle women of this exposure to national conferences and favorable publicity, it could not have hurt local women's groups when the *Post-Intelligencer* told its readers: "Women out here seem to be living for the good they may do; they are in the industries; they are in business; they are factors of great force in charity work, in education, and in all movements which make for the civic and moral betterment of life's conditions in this section. . . . They honor Washington; the state is proud of them, and grateful for the helpful work they are doing."[19]

Locally, club memberships did not skyrocket, but they continued to climb gradually, as they had since the turn of the century and would continue to do until the Depression devastated dues payers in the early 1930s. Eventually the suffrage victory, the culmination of a twenty-one-year struggle in the state, created a euphoria regarding the extensive work women had already done and had yet to do. Seattle women were bound to continue their reform efforts, assisted by the newly won ballot and by a winning technique—their cooperative womanhood.

When the fair closed in the fall of 1909, women students were handed the Woman's Building, along with the charge to forward cooperation among women. According to agreement, the structure was adapted for campus use. At the time, no doubts were raised, no cautions voiced about the long-term effectiveness of the apparently winning technique of women's separatism. For several years, it indeed appeared that women could thrive handily in their own building.

In January the building was reopened as a student center, and women students held a modest open house to show off the new reading and luncheon rooms on the first floor. In June an upstairs suite was prepared for the new dean of women, Isabella Austin, who presided over the women's activities. Like her predecessors, she supported women's club life, maintaining membership in the DAR, the Women's University Club, and the Association of Collegiate Alumnae.[20]

Just as Washington's clubwomen had hoped, the space became the hub of women's activities on campus and a link with Seattle's women's groups. The YWCA retained its lunchroom, serving women faculty, visiting community clubwomen, and women students, who were relieved to eat their lunches in comfortable quarters rather than university stairwells. The "Y" also kept its library in the building and held devotional meetings there. The women who ran city philanthropic institutions, such as Washington Children's Home, the Industrial Home for Girls, the Wayside Emergency Hospital, and the Kenney Home for Old Ladies, began to recruit volunteers there. The new campus building also became Women's League headquarters. A variety of information for women students was available, and women's programs, such as the Tolo Club (the Woman's Senior Honor Society), met there, as did the two women's debating teams. Emergency loans, from the Faculty Women's Club and Association of Collegiate Alumnae of Spokane, were advertised. Kla-How-Yah, a club for nonsorority women, was founded there. Vocational conferences and Founders' Day receptions with alumnae took place in the building, as did meetings of the Sororia Society, a campus organization for mature women resuming studies. The call for increased services and departments for women students by *Pro Bono Publico*—"Is Washington Just to Its Women"—in the *Washington Alumnus* of March 1911, may well have reflected the fact that the Woman's Building could no longer hold all its programs.[21] The space had indeed contributed to the launching of an impressive number of women's activities.

It was so widely assumed that the meeting space facilitated the cooperation that enabled important projects to be devised and carried out that community women followed suit. Turning the tables on the original plan for mature women to mold the coeds, alumnae were inspired to emulate the campus women by building structures in which to strengthen their own organizational work. In 1914, Mrs. LeRoy M. Backus called together university women from a wide variety of colleges to establish a Women's University Club in Seattle. By May, they had built a one-story building with parlor, dining room, and kitchen, that allowed women to broaden their acquaintance among the college women of Seattle, maintain their interest in the liberal arts and the sciences, stimulate and advance the cause of general education, and encourage cultural and social activities.[22]

Soon women all over Seattle ensured a revitalized collaboration by creating better environments in which to operate. The Sunset Club was founded in March 1913, and built a meeting place in 1915. The First Presbyterian Church nursery, supported by women, outgrew its old quarters and moved to the Kenney Home. In 1911, the Children's Orthopedic Hospital abandoned its six-bed ward in Seattle General Hospital and financed a hospital of its own, through guild members'

dues, contributions, and fund-raising fairs. The YWCA at last built
its new quarters downtown in 1914.

The DAR emulated the Washington State Federation of Women's
Clubs closely by building a sorority house near the university campus
for its young recruits. Convinced of the wisdom of tutoring young
women in sisterly cooperation, various state chapters contributed
furnishings, decorations, financial aid, and supervision at the girls'
social events.[23]

Town and gown women collaborated in many mutually beneficial
ways during this era, maintaining a pattern that increased their power,
influence, and respect in Seattle. But the town and gown liaison women
formed in 1913 to urge legislative support for more adequate university women's facilities was far less successful. Despite the presence
of the first women legislators in Olympia, political support was in-
adequate to overcome Governor Lister's veto of the proposal. Wom-
en's close cooperation among themselves could create a powerful
pressure group, but the strategy had its limits. Until women could
infiltrate the political structure in sufficient numbers to define policy,
they remained at the mercy of external forces. The community's clubwomen, who dreamed of winning better campus facilities through
the next legislature, saw no such plans resurface in 1915.[24]

In fact, their original coup, the Woman's Building, was itself now
in serious jeopardy because of their very distance from the administration's decision making. The death of the dean of women, Isabella
Austin, in August 1915, left the second floor unoccupied, and the
loss of her moral support for the Woman's Building and sisterhood
was deeply felt.[25] At the same time, two further threats to the autonomy of the Woman's Building were forming. On November 21,
1916, the U.S. secretary of the interior, Dr. Franklyn K. Lane, designated the University of Washington as the site of one of the ten
mining experiment stations in the country, if space could be provided.[26] In the same year, the university's new Home Economics
Building opened. This large and modern facility was seen as a place
that should accommodate all of women's needs, even though, from
the start, crowding necessitated that the space be shared with Ger-
man and education classes and that the basement be used as the
Commons cafeteria.[27] Finally, the war in Europe accustomed women
students, like the community at large, to sacrifice. While the males
on campus marched, the females sewed and knitted garments and
rolled bandages to send to France.[28] In this context the Woman's
Building was appropriated for the mining station in 1916. The women
moved out. It is not known what became of the furnishings they had
provided.

At first, women responded to the loss with a stoic wartime self-lessness. They coped with their eviction in a resourceful manner, scrambling to maintain the services once housed in the Woman's Building. They found another place for their war work and their fund-raising bazaars for the war effort. The Woman's League Tea was held in the Home Economics Building, debating tryouts in Denny Hall,[29] and cultural events in Meany Hall. Women also won permission to meet in the Men's Building, a luxurious clubhouse appropriated after the fair for developing "the gentle art of being a good fellow . . . of immense importance to every man who has to rub against the world." Reputedly the most elegant quarters on campus, to prevent the corruption of young men who might otherwise wander down-town fcr illicit pleasure, it humbled the Woman's Building in com-parison.[30] It must have been a bitter irony for women who had so painstakingly planned and furnished their own small building to see the space in these lavish clubrooms bestowed on male students by a generous university administration. The contrast provided tangible proof of the favors reserved for constituencies with advocates in high places.

For a time, the war masked the significance of the loss of the Wom-an's Building. The drafting of male students left vacancies the women were eager to fill. Women now ran student government, edited the *Daily,* dominated the dramatics association, the musical club, and the debating teams. One even coached the football team. New build-ings became available to them for their work. Women found ample workspace in fraternity buildings vacated by drafted students.[31]

Like their sisters all over America, University of Washington women enjoyed the exhilaration of mastering new and important skills for a patriotic purpose. The emergency seemed to forecast a new era in which women would be equal with men in the public sphere. No longer would there be a need to cultivate a separate sphere of influ-ence. After the war was over, however, university women realized that a designated woman's building was still desirable if the growth of women's roles was to continue. The men returned to their fra-ternities, gymnasiums, newspaper, and debating societies, leaving women no place in the institution from which to work. Only belat-edly, then, did campus women realize they had also lost their base for alternative routes to influence. Their previously effective coop-eration at the Woman's Building was now undermined.

One might have supposed that advocates of the restoration of a Woman's Building on campus would have found a friend in Ruth Karr McKee. In 1917, Governor Lister appointed her to the Board of Regents. She was the first woman to hold the position. When she

assumed the board presidency in 1923, she was the first woman to
hold the office at any major university. McKee, an alumna, was also
a clubwoman. She held office in the Hoquiam Woman's Club and
the Grays Harbor Federation of Women's Clubs. She presided over
the Washington State Federation of Women's Clubs from 1913 to
1915, was appointed a member of the State Council of Defense's
Division of Women's Work in Wartime, and became state vice-regent
of the DAR. Schooled in the tradition of separate spheres for women,
she now moved into the male-dominated hierarchy of power with
the assumption that female systems for collaboration were obsolete.[32]

McKee failed to return the Woman's Building to the students, even
though the progress of her own career clearly represented the effectiveness of women's collective action in making change and building
influence. Her clear break with the separate sphere ideology signaled
that the war and the granting of woman suffrage had effected great
change, the creation of a whole new strategy for women's rights. A
century of sisterhood, within a woman's separate world, paled into
insignificance. Instead, women's equality with men in the public sphere
became a primary concern. The entrance of some women into standard routes to influence—professional schools, careers, and sports—
seemed to nullify the need to cultivate cooperation among women.

On campus there remained some women who continued to value
the sisterhood that the building had fostered, and they would not
relinquish it without a fight. In January 1920, Dean of Women Ethel
Hunley Coldwell, acting on now outmoded principles, sent a letter
to the university's Board of Regents, seeking permission to initiate a
fund-raising campaign among women students, alumnae, and wom-
en's organizations to replace the Woman's Building. When no action
was taken, she appeared before the board in person. In her presence,
the board moved "that construction of a temporary woman's building be referred to the committee on Building and Grounds for investigation and report." When she left the meeting, however, the regents raised the question of policy on permitting student organizations
to have a building on campus, despite the existence of a Men's Building. The regents carried a motion affirming "the general policy not
to permit the erection on campus of buildings for use of student organizations with limited membership."[33]

The mood was clearly uncongenial to the reestablishment of the
original facilities for women, but in November a second effort was
made. A stubborn "deputation of ladies," unwilling to relinquish their
dreams of instilling sisterhood in upcoming generations, called for
expanded women's facilities, including a gymnasium. In response,
President Suzzallo submitted "an exhaustive array of facts and fig-

ures showing [the university's] total inability to erect and equip it." By January 1921, the women presented a counterproposal, an ingenious plan to win women's facilities on campus without expense to the university. Alumnae appeared before the board to ask permission for a site on which to build a new woman's building, larger and better, at the women's own expense. Told to put the request in writing, the women hoped to win permission at the March 12, 1921 board meeting. Instead, the regents objected to the plan, tabling it until the highly touted "stadium indebtedness has been reduced to such an amount as to be proportionate to the ability of the Associated Student Body to pay." The rejection carried unanimously, and the effort to reestablish a woman's building died.[34]

In the short term, the plan was a victim of low priority in comparison with the sports stadium and its financial problems. More important, it had been buried by the weakening of the ideology of female separatism, in the face of the "new woman's" hopes for equality. The Woman's Building, a physical and symbolic tribute to Seattle women's early sisterhood, in the end became a casualty to a newer wave of women desiring independence and integration into the public realm. Mature women, from clubs and alumnae associations, had fought a hard fight, but their dreams of perpetuating women's cooperation were no longer universally shared. Their old-fashioned and unpopular ideals ultimately succumbed to an overly optimistic illusion that new opportunities for some women portended success for all.

The essence of this debate continues: is it more important to integrate women into male-dominated worlds or to encourage women to devise their own separate foundations from which to seek change? Sixty-two years passed before the Seattle building enjoyed a much-needed facelift for its rededication on May 10, 1983, as Imogen Cunningham Hall, the new home of the University's Women's Information Center. The mandate of this bureau—to link campus and community women—is reminiscent of the mandates of the early deans of women, signaling a renewed respect for women's special abilities to collaborate to rectify injustices against their sex.

Ironically, at the dedication ceremony, President William P. Gerberding was heckled by feminist demonstrators who were unimpressed by climbing admissions figures for women in professional schools.[35] They focused instead on the budget cuts that precipitated a dismantling of women-dominated programs such as textiles, dental hygiene, and children's drama.[36] In light of these cuts, picketers labeled the restoration of a woman's center as tokenism. In fact, both the building's revival for use by women and the demonstrators' respect for the woman's culture it promised to nurture, symbolized the renewed appeal of an ideology undervalued for more than half a century. The old formula, which called for sisterly cooperation in Seattle as elsewhere, was revitalized.

Notes

1. Estelle Freedman identifies the importance of female institution building in "Separatism as Strategy: Female Institution Building and American Feminism, 1870–1930," *Feminist Studies* 5 (Fall 1979): 512–29.

2. Opposition to club work can be found in Grover Cleveland, "Woman's Mission and Woman's Clubs," *Ladies Home Journal* 22 (May 1905): 3–4; Edward Bok, "My Quarrel with Women's Clubs," *Ladies Home Journal* 27 (January 1910): 5–6.

3. Karen J. Blair, *The Clubwoman as Feminist: True Womanhood Redefined, 1868–1914* (New York: Holmes and Meier, 1980).

4. Washington State Federation of Women's Clubs, 1908–9 *Report;* Minnizelle George, "The University and the Alaska-Yukon-Pacific Exposition," *Washington Alumnus* 1 (June 1908): 7.

5. Washington State Federation of Women's Clubs, 1908–9 *Handbook,* p. 43; "Nurses Decline to Fight for Ballot," *Seattle Times,* June 16, 1909.

6. Washington State Federation of Women's Clubs, Handbooks, 1900–1909.

7. Charles M. Gates. *The First Century at the University of Washington, 1861–1961* (Seattle: University of Washington Press, 1961), p. 105.

8. Margaret Hall, "Women Faculty at the University of Washington, 1890–1970," Ph.D. diss., University of Washington, 1984.

9. Rose Glass, "Washington Alumnae Organize," *Washington Alumnus* 2 (December 1908): 6–7.

10. University of Washington Alumnae Club, *1980–81 Directory,* p. 2.

11. "Organization of Alumnae," *Washington Alumnus* 1 (June 1908): 28.

12. "The Needs of Women in the University," *Washington Alumnus* 1 (June 1908): 13–14.

13. Washington State Federation of Women's Clubs, 1908–9 *Report; Washington Alumnus* 2 (February 1909): 21; Board of Regents Minutes, 4:565, June 24, 1908.

14. "State Delegates Attend Busy Session," *Seattle Times,* June 24, 1909; Washington State Federation of Women's Clubs Handbook 1909; "Clubwomen to Urge Legislation for Clean Food," *Seattle Post-Intelligencer,* June 20, 1909; "Would Train Girls for Motherhood," *Seattle Post-Intelligencer,* July 13, 1909; "Resolutions Made by Club Women," *Seattle Times,* June 25, 1909; "Miss Janet Moore Chosen President," *Seattle Post-Intelligencer,* June 25, 1909.

15. "National Council Is for Suffrage," *Seattle Post-Intelligencer*, July 17, 1909.
16. "Grand Old Man in Cause of Suffrage," *Seattle Post-Intelligencer*, July 7, 1909; "Women of Nation Begin Sessions," *Seattle Post-Intelligencer*, July 5, 1909.
17. "Suffragists Heard in Churches and at Fair," *Seattle Times*, July 5, 1909.
18. "Editorial: Votes for Women," *Seattle Times*, June 30, 1909; "Suffragists Guard Against Imposters," *Seattle Post-Intelligencer*, July 14, 1909; Ruth Bordin, *Woman and Temperance* (Philadelphia: Temple University Press, 1982).
19. "Editorial: Women of Washington," *Seattle Post-Intelligencer*, June 23, 1909.
20. Dr. Thomas F. Kane Papers, "A" Misc. Records, Aug. 2, 1909, in University of Washington Archives; "Women's League to Give Housewarming," *University of Washington Daily*, Jan. 7, 1910 (hereafter *Daily*); Board of Regents Minutes, June 14, 1910; University of Washington Catalog, 1909–10; "Will Be Dean of Women at University of Washington," *Seattle Post-Intelligencer*, June 29, 1909.
21. "Soria [*sic*] Society," *Seattle Woman*, December 1924, p. 55; "Women's League Handbook, 1912–13" (University of Washington Print Dept., n.d.); "Women Frame Laws for New Athletic Club," *Daily*, Jan. 14, 1913.
22. History and Traditions Committee, "The Women's University Club of Seattle: Historical Highlights, 1914–1980," 1980; C. T. Conover, "Women's University Club Plays Full Role in City's Advancement," *Seattle Times*, n.d. (Pamphlet file: Seattle-Clubs and Societies, Women's Clubs, in Northwest Collection); Dorothy Brant Brazier, "Women's U. Club Growing Old with Charm, Dignity," *Seattle Times*, Feb. 2, 1949.
23. Washington State Daughters of the American Revolution, *History and Register 1924* (Seattle: Washington State DAR, 1924), pp. 83, 108.
24. "Getting the Women's Building," *Washington Alumnus* 6 (March 1913): 5; "Women's Building Bill Vetoed," *Washington Alumnus* 6 (March 1913): 5; "Two New Buildings Sought," *Washington Alumnus* 6 (January 1913): 5.
25. Board of Regents Minutes, 5:270, Aug. 20, 1915; "Dean of Women at University Passes Away," *Seattle Post-Intelligencer*, Aug. 9, 1915.
26. Milnor Roberts, *History of the College of Mines* (Seattle: University of Washington Press, 1936), pp. 23–24, and Board of Regents Minutes, 5:347, Aug. 16, 1916.
27. "New Building Is Essentially for Women," *Daily*, Sept. 13, 1916.
28. "Faculty Women Sew for the Troops," *Seattle Times*, June 24, 1917; "The University at War," *Washington Alumnus* 10 (May 1917): 9; "Thinks Women Can Make Guns for Soldiers," *Seattle Times*, July 1, 1917.
29. "Sacajawea Institutes 20 New Debates," *Daily*, Nov. 22, 1917; "Wednesday Tea Resumed," *Daily*, Nov. 20, 1917; "Members Chosen for Athena Debate Club," *Daily*, Oct. 17, 1917.

30. "League Will Meet in Men's Building," *Daily,* Nov. 19, 1917; "ASUW Takes Arctic Building," *Daily,* Dec. 17, 1909; John T. Condon, "The Men's Club," *Washington Alumnus* 3 (Dec. 22, 1909): 6; "Smoker Will Warm Home of Men's Club," *Daily,* Jan. 14, 1910; W. E. Parker, "The Men's Club," *Washington Alumnus* 2 (November 1909): 9; "Men's Club Building," *Washington Alumnus* 3 (March 2, 1910): 3.

31. "Women's League Has War Relief Division," *Daily,* Oct. 3, 1917; "U of W Girls Who Are Taking Men's Places," *Seattle Times,* Oct. 7, 1917; "Sororities Gain as Fraternities Give Up Their Homes for War," *Seattle Times,* Sept. 30, 1917; "Athletic Movement for Women Started," *Daily,* Oct. 2, 1917.

32. "Mrs. McKee, Former U.W. Regent, Dies," *Seattle Times,* March 8, 1951; Washington State Federation of Women's Club Presidential File, *Who's Who in America, 1923;* Washington State Federation of Women's Clubs, *Bulletin* 6 (September 1922): 25.

33. Board of Regents Minutes, 5:628, Jan. 16, 1920; 5:655, Feb. 10, 1920.

34. Board of Regents Minutes, 5:753, Nov. 26, 1921, and 5:761, March 12, 1921. For the popularity of the stadium see the entire issue of *Washington Alumnus* 11 (Apr. 19, 1920); Board of Regents Minutes, 6:386, March 12–13, 1926, and 6:475–76, Oct. 16, 1926.

35. William P. Gerberding, "President's Annual Report to the Faculty," May 23, 1983.

36. Sally Macdonald, "Irony at the U: Late, Great Alumna Is Lever for Feminism," *Seattle Times,* May 7, 1983; Julie Reimer, "Imogen Cunningham Hall Dedication Protested," *Daily,* May 11, 1983; Brian Haughton, "UW Honors for Famous Woman Set Stage for a Feminist Protest," *Seattle Post-Intelligencer,* May 11, 1983.

Bertha Knight Landes:
The Woman Who Was Mayor

Doris H. Pieroth

With her election as mayor of Seattle in 1926, during a decade that promised more for women in politics than it delivered, Bertha Knight Landes became the first woman mayor of a major city in the United States. She has been largely ignored by historians or depicted as a prohibitionist killjoy, a figure of ridicule whose term in office can be dismissed simply as "two turbulent years of 'petticoat rule.'" This essay is a look past the caricature to the woman whom the Seattle voters trusted enough, and with whom they were sufficiently comfortable, to elect to public office.[1]

She belongs to the progressive tradition, that seeming paradox of altruism and pragmatism that, for all the diversity of its reform efforts, was intent on the moral regeneration of a society becoming increasingly urban, industrial, and multicultural. She was thirty-two years old in 1900—a nineteenth-century woman who, in her twentieth-century career, espoused moral uplift, public decency, and effective civic management in such areas of urban life as health, safety, and wholesome recreation. She championed the city manager form of government and municipal ownership of utilities. Her public career came during the life of the Eighteenth Amendment, and for good or ill, her reputation became inextricably tied to enforcement of the prohibition laws. She was dedicated to duty and service, guided by science and reason—a practical, law-abiding, and moralistic woman who operated under an internal restraint that was reinforced by contemporary culture.

Her political career began in 1922. She and Mrs. Kathryn Miracle broke the all-male barrier to city government that spring with their election to the Seattle City Council, Mrs. Landes by the unprecedented plurality of 22,000 votes. She came to office as a "nonpolitician," backed primarily by women's organizations and an informal network of establishment groups and individuals. Although she grew as a politician and became more politically astute, she failed to strengthen or broaden her power base and to fashion a strong political organization of her own. She appears to have lacked one thing necessary to have made a truly productive and lasting contribution

This chapter appeared in *Pacific Northwest Quarterly*, vol. 75 (July 1984).

to municipal reform—personal political ambition. Or, if she possessed it, she suppressed it. By the time she glimpsed some vision of her political possibilities, the door had closed on them and she was denied reelection as mayor.

She brought to the role of public servant fifty-three years of previous experience as daughter, sister, student, wife, pioneer, mother, community leader, and club woman. She was born Bertha Ethel Knight on October 19, 1868, in Ware, Massachusetts, the daughter of Charles Sanford Knight and Cordelia Cutter Knight. She was the youngest of nine children, the sister of two boys and six girls. On her father's side there was said to be a "dash of French Huguenot," which showed itself "in the olive complexion, dark hair and big black eyes of his children." In 1926 the *New York Times* described Bertha as "below medium height with olive skin and drab brown hair," noting that "the keen brightness of her eyes is her most arresting feature."[2]

Although both the Knights and the Cutters could trace forebears to early Massachusetts Bay, there is little to suggest great family wealth. Her father worked as a painter in the village of Ware after his discharge from the Union Army; he moved the family 20 miles east to Worcester and entered the real estate business when Bertha was five years old.[3]

Worcester, an industrial center with a population of 41,000 in 1870, had been, before the war, a center of militant resistance to the Fugitive Slave Law. It was also an important nineteenth-century educational center, the home of Worcester Polytechnic Institute, Holy Cross College, a state normal school, and Clark University.[4]

Bertha Knight grew up in that city, in a family later described as providing "the best of home influences, a father and mother of old American stock, of that sterling uprightness, and devotion to duty, that 'plain living and high thinking' that has produced so many of our best in literature, arts and statesmanship." While the Knight children "were rigidly taught to abide by the law," the family was evidently close, secure, and loving. Bertha thought her mother the most wonderful woman she had ever known; she especially admired her devotion to the nine children and to the care of her husband, whose Civil War wounds had left him an invalid by the time Bertha turned eight.[5]

Indications of a close family with a strong sense of family obligation are apparent in Bertha's years as a young adult. She had graduated from Classical High School in Worcester and was living at home in August 1887, when her sister Jessie married David Starr Jordan, who was then the president of Indiana University. In the fall of 1888, just shy of her twentieth birthday, Bertha went to Bloomington to live with the Jordans and to enroll as a student at the university. She was there that October, undoubtedly providing help and support when Jessie's first child was born into a household that also included Jordan's two children by his first wife.[6]

Following her graduation from Indiana in 1891, Bertha returned to Worcester to live with her mother and to teach until her own marriage three years later. In Bloomington she had met and become engaged to Henry Landes, a geology student from Carroll, Indiana, who had gone on to Harvard for a master's degree.

Bertha seems to have chafed somewhat in the role of single daughter under her mother's roof and she perhaps anticipated difficulty breaking away. In a long and eloquent letter written in the last summer of their long engagement, her fiance reacted to the latest word from her:

> I am so glad that you find your life happier than you had expected. It takes a load off me when I find you cheerful. . . . You must not be blue dearie, it don't pay. Your letter was not blue by any means— but very cheerful. I am very sorry that mother is ill, and that you have to work so hard. Please do not do too much, but keep as strong as you can. . . . I am very much surprise[d] at the turn Charlie [her brother?] and May have taken. I should think that if they came over they would . . . stay there permanently. It certainly would be a nice thing all around. And how easily it will be for you to leave home when you can. It will very [e]ffectively settle your dilemma. Now if other things would only shape themselves in such good fashion we might get married before many months after all. . . . I know but little more than I did a week ago. You must expect developments very slowly.

The "other things" included his finding a job at the end of that summer, which he had spent with a United States Geological Survey team. Despite the precarious state of the nation's economy in 1893, he did secure employment that fall, classifying and arranging the geological collection for the New Jersey State Museum. They were married on January 2, 1894, and made their first home in Trenton.[7]

At Indiana, Bertha Knight and Henry Landes had attended a university that was experiencing an intellectual renaissance and enduring political and economic stress. Its student body of fewer than 300 included between 30 and 40 women. Bloomington, with a population of 3,500, "was still a backwoods court house town," with flickering electric lights and muddy streets; it had no registered saloon, but it boasted twelve churches. Founded in 1820, Indiana University had known only clergymen as presidents prior to the appointment in 1885 of biologist David Starr Jordan, who helped the school redefine its mission within the context of the humanities and the social and phys-

A youthful Bertha Landes, Indiana University class of 1891, emphasized the study of history and politics as an undergraduate. *(Courtesy University of Washington Libraries)*

ical sciences. There was extensive curriculum revision, and emphasis on physical science led Henry to a career in geology, while Bertha studied for her degree in the new Department of History and Political Science, whose young chairman, influenced by the Johns Hopkins Seminar, stressed American history and politics.[8]

David Starr Jordan touched the lives of thousands of students, and his influence on Bertha and Henry Landes is readily apparent. Although a "Darwinian extrovert among Hoosier fundamentalists" at Indiana, the liberal scientist was still somewhat old-fashioned and strongly opposed to drinking. His sister-in-law was seventeen years his junior, and in her years as a student, living for a time in his home, she had ample opportunity to be exposed to his ideas and style, his commitment to science and reason, and his politics. They corresponded after the Jordans had moved to California, where he served as the first president of Stanford, and she traveled occasionally to the Bay Area during her years in public office. He consoled her following her defeat in 1928, telling her he was not surprised at the election's outcome and asking, with Thoreau, "When were the good and true ever in the majority?"[9]

It is quite likely that conversation at the Jordan dinner table in Bloomington included politics, both civic and academic. The university was always faced with appropriations struggles and battles with legislators who at one time wanted "not only to cut the University's . . . funds but even to close the institution." Bertha Landes's experience on a campus pressed politically and financially, and whose administration she had observed from a unique vantage point, came with her to the role of faculty wife the year after her marriage. Henry Landes, on Jordan's recommendation, was appointed professor of geology at the University of Washington, and the Landeses arrived in Seattle in the fall of 1895. Newly occupying its present campus, the school was on the threshold of growth and improvement. Its immediate future was stormy, however; a Populist legislature, elected in the sweep of 1896, cut the university's requested appropriation from $90,000 to $78,000, and faculty salaries were among the nation's lowest. During the Landeses' first seven years, the university saw a succession of four presidents. A fifth, Thomas Kane, served until January 1914, when he was replaced by an acting president—Henry Landes.[10]

The Landeses rightly qualify as Seattle pioneers; the university's new location was on a heavily wooded site well beyond the city, and they were among those university people who chose to live near the new campus and become active participants in the life of the community. They built their home at the pivotal intersection of Brooklyn

Avenue and Northeast 45th Street; it was a large, two-story frame house with a hospitable and inviting front porch.[11]

The Congregational Church, long the only church in the district, was a center of community activity; geared intellectually to serve university families, it became a focal point for the Landeses, who had joined the fledgling congregation early on their arrival. By 1899, Henry had become its treasurer and a trustee, and Bertha was to serve two terms as president of its Women's League—in 1903 and again in 1918. Dean Frederick Padelford later described their community at the time of his own arrival:

> In 1901 the University District was distinctly a town in the making—a few unpaved streets, wooden sidewalks, cottage homes, bits of lawn on which the cows from the Green Lake farms were daily trespassers, a cluster of stores at the corners, and a little community church, bare and graceless as frontier churches are wont to be. But it was a warm-hearted and strictly democratic community, almost entirely made up of people in their twenties and thirties, all of them from somewhere else, and all ambitious and confident of achievement. The atmosphere was electric, charged with youth and energy. The environment, both physical and social, was flexible, and with singular unanimity the members of the community went about the task of molding it into something fine and worthy. . . .[12]

In such an environment and among such people, the Landeses reared their family. Bertha bore three children; the first, a daughter, Katherine, was born when her mother was twenty-eight. She was a beautiful and talented child, and her death in 1905 at the age of nine from complications following a tonsillectomy can only have been a crushing blow. There were two sons—Roger, who did not survive infancy, and Kenneth, who followed his father's career choice to become professor of geology at the University of Michigan. Two years after Katherine's death, nine-year-old Viola was adopted into the family, whose circle for many years included a blind and aged uncle of Bertha's. She devoted the years prior to World War I to home and family. Her outside activities were related to the church, to schools and PTA, to social services such as the Red Cross, and to women's clubs.[13]

During the year of the acting presidency, the Landeses entertained students and faculty on frequent occasions, giving the first alumni homecoming reception, which was attended by more than four hundred people. Bertha Landes's home was once again that of a university president awash in politics, and in the spring of 1914 there was speculation that Landes would be named to the presidency permanently. The speculation ended with the appointment of Henry Suzzallo.[14]

For any woman carving a career, Henry Landes would have been an exceptional husband; he gave his wife unwavering support. She fully appreciated this and said at one time that he "is as interested in having me live a full, rich life as he is in having one for himself." He understood and acknowledged the contributions of women, and as dean of the College of Science at the university, he provided a source of counsel and support for women on the faculty. Both the nursing and home economics departments considered him one of their best friends. He was described by a long-time friend as "always happy, gallant and gay," and a student who ran afoul of the faculty and was dealt with by Landes said that he was "a man of inflexible honor and exalted ideals. . . . Moreover, he possesses infinite tact, a rare sense of justice, and a rarer sense of humor."[15]

It was widely speculated during Bertha's campaign in 1922 that *he* would be the councilman in truth, and letters to the editor asked such things as "Will she do as Henry tells her—if elected?" There is no evidence that he controlled that council seat, although he obviously was her staunch ally and a chief adviser. She said that he was "a tower of strength in times of stress and made many sacrifices without complaint that I might give my time and strength to my civic service." One such sacrifice by the former Indiana farm boy could have been the postelection move from their home (then at 4511 18th Avenue N.E.) to an apartment in the Wilsonian Hotel, a move that lightened her domestic duties, some of which she continued to carry even while mayor.[16]

Both Landeses saw her career as duty and service rather than an opportunity for fulfillment of her own ambition, and they both justified her political activities within the context of woman's proper place. In 1926, Henry Landes found nothing "revolutionary" about his wife's election as mayor, saying, "It's simply the natural enlargement of her sphere. Keeping house and raising a family are woman's logical tasks, and, in principle, there's no difference between running one home and a hundred thousand." The city as simply a larger home was a theme of many of her speeches and public comments; one of the nationwide lecture tours that she made was called "Adventures in Municipal Housekeeping." Throughout her public career she held to the old values, and she sought to reconcile woman's "proper place" with her newly emergent opportunities in a wider sphere.[17]

In 1921 Mrs. Landes was president of the Seattle Federation of Women's Clubs; she was involved in university community affairs, active in campus circles as a faculty wife, and a leader in the University Congregational Church. The quintessential clubwoman, she had honed her skills in public speaking and parliamentary procedure during years of active leadership in such clubs as the Woman's Century Club and the Women's University Club. As federation president, she was a driving force in planning and directing the highly successful week-long Women's Educational Exhibit for Washington Manufacturers. This exhibit of Washington State products was staffed by more than one thousand clubwomen who had become enthusiastic supporters of local industries at a time when the city and the region were in the throes of economic depression and severe unemployment. The business community was impressed with the women's efforts in behalf of the state's economy and the Seattle Chamber of Commerce president praised Mrs. Landes for her role, telling her that he was "particularly impressed with the character of the interviews you have given out, showing as they do that you have caught the great vision of civic usefulness and responsibility."[18]

That year, Mayor Hugh Caldwell created a five-member commission on unemployment to deal with the city's problem, and he appointed one woman—Bertha Landes. Another member of that commission urged her to run for the city council. She had successfully bridged the gap between woman's traditional world of home, church, and club and the world of business and civic service; she was now a strong, serious, and worthy candidate for public office.[19]

She couched her 1922 council campaign in perfectly acceptable terms for a woman. While asserting that the time had come for women to be represented in governing bodies, she stated clearly that woman's first duty was to home and family. Many of her campaign statements seemed aimed at reconciling those two points, and they frequently smacked of apology for a candidacy justified as duty and service and for a candidate who disavowed any political ambition. As she filed for office she said, "It is not only the right, but the privilege and duty, of women to take part in the administration of public affairs." She stressed time and again the right of 40 percent of the voters to representation on the council, and said that if elected she would "support the moral and welfare projects in which women are primarily interested."[20]

During the campaign, noting the large number of women candidates in the country, she said, "This woman's movement is the logical outcome of two things: 1. Suffrage [and] 2. Commercialization of many of the activities which formerly centered in the home, such as the laundry work, baking, sewing and so forth." She also thought, though, that women might not be so anxious to demand the right to representation, which suffrage gave them, if men had "been able to interpret and express women's viewpoint on matters relating to the home, the welfare of women and children and the moral issues." The viewpoints of both men and women, she believed, were "as necessary for a well-balanced theory of city government as for a well-managed house. Home standards should be city standards, and this man has not realized." Since technology had ended much household drudgery, women had more time for outside activities, and "if [a woman] is not to be a parasite, something abhorrent to her nature, she must turn her energies to public service of some kind." While Mrs. Landes emphasized that woman's task is "to make the home and rear the future citizens," she urged civic involvement for the woman "who has reared her family and has . . . a trained intelligence to offer in service to her country . . . and who can render it without detriment to home or family interest."[21]

That first campaign and its organization were considered "absolutely unique in the political annals of the city." It was run by a group of five women—Mrs. Landes and four staunch backers from among the city's clubwomen, who were described as "typical Seattle housewives." One of them, Mrs. R. F. Weeks, said, "We wanted political experience; we were all amateurs." She stressed that they had run a low-budget operation in order to avoid "slush funds [which] mean either paid campaign workers or promised jobs"; they wanted Bertha Landes to enter office with clean hands, beholden to no faction.[22]

On May 2, 1922, the day of the general election, the candidate issued one final statement: "Our campaign is over. It has been strictly a women's campaign to elect a woman to the city council without entangling alliances, to represent woman's thought and viewpoint. . . . Our idea was to serve the best interests of the city; not to further the political ambitions of any one woman."[23]

From her seat on the council license committee, Mrs. Landes spearheaded the move for an ordinance that provided for the tighter regulation of cabarets and dance halls. In June 1924, she was elected council president and became acting mayor when Mayor Edwin J. "Doc" Brown was in New York attending the Democratic National Convention. She caused a furor and received attention in the national press when she fired Brown's police chief, William Severyns, for failing to rid his department of corruption, which he himself had widely publicized, and for his insubordination in an exchange of letters with her. She won reelection to the council in 1925 by a margin well below her phenomenal showing of 1922, but as muncipal election time approached the following year, her name cropped up as a potential mayoral candidate.

She was extremely reluctant to run for mayor and saw herself as a candidate only if none other emerged with a chance of defeating Doc Brown. It was not until the last day of filing, during which she changed her mind several times, that she made her final decision. She was heavily influenced by leaders in women's organizations that had been the backbone of her council campaigns and by pressure from backers of an initiative—also on the ballot—to establish city manager government in Seattle. In favor of the city manager plan and optimistic about its passage, she perhaps felt less diffident about entering the race because of the likelihood of the mayor's office being superseded.[24]

Her mayoral campaign occurred against the backdrop of the celebrated "Rum Trial" of the Seattle policeman-turned-bootlegger, Roy Olmstead, a coincidence that kept the spotlight on Mrs. Landes's concern for morality and law enforcement. The trial tended to substantiate links between Brown and bootleg interests and to corroborate assertions she had made during the Severyns firing in 1924. She was elected on March 9, by a margin of just under 6,000 votes in what was then a record voter turnout.[25]

As mayor she sought strict law enforcement, sound management for the municipal electric utility (City Light), a firmer financial base for the troubled street railway department, improved traffic safety, and quality appointments based on merit. She could and did take pride in such accomplishments as enhanced and expanded recreational programs in the park department and the return to profitable operations for the streetcar system. Although she had assured the Municipal League that as mayor she would "attend to other duties than 'greeting actresses at incoming trains,' " Mrs. Landes was gracious in her ceremonial tasks; notable among them was welcoming to Seattle both Charles A. Lindberg, recently returned from his Atlantic flight, and Queen Marie of Rumania, on her widely heralded tour of the United States.[26]

In 1928, the once reluctant candidate was being touted in some quarters as a candidate for governor, but she wanted to be reelected mayor. A two-year term was, according to the incumbent, "not long enough to work out and put in effect a constructive program." She told reporters, "Frankly, I like being mayor. I haven't seen any reason, since taking office, why a woman can't fill it as well as a man." Another thing that appealed to her as a woman was a "hope to show that a woman could not only get an office, but could 'make good' and win indorsement of voters for a second term."[27]

She began her reelection campaign armed with a good record in office and the same type of support she had commanded since 1922. But, "within the space of a short election campaign, the incumbent mayor went from a betting odds' favorite . . . to resounding defeat." She lost to Frank Edwards, a man completely unknown politically and without any record of public serivce or community involvement.

In performing her ceremonial duties, Mayor Landes frequently greeted visiting dignitaries. Here she welcomes naval officers during a fleet visit to Seattle, perhaps a doubly pleasant task for the sister of Rear Admiral Austin M. Knight, who had commanded the U.S. Asiatic Fleet during World War I. (*Courtesy University of Washington Libraries*)

The conventional explanation for her ouster has been that by pressuring the police department into making liquor raids she lost valuable support and that by 1928 "Seattle was tiring of reform and of Mrs. Landes."[28]

Although enforcement of prohibition was without doubt a factor in the election, it was not the whole story. She herself attributed her defeat to a combination of "a nine months' campaign on the part of my opponent, excessive expenditure of funds, and sex prejudice."[29]

Indeed, the Edwards campaign was of unprecedented length and cost; it had started the preceding summer and utilized hundreds of paid precinct workers, citywide billboards, and film footage of the candidate at City Light projects on the Skagit River. Edwards's reported expenditures failed to include much of that, prompting the prosecuting attorney to consider an investigation of his funds. However, such a probe could be initiated only by the defeated candidate, and she never did request an investigation.[30]

Lacking the facts, which might thus have been uncovered, speculation as to the source of Edwards's money centers on those favoring a more open city and less stringent law enforcement and on private power interests. Both groups had long-standing cause to oppose Mayor Landes.

A backer of municipal ownership of utilities throughout her career in public office, the mayor sided with J. D. Ross, the popular and increasingly powerful head of City Light, in his plans for developing the power potential of the upper Skagit River. Although overshadowed by her sensational dismissal of the police chief, two other actions Mrs. Landes took as acting mayor in 1924 may have earned her the opposition of private power. One was the signing of a new contract for Ross, which had been held in abeyance by Mayor Brown for six months, and the other was proclaiming June 18 as Power Day, in support of the drive to gain ballot qualification for the Bone bill, an initiative that would authorize expanded opportunities for public utilities.[31]

The financial woes of Seattle's street railway system, the city's $15 million white elephant inherited from Mayor Ole Hanson's glory year of 1919, brought Mrs. Landes face to face with the firm that had sold the city the system—Stone and Webster, parent company of Puget Sound Power and Light. The refusal of banks in the Seattle Clearing House Association to honor railway warrants in December 1927 forced the mayor to go beyond measures that cut operating expenses and to negotiate refinancing of the system. The success of this depended on state enabling legislation, and while making the city's case before the lawmakers in Olympia, "she clashed with private power company officials over the bill's contents."[32]

Activities of the Civil Service League also contributed to her ouster from office. That organization of municipal employees actually sought out Edwards and encouraged him to run, and "firemen and policemen openly compaigned for him while on duty." The mayor had alienated many streetcar men by making deep cutbacks in personnel in order to ensure the system's solvency.[33]

Sex prejudice, as Mrs. Landes put it, looms as no small factor in her defeat. In her study of the 1928 election, Florence Deacon stresses the pervasiveness of the issue and sees it as both an overt and a subtle factor. She characterized the successful Landes campaign of 1926 as a "nonthreatening" one in which the candidate "did not step out of the traditional woman's role: she was simply to be a municipal housekeeper." In contrast, for the reelection race, the mayor "was too busy running the city to present an adequate campaign. She didn't take time to play up the role of 'little woman' and housewifely mother." Deacon concludes that the voters would not accept Mrs. Landes in other than the traditional role. Her opponent stressed his experience as a business*man* and much of his literature promoted "Frank Edwards, the *man* you would be proud to call mayor." The issue of a woman mayor was a constant theme in the press, pro-Landes papers decrying the fact that the only criticism of the incumbent was that she was a woman. It was implied at every turn that a city of Seattle's stature really needed a man for mayor. The Portland *Oregonian* chided the city for defeating a mayor considered the superior of most of her predecessors:

> We suspect . . . that Mrs. Landes was defeated solely because Seattle wishes to be known as a he-man's town. . . . [I]t wants a mayor's office where one can put one's feet on the desk. . . . [The Commercial Club] wants a mayor whose presence does not call also for letting everyone's wife in to the festivities. . . . [I]t is the fashion for cities to personify their dignity and importance through the male sex. . . . Yet out here in the far west where men are reputed to be men a proud and hustling city was mayored by a woman. Many a bearded cheek in Seattle has blushed in the last two years over this imagined shame upon a he-man's town.[34]

If the public woman was beset by the he-man factor, the private woman seemed beset by an inner restraint that kept her from using her political power effectively and to her own advantage. Nonetheless, Bertha Landes held strong convictions about the role of government and the place of women in relation to government, and she was firm in her commitment to progressive measures.

The mayor's progressivism suggests the influence of David Starr Jordan, whose abiding interest in politics comprised a strong opposition to the spoils systems and an ongoing concern for civil service reform. Jordan and Theodore Roosevelt, who met when Roosevelt spoke on the Indiana campus in 1888, shared political convictions, and the views of the two men informed those of Bertha Landes. Her appointment policy as mayor was one Jordan could approve—one intended, in Roosevelt's words, "to take politics out of politics." A forgotten element in her clash with Doc Brown in 1924 was his alleged abuse of civil service regulations; after her brief tenure as acting mayor she continued to serve on the council's efficiency committee, which conducted a wide-ranging investigation of the Civil Service Commission.[35]

Mrs. Landes preserved the reprint of the text of a speech Roosevelt gave in 1893, and she quoted from it to advise the 1927 graduating class of Yakima High School to become involved in civic affairs. In choosing to avoid politics, she warned, "You are simply saying that you are unfit to live in a free community." That particular Roosevelt speech could almost have served as her political credo:

> The first duty of an American citizen is that he shall work in politics.
> . . . [He should remain in political life] only as long as he can stay
> in it on his own terms, without sacrifice of his own principles. . . .
> [W]hen a public servant has definitely made up his mind that he will
> pay no heed to his own future, but will do what he honestly deems
> best for the community, without regard to how his actions may affect
> his prospects, not only does he become infinitely more useful as a pub-
> lic servant, but he has a far better time. He is freed from the harassing
> care which is inevitably the portion of him who is trying to shape his
> sails to catch every gust of the wind of political favor.[36]

She presented her views on municipal government, home, and womanhood in a speech prepared for delivery shortly after her election as mayor. Echoing Frederic C. Howe, she noted that the city "is said to be the hope of Democracy," and deplored people's reluctance to become involved politically: "The majority of our people desire civic decency and public morality but they don't desire them sufficiently to be willing to sacrifice very much of their time, strength or money to procure them." She reminded her listeners that the family is the smallest unit of government, that "government centers around the home," and that "the underlying principle [of government] is the satisfaction of all the needs of the people." For her, the most important function of government "is creating the proper atmosphere, mental, moral and physical, for the rearing of children and the activities of adult life. The city is really only a larger household or family with its problems increased manyfold through its diversified interests and the cosmopolitan nature of its members." The city must "supervise and regulate commercial amusements within her borders—keep down vice and immorality with a firm hand and . . . control the moral conditions under which her people live." In a personal message for the women in the audience she said:

> Let me tell you . . . that though I am a public official and a so-called politician, that I am first and always a woman . . . that I am a wife and mother but a mother whose children are grown . . . that I yield to no one in my respect for wifehood and motherhood and regard those professions as the very highest ones which any woman can fill. . . . I now want to urge you to assume your personal responsibility for civic betterment. If woman is indifferent and fails to realize her responsibility . . . then is the outlook gloomy and the future uncertain. . . . [Even the mother of small children] must pay some attention to what is going on outside the walls of her home. . . . The woman of mature years who has raised her family certainly has an added responsibility for civic conditions, for which she has not only leisure but a maturity of judgment which should be used for the public good."[37]

Mrs. Landes remained firm in her belief that a woman should have raised her family before seeking office; she preferred also that a woman not be dependent on the job for a living because financial freedom encouraged objectivity and independence. This sounds naively idealistic, but though she did not change her basic belief, she did become more practical. She came to see politics as the art of the possible. While she was mayor, she spoke of the "necessity for compromise in small things in the hope of providing for greater ones," and she acknowledged the difficulty of reconciling one's ideals with reality.[38]

She had assumed that her greatest contribution on the city council would be supporting women's traditional health and welfare measures, representing others rather than intiating and leading. Two things thrust her into a leadership role—the need for a dance hall ordinance and conditions within the police department, including the insubordination of the police chief. In the former instance, she had the active and open backing of leading men in the community; in the latter, she took matters into her own hands, while a few men offered advice in the background. The episode of the police chief weighed heavily on her. She later said that she had been given power; she believed in God; she felt like a martyr; and "Oh, I didn't want to do it!" With something akin to a sense of calling, she did what she had to do, feeling somewhat victimized in the process.[39]

When the call came, or pressure was applied, to be a mayoral can-

didate, she felt no special urge to be mayor, but asked herself, "[Am]
I the person to help my city realize its possibilities?" Again, potential
power was thrust on her; she had not sought it. Once again she answered the call and did her duty. Toward the end of her term as
mayor, as she came to relish the opportunities and the power of her
office, she said:

> Municipal housekeeping means adventure and romance and accom-
> plishment to me. To be in some degree a guiding force in the density
> of a city, to help lay the foundation stones for making it good and
> great, to aid in advancing the political position of women, to be the
> person to whom men and women and children look for protection
> against lawlessness, to spread the political philosophy that the city is
> only a larger home—I find it richly worthwhile![40]

She had come to public life from among Seattle's middle-class clubwomen, but during her time in office she encountered a much broader
spectrum of Seattle's women. She came to appreciate women wage
earners and their concerns as well as the business and professional
women who made up the Seattle Soroptimist Club, of which she was
a charter member. Her expanded contacts seem to have made her
more understanding of the economic problems of women and perhaps less prone to sit in judgment. In the dance hall ordinance battle
of 1922, she softened her stand to some extent after receiving in her
home three women who worked in one of the establishments targeted
for closure and who came to plead economic necessity. She was re-
portedly determined to wipe out vice in the city, having been informed "that the same type of women are here today that were here
some years ago, when we had a wide open town, and that gambling
and all other vices of those days are again in vogue." Yet her visitors
"did not make a bad impression. We had a pleasant talk. I got their
viewpoint. It was enlightening, but I have nothing to say about it."
Two of the women were working to support their children; they could
earn $4.00 or $5.00 a night in the dance halls, in contrast to $13.45
a week in a factory or $2.40 for an eight-hour shift in a restaurant.
Whatever her reasons, Mrs. Landes did settle for dance hall regulation and supervision rather than closure in the final version of the
ordinance.[41]

She remained sympathetic to women's causes after she left office;
the Depression underscored the economic plight of women. In 1931
she was the principal speaker for a successful lobbying of the city
council that was organized by the Women's Protective Association
in opposition to a proposed charter amendment barring married
women from city employment. She headed the women's division of

the city's Commission for Improved Employment early in the Depression; its main project was the operation of three sewing rooms that provided employment for women and clothing for needy children. Mrs. Landes showed concern for the self-esteem of the women in the sewing rooms: she declared that the city, in helping such women "avoid the dole," must make "every effort to provide work and see that work is paid for so that there is no feeling of accepting charity." During her term as president of the American Federation of Soroptimist Clubs, from June 1930 to June 1932, one of that organization's major concerns was relief for older women, who as a group suffered disproportionately from unemployment.[42]

That she was a prohibitionist is a fact. But it is open to question that she merits the reputation as a "blue-nose" moralist intent on spoiling all the fun of the roaring twenties. During the mayoral race in 1926, in an effort to divert the issue from being solely "whether you want an open town or a blue law one," the *Seattle Star* said, "Bunk! Mrs. Landes isn't a blue law person. She wants only what a vast majority of our citizens want—a fair degree of decency and some dignity in public office."[43]

She never did promise to "entirely eradicate bootlegging and illegal sale of liquor." She did say, however, "that there would be no longer open and flagrant violation of any law—be it the prohibition law or any other law." She fought repeal and thought that many seeking it were "men and women who can afford financially the 'high cost of drinking' . . . [and who wish to] break down the protective law which the 18th Amendment has built around society . . . apparently in order that they may go their way unhampered and with a less guilty conscience." She herself personified restraint and self-control, and at the heart of her prohibitionism was her contention that "all prohibitive laws have arisen as a result of a lack of personal restraint on the part of individuals and the placing of an over-emphasis on the right of personal liberty."[44]

While she cannot be classified as a civil libertarian, neither should she be thought a bigot; in the context of her times, on occasion she appears comparatively enlightened, and her activities and statements indicate an objective and rational approach to race relations. She was a member of the board of directors of the city's Soroptimist Club, which took the lead in eliminating the "white only" restriction for membership in that organization; she was president of the national organization when all reference to race as a membership qualification was deleted from its constitution. Her reported opposition in 1921 to interracial marriage was based on the ground that "where the two races are so different, the result could mean nothing more than incompatibility." That is a rational note for an era marked by agitation for immigrant exclusion and by virulent racism—a time in which fifty hooded and robed members of the Ku Klux Klan could be seated in a body for Sunday services at Seattle's First Presbyterian Church and be described by the Reverend Mark Matthews as worshipping "reverentially."[45]

Bertha Landes was blessed with a sense of humor, even in regard to liquor. She saved the printed lyrics of a song parody that had been sung to her while she was mayor. Set to the tune of "Maryland, My Maryland," it went:

> You took our booze and took our gin,
>   Mayor Landes, mayor dear!
> And made it hard for us to sin,
>   Mayor Landes, Mayor dear!
>
> When we had Doc and Roy and Bill
> We felt quite safe to drink our fill;
>   Now hooch there ain't, though we be ill—
> Mayor Landes, mayor dear!
>
> Now, kindly woman that thou art
>   Mayor Landes, mayor dear!
> Please, prithee, show a woman's heart,
>   Mayor Landes, mayor dear!
>
> Let down the bars, we'll stand in line;
> Fill once again ou[r] empty stein;
>   We'll vote for you; we like you fine—
> Mayor Landes, mayor dear!

In her ill-fated campaign for reelection, unable to get her opponent to meet her in debate, she staged mock debates with an empty chair. The *New York Times* reported that "she laughs as she conducts these one-sided debates and appears to get as much 'kick' out of them as her hearers, and the audience is usually in an uproar."[46]

She met defeat in 1928 in much the same manner that she had encountered other developments in her life—realistically and without false modesty; stoically but with some humor. The day after the election she told the Rotarians, gathered for their Citizenship Day luncheon, that they were "imposing a severe test upon her to laud voters for 'intelligent citizenship' in view of their decision of the previous day." She took pleasure in the knowledge that she could leave office with the conviction she had given Seattle a "constructive administration" and that the city was cleaner than it had been for years.[47]

Later, however, she indicated that she had been abandoned by her supporters. Although she avowed no regrets, there is disappointment in her words:

> The people who had put a woman into office to house clean for them "rested upon the comfortable assurance that all was going well and they could rest upon their oars." . . . So . . . they left their woman mayor to the wolves . . . an unguarded sheep. . . . Then the wolves came down *en masse* and, to all practical purposes, devoured her. They sent her back, providentially, to private life. She had worked day and night with very few play days for two years. . . . She was not exactly weary in well doing, for she fought long and hard to win, but at the same time she took her defeat with a certain sense of relief and without bitterness or deep regret.[48]

Reflecting on her performance in office, she once said, "I tried to uphold the ideals of womanhood." For her, that meant exhibiting strength, intelligence, and courage, and taking the slings and arrows stoically. Her formula for political success for women included "courage without tears . . . personal charm . . . poise . . . endless physical energy . . . a sense of humor . . . but most of all—no tears." An overly sensitive woman would "be hurt by the many unpleasant things people do and say. And before she knows it she [would] be in tears, which would bring disgrace on womankind!"[49]

She had wanted full equality in name and in truth, once saying she was a councilman, "not a council woman, please note. And I threaten to shoot on sight, without benefit of clergy, anyone calling me the mayoress instead of the mayor. Joking aside, I am fighting for a principle in taking that stand. Let women who go into politics be the real thing or nothing! Let us, while never forgetting our womanhood, drop all emphasis on sex and put it on being public servants."[50]

In the summer of 1933, she and Dean Landes conducted the first of a series of University of Washington sponsored study tours to the Far East, and they led a group during each of the next three summers. On the return trip in 1936, Henry Landes became ill, developed bronchitis, and died shortly after arriving back in Seattle. The former mayor agreed to lead the tour alone the following year, but this was among the last of her public activities. Even though by 1939 her own health had become a problem, she continued to live at the Wilsonian, and she maintained her independence. During those later years, she encountered the thinking of the Unity School of Christianity, the Kansas City based organization that stressed faith healing and a sort of self-help, matter-of-fact approach to the spiritual. That Mrs. Landes would turn to it seems quite in keeping with her character, and it is not surprising that among the Unity School literature that she kept was the motto: "I meet every situation in my life with perfect poise, for

Henry Landes, shown here with Bertha in China, was his wife's unfailing ally during her years in public office. *(Courtesy University of Washington Libraries)*

I am secure in the realization that God guides, protects and prospers me." In 1941, in part because of poor health, Bertha Landes moved from Seattle to Pacific Palisades, California. She died November 29, 1943, at the age of seventy-five, at her son's home in Ann Arbor.[51]

Bertha Landes graduated from college at the dawn of the progressive era of political and social reform, but she was not enfranchised until the age of forty-three. Although a leader in church, club, and community, she remained on the sidelines politically until, as a woman whose personal identity was first and foremost wife, mother, and homemaker, she was called upon at fifty-three to begin a new career in elective office.

Her political career had strong overtones of the progressive tenets of efficiency and regulation in public affairs, but her term as mayor did not mirror institutional reorganization that had taken place under progressives elsewhere, nor did it produce any lasting social change. It seems rather that she fought a rearguard action in which she tried to reestablish in the city a rational and efficient approach to civic affairs, to strengthen municipal utilities, to improve services and programs for the betterment of the people, and to enforce the laws that she considered essential for the health and welfare of all.

Unlike other and earlier progressives, Mayor Landes built no political machine of her own. The short, two-year mayoral term worked against her enlistment of able, and younger, strategists with long-range goals and ambitions of their own, and her reliance on a core group of women supporters, amateurs all, who lacked political staying power, added neither strength nor breadth to her campaigns.

She failed to effect reforms and she failed of reelection. It can be argued that the causes of the failures were the two things that made her tenure unique—her espousal of progressive measures and her sex. By the mid-1920s, a progressive was already something of a political anachronism, and her 1928 defeat may be seen as further evidence that the progressive movement had died or gone underground to await rebirth in the New Deal. As a woman she confronted the same forces, both subtle and not so subtle, that still account for gender inequality in politics; even within herself she was restrained by having been born and bred to a nineteenth-century woman's "proper place."

She reconciled the role of women-in-the-family and that of woman-in-public office by combining them. She simply proclaimed the city a larger home, a concept acceptable to her and to contemporary culture. But the attempt to achieve political success took her beyond the stereotype of municipal housekeeping to meet politics on its own terms, and she found herself, a woman beyond the home, at odds with her culture if not with herself.

Notes

1. George W. Scott, "The New Order of Cincinnatus," *Pacific Northwest Quarterly* 64 (1973): 137 (quotation). Two exceptions to this treatment are Florence J. Deacon, "Why Wasn't Bertha Knight Landes Re-elected?" M.A. thesis, University of Washington, 1978, and *Notable American Women, 1607–1950,* s.v. "Landes, Bertha Ethel Knight."

2. David Starr Jordan, *The Days of a Man,* 2 vols. (New York, 1922), 1:326 (quotations); *New York Times,* March 28, 1926.

3. *Notable American Women,* s.v. "Landes"; *Biographical Cyclopaedia of American Women,* vol. 2, s.v. "Landes, Bertha E. Knight."

4. *Encyclopaedia Britannica,* 9th and 11th eds., s.v. "Worcester, Massachusetts."

5. *Biographical Cyclopaedia,* s.v. "Landes" (first quotation); Blanche Brace, "Well . . . Why Not?" *Woman Citizen* 11 (September 1926): 9 (second quotation); Julia N. Budlong, "What Happened in Seattle," *Nation* 127 (Aug. 29, 1928): 197.

6. Jordan, *Days of a Man,* 1:326–27.

7. Henry Landes to Bertha Knight, July 9, 1893, box 1, Bertha K. Landes Papers, University of Washington Libraries, Manuscripts Section; G. E. Goodspeed, "Memorial of Henry Landes," *Proceedings of the Geological Society of America for 1936* (June 1937), pp. 207–13.

8. Thomas D. Clark, *Indiana University: Midwestern Pioneer,* 4 vols. (Bloomington, 1970–77), 1: 214, 219–20, 236 (quotation), 237.

9. Ibid., pp. 211 (extrovert) and 239; Jordan to Bertha Knight Landes, March 14, 1928, box 1, Landes Papers.

10. Clark, *Indiana University,* 1:212 (quotation); Charles M. Gates, *The First Century at the University of Washington, 1861–1961* (Seattle: University of Washington Press, 1961), pp. 60, 62, and 123.

11. Photographs, box 1, Landes Papers.

12. Frederick M. Padelford, "The Community," *University Congregational Church Fiftieth Anniversary Program* (1941). In 1928, Bertha Landes became the first woman to serve as moderator of the Washington Conference of the Congregational Church.

13. *Pacific Wave* (Seattle), April 7, 1905; "Memorial of Henry Landes"; Matthew O'Connor, "Biography of Bertha Knight Landes," (typescript), box 1, Landes Papers; Budlong, "What Happened in Seattle," p. 197.

14. *University of Washington Daily,* Nov. 30 and Feb. 20, 1914 (hereafter *Daily*); Gates, *First Century,* p. 142.

15. Clipping, Feb. 9, 1927 (Landes quotation), box 2, Landes Papers; Cora Jane Lawrence, "University Education for Nursing in Seattle, 1912–1950," Ph.D. diss., University of Washington, 1972, p. 75. Grace Denny to Landes, Sept. 1, 1936, Effie Raitt to Landes, 1936, and Eva Ronald Benson to Landes, Aug. 28, 1936 (friend's quotation), box 1, Landes Papers; *Daily,* Feb. 25, 1914 (student quotation).

16. *Seattle Star,* April 15, 1922 (campaign quotation); typed fragment

(n.d.) (Landes quotation), box 1, Landes Papers; "Interesting Westerners," *Sunset* 58 (February 1927): 46.

17. *New York Times,* March 28, 1926.

18. *Seattle Spirit,* (April 28, 1921); Robert S. Boyns to Bertha K. Landes, April 19, 1921 (quotation), box 1, Landes Papers.

19. Bertha K. Landes, "Does Politics Make Women Crooked?" *Collier's* 83 (March 16, 1929): 36.

20. *Seattle Star,* March 2, 1922 (first quotation); *Seattle Post-Intelligencer,* March 10, 1922 (second quotation).

21. Bertha Landes, "Women in Government," *Seattle Star,* April 4, 1922.

22. Ibid., April 21 (first two quotations) and 5 (Weeks quotations), 1922.

23. Ibid., May 2, 1922.

24. *Seattle Times,* Jan. 23 and 24, 1926; *Seattle Post-Intelligencer,* Feb. 3, 1926. Brown was a Democrat, and it is likely that Mrs. Landes was a Republican; however, the mayoral election was nonpartisan.

25. *Seattle Post-Intelligencer,* Jan. 29 and 30, Feb. 3, 4, and 21, 1926; *Seattle Star,* March 10, 1926.

26. *Seattle Post-Intelligencer,* Feb. 3, 1926.

27. Ibid., Oct. 30, 1927.

28. Norman H. Clark, *The Dry Years: Prohibition and Social Change in Washington* (Seattle, 1965), p. 199 (last quotation); "Why Wasn't Landes Re-elected?" pp. 62 (first quotation) and 114.

29. Undated clipping fragment, box 2, Landes Papers.

30. *Seattle Times,* March 5, 10–13, 1928; Deacon, "Why Wasn't Landes Re-elected?" pp. 72–73, 93.

31. *Seattle Star,* June 13, 1924 (text of proclamation); *Oregonian,* June 29, 1924; Landes to Oliver Erickson, Aug. 11, 1927, box 87, Seattle Lighting Department Records, University of Washington Libraries; *Seattle Times,* June 27, 1927.

32. Deacon, "Why Wasn't Landes Re-elected?" pp. 47–59 (57, quotation).

33. Ibid., pp. 114 and 93 (quotation).

34. Ibid., pp. 115 (first three quotations) and 79 (fourth quotation); *Argus,* (Jan. 7, Feb. 4, and June 2, 1928); "Revolt of the He-Men," *Oregonian,* March 15, 1928.

35. Jordan, *Days of a Man,* 1:306 (quotation). As mayor, Bertha Landes appointed civil service commissioners of her own choosing, one of whom was Dave Beck, then a young, rising force on the Seattle labor scene.

36. "Yakima School Speech" (n.d., typescript), and Theodore Roosevelt, "Good Citizenship and Public Office," reprint (Jan. 26, 1893), box 1, Landes Papers.

37. Text of speech, "The Problem of the Large City," pp. 1, 5, 6, 7, 12–14, box 1, Landes Papers.

38. *Kansas City Times,* Dec. 2, 1937, clipping, box 2, Landes Papers; *Soroptigram,* March 1927 (mimeographed) (quotation).

39. Budlong, "What Happened in Seattle," p. 197.

40. Bertha Landes, "Steering a Big City Straight," *Woman Citizen* 12 (December 1927): 7 and 37.

41. *Seattle Post-Intelligencer*, Oct. 14 (first quotation) and Oct. 16 (second quotation), 1922.

42. Ibid., Dec. 2, 1931; Lois Jermin to Bertha Landes, Dec. 3, 1931, box 1; box 1 (re: Commission for Improved Employment) and box 2, undated clipping (quotation) and clipping, May 31, 1933, Landes Papers; *American Soroptimist*, September 1962, p. 10.

43. *Seattle Star*, March 2, 1926.

44. Statement by Bertha K. Landes at a hearing before the House Judiciary Committee, March 12, 1930, box 1, Landes Papers.

45. *Soroptimist Yearbook*, December 1925, p. 8; 1926, p. 2; 1932, p. 40. Ruth Bachtel, "President's Report," read at Soroptimist Founder's Day Meeting, Seattle, Oct. 8, 1980; *Seattle Star*, Dec. 29, 1921 (quotation) and April 3, 1922. The allegation was made in "Recollections," *Puget Soundings*, June 1976, p. 15, that Mrs. Landes was "very prejudiced" and that she "instigated a program of cataloguing people" by color for the purpose of restricting the movements throughout the city of people of darker color. I have been unable to find any evidence to corroborate such a claim.

46. "Mayorland, Dry Mayorland," box 1, Landes Papers; *New York Times*, Mar. 11, 1928.

47. *Seattle Post-Intelligencer*, March 14 (constructive) and March 15 (severe test), 1928.

48. Bertha Landes, "An Alumna in Politics," *Indiana Alumni Magazine*," April 1939, box 1, Landes Papers.

49. Undated clipping (first quotation), and clipping from Honolulu *Advertiser*, ca. 1938 (quotations), box 2, Landes Papers.

50. Landes, "Steering a Big City Straight," p. 7.

51. *University District Herald* (Seattle), June 6, 1941; *Seattle Times*, Nov. 29, 1943; "Society of Silent Unity," p. 5 (motto), box 1, Landes Papers.

The Job He Left Behind:
Women in the Shipyards During World War II

Karen Beck Skold

During the Second World War, Portland, Oregon was one of the major centers of the American shipbuilding industry. Hundreds of Liberty ships, tankers, aircraft carriers, and other ships were built between 1941 and 1945 by a labor force numbering 125,000 at its peak. What was remarkable about this army of workers was that one-fourth were women. They were welders, burners, electricians, and shipfitters, working in jobs once the exclusive domain of men. Climbing scaffolding on the hulls or descending into the ships' holds, they earned the same pay as the men, wages that were the highest of any industry at the time. The importance of women's labor was recognized in the media campaigns recruiting more women, and by the creation of child-care centers at the workplace.

The boom in shipbuilding was short-lived. Yet women gained access during the war years to skilled trades and high wages from which they had traditionally been excluded. What was the meaning of this experience? Was a model of equality between women and men in the labor force briefly created? How much change really occurred in the definition of "women's work" and "men's work" under the pressure of the war emergency?

This essay shows, first of all, how and why women entered the shipyards, and what the process meant in terms of increased opportunities. Second, it compares the actual work done by women and men. And, finally, it examines women's postwar plans and what happened to them when the shipyards closed.

WOMEN ENTER THE SHIPYARDS

The sudden, rapid growth of the shipbuilding industry changed Portland from a quiet, provincial city into wartime boomtown. Three huge shipyards built and operated by the Kaiser Corporation dominated the industrial life of the area. Here ships for the U.S. Maritime Commission were built at record-breaking speed. In addition, several local companies built small craft for the Navy. The first of the Kaiser yards, the Oregon Shipbuilding Corporation, was built in 1941, and

Reprinted from Carol R. Berkin and Clara M. Lovett, eds., *Women, War and Revolution*, by permission of the publisher, Holmes & Meier Publishers, Inc., 30 Irving Place, New York, NY 10003. Copyright 1980 by Holmes & Meier.

absorbed most of the area's supply of unemployed men. Shortly after Pearl Harbor, Kaiser was granted a contract to build a second yard across the Columbia River from Portland in the small town of Vancouver, Washington. Then, in March 1942, a third Kaiser yard began at Portland's Swan Island.[1] The demand for labor thus increased sharply at the same time that the supply of healthy young men was being decreased by the draft.

Beginning in the summer of 1942, Kaiser recruiters sought unemployed men in cities such as Minneapolis and New York, promising to pay their transportation costs as an advance on wages. Before long a housing crisis developed in Portland, as migrants arrived faster than the war housing projects were built. The bottleneck in housing was broken with the construction of Vanport, the "world's largest housing project," built in 110 days by Kaiser and other construction firms on swampland midway between the three Kaiser yards. A year after ground was broken, Vanport was the second largest "city" in Oregon, with 40,000 residents. Between 1940 and 1944, nearly a quarter of a million migrants came into the Portland-Vancouver area.[2] The consequent strain on schools, housing, transportation, and other services was typical of defense industry centers. War industries were not built with the location of adequate labor supply in mind. Workers had to move to the jobs, given the inducement of high wages.

Meanwhile, another source of labor had begun to be tapped. Plans were made quite early to hire women in the Kaiser yards. In January 1942, the Vancouver school board learned that women would be used to help "man" the shipyard, barely under construction, and it decided to admit ten women to the school district's defense training classes. In April, when Oregon Ship hired two women as welders on the outfitting dock, it became the first of the nation's Maritime Commission yards to employ women in production work. As word spread, first private, then public welding schools began sending more women to the yards.[3]

The women who began to enter the yards in 1942 were not the only workers new to the industry. The Kaiser company estimated that only 2 percent of its workers had ever built ships before.[4] The incorporation of masses of inexperienced workers, necessary because of the vast expansion of the industry, was made possible by changes in the organization of work. Before the war, shipbuilding had been a small industry; ships were individually built by skilled workers who served long apprenticeships to learn all aspects of their trades. The war brought standardization of products to the industry, and made preassembly of ships practical. Welding replaced riveting as the means of joining steel plates, because it was faster and easier to learn. These changes, combined with the specialization of tasks, made possible the use of unskilled labor. Detailed planning by management split apart the forty to seventy skills that made a craft, so each could be learned with a brief period of training. Specialization in the preassembly phase meant that a crew of workers built the same section of a ship over and over. But there were limits on skill breakdown in shipbuilding. The basic skills of cutting, shaping, and joining steel could not be learned as quickly as assembly-line jobs. As F. C. Lane notes: "There was still a considerable range of skills in the shipyards even after scientific management had broken down the jobs."[5]

The unions did not oppose the dilution of skills, because neither wages nor union status was threatened by the change. Craft rules were relaxed to permit workers with limited training to do jobs traditionally reserved for the "first-class mechanic," provided they got the same wages and joined the union. The dues of the new members enriched union treasuries, and closed-shop agreements prevented management from using the job breakdown to undermine the unions. In addition, the old-time craftsmen moved rapidly into foreman and supervisory positions.

Government-funded War Production Training, administered by state and local school boards, enabled new workers to learn specific skills in a short period. Free defense training classes were offered by Portland and Vancouver vocational schools. Soon welding schools were opened in all the major shipyards, and paid trainee programs began in March 1943 to help meet the critical need for more welders. At the peak of the training program, government agent Augusta Clawson enrolled in the Swan Island welding school to discover ways of improving training and reducing turnover, especially among women. At her suggestion, an orientation program for the newly hired was started, which included a special session for women workers conducted by the women's counseling department. A few months later, the turnover rate for women production workers dropped to just slightly above that of men.[6] The training program, coupled with the breakdown of crafts into component parts, made it easy for women and other inexperienced workers to enter shipbuilding.

Another barrier to the employment of women fell when unions admitted women to membership. Workers in the Portland yards, as in most West Coast shipyards, were represented by the American Federation of Labor (AFL) craft unions. Even those conservative unions soon recognized that if women had to be hired in the shipyards, it was preferable that they work under union jurisdiction. In September 1942, the Boilermakers Union, which controlled two-thirds of all shipyard jobs, voted to admit women. This decision came a few months after the first women welders were hired in Portland.[7]

Increasing rapidly from dozens to hundreds to thousands, women became a significant part of the overall labor force in the shipyards. From only 3 percent of the total payroll in January 1942 (all office workers at that point), women grew to 15 percent by January 1943 and to 28 percent a year later. Both total employment and women's employment rose steeply through the end of 1943. During 1944, employment fluctuated because of uncertainty about the future of shipbuilding contracts. The Kaiser yards lost 10,000 workers in the first half of the year, but the percentage of women remained high. A production drive at Oregon Ship and Vancouver in the latter half of the year brought employment up again, and women made up as much as 30 percent of the work force. At this point 28,000 women were working in the Kaiser shipyards and several thousand more in smaller Portland yards.[8]

Women were hired earlier and in greater numbers in Portland than in most of the nation's shipyards. When the U.S. Women's Bureau made visits to forty-one shipyards in the fall of 1943, few had employed women as long as one year, and six had yet to hire women. But in the three Portland-Vancouver Kaiser yards, 27 percent of the employees were women by April 1944; on Swan Island the figure was 32 percent, compared with 18 percent in Kaiser's Richmond, California yards, and 8 to 10 percent at most eastern shipyards.[9] The main reason was that the sudden growth of shipbuilding in a low-population area created a greater labor shortage than in other areas of the country. Male workers were always the preferred labor force, and women were hired only when it was clear that sufficient men were not available. This point was simply reached sooner in Portland, a small city in a rural state. The eastern shipyards were located near highly populated areas, and they also had most of the nation's trained shipbuilding workers since many of the yards dated from prewar times.

Women entering shipbuilding gained access to high wages, to equal pay, and to jobs from which they had formerly been excluded. Wages in shipbuilding were the highest of any defense industry, averaging $63 a week in September 1943. This reflected the importance of the industry to the war effort. Shipbuilding was also noted for its high proportion of skilled to unskilled workers. Sixty percent of the workers were journeymen, who earned $1.20 an hour as a basic rate. The rest were mostly helpers, earning 95 cents an hour. Wages were set by the job, so women and men in the same job category earned the same pay.[10] Despite the skill breakdown, the crafts that women workers entered involved more interesting and varied work than most jobs available to them in the past. Even the simplest welding job, that of tacking, required two weeks to learn and longer to master; it could provide a sense of accomplishment greater than cleaning houses, waiting on tables, or filing letters. Workers were not tied to one spot, as on an assembly line, but moved about as the work demanded. In addition, women did not enter the industry at the bottom, as is often the case when they move into a formerly male job. The first women hired were welders; only later did women branch out into unskilled helper and laborer jobs, as well as into other crafts.

Recruitment campaigns stressed high wages and the capabilities of women workers. A major mobilization campaign was held in Portland in June 1943, under the auspices of the U.S. Employment Service, the War Manpower Commission, and the Office of Civil Defense. The mayor declared Working Women Win Wars Week, and a door-to-door canvass to find women able to take war jobs was publicized by the local media. Women war workers demonstrated their skills on lathes and other machines in the display windows of downtown department stores.[11] The Kaiser employee publication urged shipyard men to "help your yard lick the manpower problem" by recruiting their wives: "If your wife, or any woman of your acquaintance, is between 18 and 35, not employed in essential industry, active, in good physical condition, and not overweight, tell her about these well-paid welding jobs." Starting at 95 cents an hour during training, welders could earn from $62 a week on day shift to $72 on graveyard.[12]

The importance of women's labor to the war effort was recognized by the creation of government-funded child-care centers. Community-based centers, funded through the Lanham Act, were opened in Portland, Vanport, and Vancouver. Of greater importance to shipyard mothers were the two Kaiser child-service centers, nationally known for their quality and innovations in workplace childcare. Located at the shipyard entrance, so parents could drop off their children on their way to work, the centers operated on all three shifts, and could accommodate up to 350 children each. The best child development experts were recruited to run the centers, which became a showcase proving that young children could thrive in group care for long hours. Meals and snacks were planned by a well-known nutritionist, and an infirmary cared for mildly ill children. Another notable feature was "home service food," precooked meals which workers could purchase at the child-care centers, take home, and reheat for dinner. High quality child care was made possible by the unusual method of funding: the cost of child care was absorbed by the Maritime Commission when it purchased the ships.[13]

The shipyard child-care centers were a result, not a cause, of the high percentage of women workers. The child-care centers did not open until November 1943, after the period of greatest increase in the female labor force. Although the centers were reputed to be the largest in the world, the number of children cared for was small compared with the total number of women workers. At their peak in the summer of 1944, the Swan Island and Oregon Ship centers cared for a total of over 700 children. But there were roughly 16,000 women workers in these two yards. The centers provided much-needed services to many shipyard mothers, but could not have affected the total number of women workers very much.

Women were attracted to shipyard work for a combination of reasons, but high wages was the most important. Many women learned of opportunities for shipyard jobs from their husbands or other friends and relatives already working in the yards. One woman said that she worked in the shipyard "to make money. My husband was working there. We hadn't been married too long, and we decided that if I was going to work I might as well work where the pay was a little more."[14] Women who were the sole support of their families were especially interested in the high wages. A divorced mother of two was working on a Work Projects Administration (WPA) job when the program was phased out because of the war. She was given a choice of training for a shipyard job or of working in a child-care center. She inquired about the pay, found that child care paid $35 a week compared with $62 a week in the yards, and said "I'll take the shipyards."[15]

For some women, the chance to do different or more interesting work was as important as the high wages. One young mother of three followed her husband to Portland from Nebraska when he found a railroad job there. Explaining her interest in welding, she said: "Dad had a blacksmith shop. We lived in the country. I was always around metal and fire burning, drills and the whole bit. I really liked it. Even as a child I'd rather be outside than inside."[16] Another woman was working as an egg candler in Portland when she heard from her husband, a welder, that women were being hired for shipyard work. "I just thought I'd like to weld," she said. "That was the reason I went. I just wanted to."[17]

Concern about the war was also a factor, especially for those women who had relatives in the service. A woman from Oklahoma said, "I came out here because I had three sons and a son-in-law in service and I felt like I should be doing something to help." But she also noted that the wages were much higher than in her factory job, and that it was a chance for her to make a change in her life: "I wanted to get away. I was a widow, my family was raised. I thought this would be a good opportunity for me to do something different."[18]

WOMEN'S WORK IN A MAN'S WORLD

Women's entry into shipbuilding challenged the sexual division of labor and traditional notions of femininity. The first woman office worker at Oregon Ship recalled in a 1944 interview that "for more than a year, no woman was allowed to walk along the ways or in any construction area for fear she would be injured." A cartoon in the shipyard newspaper in the spring of 1942 ridiculed the notion that women might be hired in production work, picturing housewives in aprons and high heels ineptly handling machinery.[19] Although some men had declared they would walk out if women were hired, no one actually did. The first women welders were stared at, whistled at, and then grudgingly accepted as a war necessity.

But uneasiness about women's new work roles remained. Rumors that welding caused sterility in women were persistent, reflecting a concern that women were losing their femininity. Strict dress regulations for women were based as much on "principles of concealment and sexless propriety as on concern for safety," according to Katherine Archibald, a sociologist who worked in a California shipyard for two years. "Like soldiers infiltrating enemy lines, women in the shipyards had to be camouflaged lest the difference in sex be unduly noted and emphasized," she wrote.[20]

Regardless of how men felt about it, women were doing men's work, and doing it quite well. Only six months after the first women welders were hired, a study comparing male and female welders in all seven Kaiser shipyards showed that women nearly equaled men in productivity. In the fall of 1942 the shipyard newspaper described a woman who had outwelded all the men on her crew doing difficult overhead welding on the hull of the ship. Women soon entered other jobs in the yard. By the end of 1942, women at Oregon Ship were working as burners, crane operators, duplicators, electricians, expediters, machinists, reamers, riggers, shipfitters, laborers, and helpers in eleven different crafts. In June 1943, they were rapidly replacing men as truck and delivery car drivers. Soon there were few job categories without women.[21]

Although barriers were clearly broken, it is necessary to ask a further question: To what extent were women doing the same work as men? Studies have shown the prevalence of segregation by sex in the labor force, and its remarkable persistence over time, despite changes in the occupational structure and in the sex composition of particular jobs.[22] As the shortage of male labor pulled women into the shipyards, were they hired in the same jobs as men? Or were they channeled into some types of work and not others?

Sona Murphy, a welder in assembly building, Oregon Shipbuilding
Corporation, November 1942 *(courtesy Oregon Historical Society)*

The extent of difference between women's and men's jobs can be measured by an index of segregation. This index compares the occupational distribution of the two groups, and tells the percentage of the labor force that would have to change jobs in order to create an equal distribution of jobs by sex. For example, in a situation of equality, if 20 percent of the men were welders, then 20 percent of the women would be welders also. An index of segregation was calculated for each of the three Kaiser shipyards, based on data collected by the War Manpower Commission in 1942 and 1943. The amount of segregation was substantial. Approximately half of all women or all men working in the shipyards would have had to change jobs in order to equalize the occupational distribution of women and men.[23]

In order to understand why this occurred, it is necessary to look at the kinds of jobs women held. A careful examination of the data for all three yards revealed that in general women were overrepresented as welders and underrepresented as journeymen in the other major crafts. Women were overrepresented as helpers and laborers; in some of the unskilled jobs, nearly all the workers were women.

The reasons so many women were welders are fairly clear. As the War Manpower Commission report put it, "Welding is the craft that has absorbed most women—mainly because of the urgent need for thousands of welders in modern shipbuilding, but also because women can be trained for welding more easily than most other shipbuilding jobs" (WMC 1:51). The demand for welders was always high, because virtually all joining of steel was done by welders. Speed of production thus depended more on the availability of sufficient welders than on any other group of workers. The skill breakdown and the paid, in-plant trainee program made it easy to recruit and train women in this craft. After two weeks of training, novice welders could be put to work in the yard as tackers, making temporary welds to hold pieces in place until the seams were fully joined by production welders. It was the demand for more welders that first opened shipbuilding work to women, and at first women were hired only for this job. Thus it is not surprising that women were highly concentrated in this craft. Although women were a significant percentage of all welders, (over 40 percent at Swan Island in the summer of 1943), welding was never a predominately female job. A comparison of data for the three yards, collected at different times, shows that the overrepresentation of women as welders decreased as the number of jobs in which women were employed increased.[24]

When women entered crafts other than welding, they remained a small percentage of their craft and of all women workers. The reasons for this are less clear-cut, but some examples of women working

Commercial Iron Works electric shop, Alberta DeLano and Orrel Weichman at the drill press, March 1943 *(courtesy Oregon Historical Society)*

in crafts that remained overwhelmingly male suggest possible explanations. It was very easy for women to become welders, but to enter other crafts sometimes required a great deal of persistence and initiative on the part of the woman, and in some cases the cooperation of male co-workers.

The first full-fledged "loftlady," promoted to her job in December 1943, was an example of persistence as well as special ability. A former housewife, she went to shipfitting school and did so well that she was encouraged to take courses in loft training. After one day in the mold loft (where templates, or patterns for pieces of the ship were made), she decided she needed more training. After 200 additional hours of training at Vancouver High, she went back to work in the loft. The superintendent assigned her to the office for some time, where she checked detail prints with structural changes. She showed such ability that she was promoted. It was almost unheard of for a woman to become a loftsman, according to the shipyard newspaper, because "not one woman in a thousand has become interested enough in mechanical craftsmanship to equal her ability."[25]

The only woman who did wiring atop the 50 foot masts of the Liberty ships came to the yard as an electrician's helper. She asked for the job climbing the masts, agreeing that if she failed to do the job as well as a man, they could replace her. She was still on her job, and liked it, over a year later. This confident young woman lived on a ranch with her parents, and hoped for a career in aviation after the war. An article entitled "Slender Blonde Does Good Job as Rigger" told the story of another atypical woman, one of only three who had successfully tackled that job. Riggers were usually "husky ex-lumberjacks," and their job was to attach loads to cranes and then guide the crane operator with hand signals. She attributed her success to the cooperation of a fellow worker. "I never could have made the grade if it hadn't been for Joe Harris, the other crew member. He taught me a lot of tricks in rigging to take the place of the brawn a woman rigger doesn't have."[26] Presumably, women not fortunate enough to work with a "good Joe" had a more difficult time.

Hierarchies of pay and of responsibility may also have played a part in limiting women's access to certain jobs. While most journeymen earned a basic rate of $1.20 an hour, in some crafts, presumably those requiring greater skill, the pay was $1.33. Loftsman was one such job, and as the example cited above shows, only a woman of exceptional ability and persistence was able to break the barrier to this craft. A similar job was layer-out in the mold loft, which also paid $1.33 an hour. The account of one woman who was finally able to transfer from welding to layout suggests that it was not a lack of

ability that kept women out, but a desire to maintain a male monopoly on a good job. She described the work as follows: "They have
patterns and you lay them out on steel, then trace around them to
cut out parts for the ship. It's just like making a dress." She needed
no extra training to do this job well, because she found her high
school home economics background in pattern making sufficient. As
she put it, "patterns are patterns." The mold loft would have been
a logical place for the shipyards to make use of women's traditional
skills. But few women worked there. The reason, according to this
woman, was that "the men who were qualified layout people felt that
they should get the jobs because they were men."[27]

Even when there was no wage differential, the work relationships
between crafts may have influenced the placement of women. In her
book based on experience working at Swan Island, Augusta Clawson
noted that welders had a "strange status" in the shipyard: "Shipfitters and shipwrights often cannot go on with their jobs until a spot
has been fixed by a chipper, burner, or welder. The consequence is
that they are always yelling for us. 'Come and tack this!'—or 'Burn
that'—or 'Chip this.' It gives the impression that we are working *for*
them although we are really on the same pay and job."[28] Frequently
the welders and burners were women. Chipping was not done by
women, but it was often done by black men. In contrast, only 10
percent of the shipfitters at Swan Island were women, and there were
no women shipwrights. Jobs that involved directing the work of others may have been considered more appropriate for men. And women
may have shared this attitude. Clawson recorded her experience
working with a woman shipfitter whom she described as a "slave-
driver."

Basically, however, in all crafts where the supply of men was sufficient, barriers to the employment of women journeyman remained.
Because welders were needed, the shipyards made it easy for women
to enter that craft; paid trainee programs were located right in the
shipyard. But training in many other crafts was less conveniently located, lasted longer, and was not paid. Women with an immediate
need for income preferred entering the yards as helpers or trainees.
Many women learned of job possibilities in other crafts only after
they had become welders, and it was often difficult to transfer. To
enter other crafts often took special efforts, skills, or good luck.

Aside from welding, there was a concentration of women in helpers' jobs. Forty-two percent of all women at Swan Island and 50
percent at Vancouver were helpers. In both these yards, the occupational data were collected at a time when the number of women
employed was approaching its peak. The data from Oregon Ship, in

contrast, represented an earlier phase. At the end of 1942, only 8 percent of Oregon Ship's production workers were women, and the majority of them were welders. At the other yards in 1943, more women were helpers than were in any other category. Thus the expansion of job opportunities for women took place in large part in the unskilled categories. While a greater variety of skilled jobs were held by women in 1943 than in 1942, most women entered unskilled jobs.

Why were so many women helpers? The reason is suggested by a quotation from the War Manpower Commission report, which noted that "women have been filling gaps in increasing numbers where men are not available or not willing to accept this kind of employment" (WMC 2:29). Apparently, as the labor shortage grew more severe, it was difficult to find male workers for the low-wage, unskilled jobs. One woman who worked as a tank cleaner commented that "the men didn't want to do menial jobs anyway. They wanted money. They'd go for electrician or welding."[29]

Some of the unskilled job categories were filled almost entirely by women. In an industry in which all work had previously been done by men, and in which women were a minority of the labor force, the existence of any job category that was predominately female is significant. It suggests that such jobs were now identified as "women's work." For example, laborers were 80 percent female at Vancouver and 90 percent female at Swan Island. A detailed job breakdown for Vancouver, in which helpers were identified by crafts, revealed eleven jobs that were over 60 percent female, and three in which women constituted over 90 percent of the workers. Fully one-quarter of all women workers were found in these three "women's jobs": painter helper, tool checker, and shipwright helper (WMC 3:22).

Why were women channeled into some unskilled jobs rather than others? Sometimes the nature of the work, not always reflected in the job title, lent itself to sex stereotyping. The job of sweeper, for example, did not appear in any occupational classification. Sweepers were hired as laborers, shipwright helpers, and boilermaker helpers. The reason nearly all laborers at two of the yards were women, and most shipwright helpers were women in another, may have been that their actual job was sweeping. Sometimes women ended up sweeping regardless of their job title or training: "In the plate shop all new women employees start with the crew of 150 women who sweep up and clean up in that area. Regardless of experience or ultimate job desired, if the new employee is a woman, her first job is sweeping."[30]

Older women were often found in these unskilled jobs. The division of labor by age may have intensified the division based on sex, since older men were more likely to have had access to some skills or training that could be useful in the shipyards. The preferred age for women welder trainees was eighteen to thirty-five, so women over thirty-five often found themselves in helper or laborer jobs. While less skilled than welding, these jobs were not necessarily light and easy. Augusta Clawson noted that a number of women in her welding class had started as laborers. "Apparently they were terribly overworked," she wrote. "They were paid 88 cents an hour and had to pick up and carry heavy metal all day. Lots of women have quit such jobs."[31] Other women, accustomed to hard work and chores considered menial by others, were proud of their endurance. A sixty-five-year-old woman who "picked up used rod and emptied skiffs on the ways" didn't miss a day's work during the hard winter of 1943–44. "I came here from my own farm in Idaho that I worked myself," she said, "and I guess I'm used to hard work and cold weather."[32] Another woman, who worked as a scaler, scraping welded seams smooth, said: "When you bring up ten children, you work hard and you do a lot of things that aren't pleasant. This job is helping to win the war, and I feel I'm doing my bit."[33]

The separation between men's work and women's work in the shipyards may have been greater than is indicated by the data on occupational distribution. Evidence suggests that within the same job categories, women and men were doing different types of work, with the women concentrated in the less-skilled, more routine aspects of the job. This is most clear in the case of welding, where the distinction between tackers and welders lent itself to a sex-based division of labor. Frequent references to tackers as women in a variety of sources suggest that women were more likely to be tack-welders, never moving on to more skilled types of welding. Most women electricians were probably wiring lights in the electrical shops, rather than installing them on the ships.[34]

There are other indications that women and men in the same jobs were doing different work. A report on labor requirements listed workers needed both by craft and by sex. Why did Swan Island need 215 *male* welders and 166 *female* welders that week, unless they were to be assigned to different types of work? (WMC 2:28). Women were typically pictured in all-women crews in the shipyard newspapers, and most women interviewed said they had worked in all-female crews. While this practice sometimes contributed to women's solidarity as they entered a male-dominated work place, it may also have reflected a difference in the type of work done by women.

Traditional distinctions between the sexes were maintained in the matter of promotion to supervisory positions. Although there was an acute shortage of supervisory personnel, women were rarely considered suitable for promotion. The War Manpower Commission report noted that "the increase in the proportion of marginal and women workers due to the draft and other causes had materially reduced the supply of leader material" (WMC 1:63). Helper and laborer leadwomen were the main exception. All forty-five leadwomen and the only forewoman at Swan Island were supervising helpers or laborers. At Vancouver, 68 percent of helper leadmen were women. The probable reason there were leadwomen over helpers and laborers crews is that they earned less than the average journeyman's wage; laborer leadmen, for example, earned $1.15 at the most.[35] In addition, they were supervising mostly women in those jobs.

Sometimes women were promoted in the crafts. Welding was the obvious job where leadwomen might be expected, since women had begun welding earlier than any other craft. A woman pictured in the shipyard newspaper in the fall of 1942 was identified as a welder leadwoman. But by the time the occupational data for the War Manpower Commission reports were collected, there were no welder leadwomen. A former welding leadman said that men objected when several women were promoted, even though they were on all-women crews. "There was quite a little friction over that," he said. "The men resented it very much. Some of them were oldtime welders and had to take a back seat to these women."[36] Other women who were interviewed recalled no leadwomen on welding crews. "There was absolutely no hope of a woman going in as a leadman," said one former welder. "That was strictly male."[37] One exception was a crew of women welders at one of the smaller shipyards which had a leadwoman and a female welding instructor. But that was not until mid-1944, and it was the first such crew in that yard.[38]

Even more exceptional was a machinist leadwoman, since few women were even journeymen in that craft. She and her crew of eight men and five women were responsible for installing locks on steel doors, and similar tasks. The shipyard newspaper pointed out that she was probably the only woman on the West Coast to hold down a job of that kind. Not surprising, she liked her job, and said, "If there is any place for me after this war is over, I'd like to continue in this type of work."[39]

In general, the pattern of job segregation may be summarized as follows: Women were overrepresented as unskilled workers, and in some of these jobs nearly all the workers were women. Women were underrepresented as journeymen, except in welding. Women were promoted to leadman only over helpers and laborers, with a few exceptions. In addition, women and men in the same job categories may have been doing different types of work. The barriers that channeled women into some jobs rather than others were not rigid, however, and women with exceptional talent or persistence could gain access to most shipyard jobs.

The labor shortage broke the barrier to employment of women, and women entered welding because of the critical demand for workers in this craft. In general, women were hired to fill gaps where the supply of men was insufficient. The gaps increasingly were in the unskilled, lower-wage jobs, some of which became "women's jobs." The skill breakdown and the training programs, which made it easy to utilize women's labor, also facilitated the development of sex-based segregation in shipyard jobs.

Despite the opportunities that shipbuilding offered to women, in the form of high wages (even as helpers), and access to new jobs and skills (even diluted skills), the pattern of men's work and women's work reasserted itself. While women welders challenged traditional conceptions of appropriate work for women, the principle that men and women are fundamentally different kinds of workers was maintained in the organization of shipyard work.

POSTWAR PLANS AND REALITIES

How did women feel about their shipyard jobs? Surveys showed that half of them wanted to keep their war jobs. In September 1943, one shipyard newspaper asked women to fill out "coupons" stating whether or not they wanted to keep their present jobs after the war. The results, reported in a Portland newspaper, revealed that "Women welders were 60 percent for staying in overalls. Other women workers, ranging from electricians to tarp sewers, were 50% for staying on the job." A sheet-metal worker interviewed by a reporter said, "I hate to think of leaving $65 a week to come back to dishes and diapers." This expressed the feelings of many women. However, neither the number nor percentage of women workers who responded to the voluntary survey was recorded.[40]

A comprehensive survey of workers at the Kaiser shipyards, conducted in January 1944, produced a similar finding. Nine-tenths of the yards' 91,000 workers were interviewed concerning their postwar plans. Of the women, 53 percent said they wanted to continue in industrial work, 8 percent were undecided, and the rest planned to seek other jobs or to return home. That fall, the women's counseling department at Oregon Ship found that 45 percent of the women wanted to continue in the same type of work after the war. They had interviewed 872 women, probably one-tenth of the total. Did the 8 percent drop represent a real change of opinion? It is difficult to know. The shipyard newspaper pointed out that the figure was quite high, considering that the yard had been on a seven-day week for the past three months. In any case, it is more important that three different types of surveys at three different times produced roughly similar results.[41]

Despite their desire to continue in industrial work, it soon became clear that there would be no place for women in "men's jobs" after the war. Shortly after V-E Day, an article in the shipyard newspaper proclaimed "The Kitchen—Women's Big Post-War Goal." What women really wanted, the article stated, was to "put aside the welder's torch" and give it back to the men. They wanted to get out of their "unfeminine" work clothes and look for a "vine-covered cottage," where they could put up frilly curtains and grow geraniums. The message was emphasized by a drawing of a woman in work clothes and tin hat racing home, reappearing dressed in ruffled apron and high heels, washing dishes and singing gaily while two angry children fought at her feet. The article was supposedly based on interviews with one hundred women in the yards. Of the sixty-five women who were working in nonclerical jobs, there were only seven who "stated flatly that the home life had no appeal for them and that they would stay in industry if given half a chance." This drastic change of opinion is understandable, however, given the conditions of the interviews. The article noted that men kept interrupting the questions to insist, "They ought to go home. Women haven't any business trying to do men's work," and that many women agreed with these remarks because it was "a time-honored way of satisfying the male ego." In general, the women were reported to be "philosophical about the fact that there will probably be no place for them in industry doing the tasks ordinarily performed by men after the war."[42]

When the war with Japan ended in August 1945, shipyard production declined rapidly. Cancellations of Navy and Maritime Commission contracts for ships led to heavy layoffs. From 65,000 workers on August 1, the shipyards were down to 25,000 by October. A year later, only 4,500 remained. Ship repair, conversion, "mothballing," and scrapping operations kept some shipyard workers employed for a while. But these jobs were reserved for men. The last three women welders at Oregon Ship got their "quit-slips" at the end of October 1945. A few women remained in unskilled jobs. A tank cleaner worked at Oregon Ship until it closed, then worked at a small shipyard through December 1946. "I was the last housekeeper there," she said.[43]

Women's work in the shipyards had come to an end. The child-care centers at Oregon Ship and Swan Island closed abruptly on September 1, 1945. The enrollment had been declining for several months, reflecting layoffs of women before the war ended. One of the centers became an elementary school, but a proposal to keep a small pre-school program was vetoed by the school board. As a result of a national campaign, government-funded centers got their support extended to March 1946. But the purpose of child-care funding was to aid production for the war effort, and the emergency was over.[44]

In the job market, old lines were redrawn. Job opportunities were clearly differentiated by sex, age, and race, and skills acquired in the shipyards were discounted. Employers were becoming "choosy." Once willing to hire anyone because of the labor shortage, many now specified "not over 45 years, male, and white." There was a demand for skilled mechanics, but employers were interested in prewar skills: "The quickly acquired skills of the lush shipyard days are a drug on the market. Inside electricians who pushed a yellow or red wire through a hole, or [those] who sprayed paint on a ship or were emergency welders are not considered skilled according to the yardstick of employers."[45] This automatically excluded women, whose only access to the skilled trades had been in the shipyards.

The jobs available to women were in traditionally female areas, at wages considerably lower than those in the shipyards. The governor's postwar planning commission noted that the war had ended at a good time, when Oregon's seasonal industries could absorb many of the unemployed: "Fruit and vegetable canneries especially favor female help." A year later, women on the night shift in the canneries earned 85 cents an hour, while men earned $1 for "harder duties." In December 1945, there were few job openings in the higher-paid brackets, but there were plenty of jobs for 65 cents an hour. At the end of 1946, women trained as stenographers, nurses, and office workers were needed. "An equal demand is for domestics and laundry workers, with few accepting those jobs."[46]

Women's unemployment after the war was dismissed as unimportant because of the convenient belief that all women were "housewives" who didn't really need to work. In September 1945, 60 percent of Oregon's unemployment claims were filed by women. As late as March 1946, it was noted that "more women than men from the shipyards are filing claims each week. This was anticipated, for housewives who worked in the shipyards or aircraft industries have returned to their domestic affairs, but they are not over-looking any checks that may be coming to them."[47] In fact, no more than 40 percent of shipyard women listed their previous occupation as housewife, and many of them needed to continue working after the war.[48] Statistics showed that "84% of American working women in 1944 and 1945 were employed because of economic necessity and were self-supporting and/or financially responsible for other members of their family."[49]

What actually happened to women shipyard workers after the war? No systematic records were kept. Unions, which lost thousands of members in a few months, did not make any checks on what had happened to their former members. It was assumed that these people had left the state, or in the case of women, had "returned to their household duties." But the pattern is clear: women were pushed back into "women's work," whether in the home or in traditionally fe-male-employing industries.[50] Examples from interviews illustrate the process. One black woman, who had been a scaler in the shipyard, was unemployed for several months after the war. She finally found seasonal work picking chickens and turkeys in a poultry factory, then worked in a laundry for the next nine years. A young mother of three had to quit welding when the night shift at her yard shut down. She and her husband had managed child care by working on different shifts. For the next five years, she was mostly at home, and had several more children, but managed to work off and on as a waitress, in a knitting mill, and in a department store. Then she found full-time work as a meat wrapper, a job she held for the next twenty-two years. A middle-aged widow, who had earned $1.20 an hour as a shipyard electrician, returned to her prewar job as an elevator operator at 25 cents an hour. She had to sell her house in order to survive.[51] The line between women's work and men's work had been reestablished; not until the early 1970s would women have access to those jobs again.[52]

The wartime demand for labor briefly opened new opportunities to women. Barriers to the skilled trades fell, and women entered shipbuilding, the highest-paying defense industry. Access to skills and high wages was especially great in the Portland shipyards, which hired women earlier and in greater numbers than most of the nation's shipyards. The importance of women's labor was recognized by the creation of model child-care centers at two Kaiser shipyards, demonstrating that high quality workplace child care was possible, given sufficient resources.

Although women's entry into shipbuilding challenged the sexual division of labor, the basic distinction between men's work and women's work was not altered. To a great extent, women and men in the shipyards were doing different types of jobs. Women filled in where men were unavailable or unwilling to work. Thus women were concentrated in welding and in the unskilled helper jobs. Within the crafts, they were often assigned to the more routine operations. The same skill breakdown and in-plant training programs that eased the employment of women also helped channel them into certain types of jobs. That job segregation by sex persisted in the midst of dramatic changes in the type of work done by women suggests its importance as a structural feature of the labor force.

Although shipyard jobs were sometimes arduous and routine, many women preferred them to their prewar work. Half of all women shipyard workers hoped to continue in industrial jobs after the war. But employers' preferences for young white men with prewar skills confined women to the low-paying jobs where they had always been found. Women's unemployment was disguised and discounted by the myth that all women war workers were "housewives" whose husbands could support them. In reality, however, the segregated job market ensured a plentiful supply of cheap female labor for seasonal industries like the food-processing plants in Oregon and for the postwar expansion of clerical and service jobs.

While the war did create some preconditions for greater equality between women and men at work, such as equal pay, child care, and access to new skills, the changes were temporary. In an economy in which full employment was possible only during a war, and in the absence of a self-conscious women's movement, or of an effective labor movement willing to defend the rights of working women, there was little chance of consolidating these gains.[53] Women were temporary substitutes for men in a labor shortage. Like farm women helping out at harvest time, women in industry could do "men's work" when necessary, but it remained "men's work."

Notes

1. U.S. War Manpower Commission, *A Survey of Shipyard Operations in the Portland, Oregon Metropolitan Area* (Portland, 1943), 3 vols, (WMC 1, 2, or 3).

2. Kaiser Industries Corp., *The Kaiser Story* (Oakland, Calif., 1968); Vanport City, Oregon Schools, *6000 Kids from 46 States* (Portland, 1946); U.S. Bureau of the Census, *Population*, Aug. 12, 1944, series CA-2, no. 6.

3. "Yards to Give Women Jobs," *Oregonian*, Jan. 30, 1942; *Bo's'n's Whistle*, May 7, 1942, p. 6. *Bo's'n's Whistle (BW)* was the employee publication for the Kaiser shipyards in Portland. "Kaiser Shipyards Lead U.S.

in Employment of Women," *Oregonian*, April 27, 1944.

4. Kaiser Industries Corp. *The Kaiser Story*, p. 31.

5. Frederick C. Lane, *Ships for Victory* (Baltimore: Johns Hopkins Press, 1951), p. 239.

6. WMC 2:45–46. See also Oregon State Board of Education, Division of Vocational Education, "Descriptive Report of Vocational Training for War Production Workers," 1945; WMC 1, 2, and 3; Augusta Clawson, *Shipyard Diary of a Woman Welder* (New York: Penguin Books, 1944).

7. Paul R. Porter, "Labor in the Shipbuilding Industry," in Colston E. Warne et al., eds., *Yearbook of American Labor* (New York: Philosophical Library, 1945), pp. 345–60; "Boilermakers to Admit Women in Ranks of Union," *Oregon Labor Press*, Sept. 25, 1942.

8. Employment in the Three Kaiser Yards," *BW*, Jan. 14, 1944, pp. 4–5; "Employment Rolls Stable in 1944: Personnel Nears '43 Peak as Workers Heed War Demands," *BW*, Dec. 29, 1944, p. 3.

9. Dorothy K. Newman, "Employing Women in Shipyards," Women's Bureau Bulletin 192–6, 1944; *Oregonian*, Jan. 30, 1942.

10. Porter, "Labor in Shipbuilding"; Oregon Shipbuilding Corp., "Occupational Codes and Classifications," 1945; "Ladies in Overalls," *BW*, Sept. 27, 1942, p. 18.

11. "Civilian Defense Leaders Open Women-in-War Drive," *Oregonian*, June 22, 1943.

12. "How You Can Help Your Yard Lick the Manpower Problem," *BW*, June 3, 1943, p. 3.

13. Carol Slobodin, "When the U.S. Paid for Daycare," *Day Care and Early Education* (Sept.–Oct. 1975), pp. 23–25; Kaiser Corp. Inc., Portland Yards and Oregon Shipbuilding Corp. Child Service Centers, "Final Report, 1943–45."

14. Interview 14, Beaverton, Oregon, May 16, 1976. The author interviewed a number of former shipyard workers in 1976. The original tapes and transcriptions of these interviews are now available at the Oregon Historical Society, Portland, Oregon.

15. Interview 7, Portland, Oregon, Feb. 14, 1976.

16. Interview 8, Portland, Oregon, Feb. 15, 1976.

17. Interview 22, Lake Oswego, Oregon, June 20, 1976.

18. Interview 6, Beaverton, Oregon, Feb. 14, 1976.

19. "OSC Yard Opening Recalled by Woman," *BW*, Sept. 29, 1944, p. 4; *BW*, March 26, 1942, p. 8.

20. Katherine Archibald, *Wartime Shipyard: A Study in Social Disunity* (Berkeley: University of California Press, 1947), p. 22. Rumors of sterility are mentioned by Clawson, and in *BW*, June 3, 1943.

21. Kaiser Co. Inc., Richmond Shipyard No. 3, "Women in Shipbuilding," Jan. 1, 1943; "Mabel Can't Do That to Us," *BW*, Nov. 5, 1942, p. 9; WMC 1:26; "Woman power in the Three Kaiser Shipyards," *BW*, June 17, 1943.

22. For example, see Edward Gross, " 'Plus Ça Change . . . ?' The Sex-

ual Structure of Occupations Over Time," *Social Problems* 16 (Fall 1968): 198–208.

23. Data from WMC 1, 2, and 3. Index based on eighteen major job categories, excluding office workers. Results were: Oregon Ship 55 percent; Swan Island, 48 percent; Vancouver 57 percent. For explanation of index of segregation, see Gross, " 'Plus Ça Change . . . ?' "

24. Comparing the percentage of all women with the percentage of all workers who were welders, women were overrepresented as welders by 28 percent at Oregon Ship in December 1942, by 11 percent at Swan Island in August 1943, and by only 2 percent at Vancouver in October 1943.

25. "Loftlady," *BW*, Dec. 23, 1943, p. 12.

26. "High Climber," *BW*, Jan. 28, 1944, p. 13; "Slender Blonde Does Good Job as Rigger," *BW*, Sept. 29, 1944, p. 4.

27. Interview 10, Portland, Oregon, May 14, 1976.

28. " 'Gus' Comes Back: Welder-Author Visitor," *BW*, May 12, 1944, p. 2; Clawson, *Shipyard Diary*, p. 123.

29. Interview 23, Portland, Oregon, July 11, 1976 (wife in a joint interview).

30. "The Story of 130 Dozen Brooms," *BW*, May 20, 1943, pp. 10–11.

31. Clawson, *Shipyard Diary*, p. 48.

32. "Hard Job 'Natural' for Idaho Woman," *BW*, Sept. 29, 1944, p. 4.

33. "These and All Shipbuilding Mothers Honored May 14," *BW*, May 12, 1944, p. 1.

34. References to women as tackers from interviews, Clawson, *BW*; to women as inside electricians from interview 5, Portland, Oregon, Feb. 13, 1976, and Postwar Readjustment and Development Commission, "Progress Report," November 1945 (PDRC).

35. Oregon Shipbuilding Corp., "Occupational Codes and Classifications," 1945.

36. Interview 23 (husband in a joint interview).

37. Interview 7.

38. " All-Women Welding Crew," *Stem to Stern*, June 2, 1944, p. 7.

39. "Machinist Leadwoman Position Unusual Job for Woman," *BW* (Vancouver), Dec. 15, 1944.

40. "Women at WISCO," *Stem to Stern*, Sept. 9, 1943; Ellen Mills Ewing, "Postwar Poser: Pants or Aprons?" *Oregonian*, Nov. 21, 1943 (magazine section).

41. Two-thirds of all shipyard workers hoped to continue in industrial work. "Workers Shy Postwar Plans," *BW*, March 10, 1944, p. 7; "Many Women Plan to Stay in Industry," *BW*, Nov. 24, 1944. p. 3.

42. *BW*, May 11, 1945, p. 7.

43. PRDC, August 1945, October 1945; Oregon State Employment Service, "Analysis of Oregon Labor Market," October 1947; "Women Welders Out," *BW*, Nov. 2, 1945, p. 8; interview 23.

44. Child Service Centers, "Final Report"; Minutes and Reports of the Day Care Committee, Portland Council of Social Agencies, 1945; Howard

Dratch, "The Politics of Child Care in the 1940s," *Science and Society* 38 (Summer 1974): 167–204.

45. PRDC, October 1945; PRDC, December 1945, p. 5.

46. PRDC, August 1945, p. 3; PRDC, September 1946; PRDC, November 1946, p. 3.

47. PRDC, September 1945; PRDC, March 1946, p. 6.

48. The figure of 40 percent former housewives is derived from the report that 11 percent of all shipyard workers listed "housewife" as previous occupation. Other listed occupations were not broken down by sex. From *BW*, March 10, 1944, p. 7.

49. Lyn Goldfarb, *Separated and Unequal: Discrimination Against Women Workers After World War II* (Washington, D.C.: Union for Radical Political Economics, n.d. prob. 1976), unpaginated, quotation from 11th page.

50. PRDC, November 1945.

51. Interview 12, Portland, Oregon, May 15, 1976; interview 8; interview 5.

52. Several women interviewed had returned to welding in Portland shipyards in the early 1970s.

53. Even a progressive union like the UAW did not defend the jobs of its women members. See Goldfarb, *Separated and Unequal.*

Part 3

RACE AND ETHNICITY

Job and other opportunities have been far more limited for women of color than they have for white women. Severe discrepancies have existed, and continue to exist, in housing, education, income, and health care. For all but a handful of women of color, leisure time to agitate for political rights or municipal reform has been almost impossible to come by. At the same time as documentation of the inequities is being amassed, however, new researchers are calling for an affirmative dimension to the history of people of color. This would celebrate the aspects of the black, Native American, and Asian cultures that are different from the patterns of the dominant culture. Furthermore, this endeavor can uncover alternate role models, particularly among the women who have shouldered the double burdens of racism and sexism.

The achievements of black women in the Northwest have yet to be fully documented, and Susan H. Armitage and Deborah G. Wilbert call for a serious look at a range of topics especially fruitful for exploration. Particularly in urban communities, where black women both raised families and worked for wages, there is a history crying for research and interpretation. In the mostly male mining towns, black women ran boardinghouses, restaurants, laundries, and hotels or provided domestic services to the miners. In addition to their roles in families and as wage earners, their community contributions need to be uncovered, especially those made through churches and clubs.

Religious institutions, the source of enormous strength, cohesiveness, and practical assistance for black people, generally owe their establishment and sustenance to unrecognized black women. So, too, the forgotten founders of temperance organizations, study clubs, and associations devoted to civic reform deserve our attention. The question of racial segregation, intensifying during World War II when the war industries brought increased numbers of black men and women to Seattle and Portland, calls for historians' scrutiny as well. Authors Armitage and Wilbert provide researchers with clues for the exploration of these neglected topics. Their broad bibliography points scholars in appropriate directions for commencing this much-needed effort.

Anthropologist Lillian A. Ackerman observes women's roles within Native American culture in "Sexual Equality on the Colville Indian Reservation in Traditional and Contemporary Contexts." She conducted forty-five interviews with elders aged sixty to ninety, in addition to interviews with more youthful members, from eleven tribes (Sanpoil, Nespelem, Colville, Lakes, Southern Okanogan, Methow, Chelan, Entiat, Columbia, Wenatchi, and one band of Nez Perces). She finds great differences between Indian women's sexual equality and that of Euro-American women. Contrasting the reminiscences of the 1920–30 era with descriptions of contempory life and tribal arrangements, she notes real changes in politics, economy, religion, and domestic life. Nevertheless, the women of both eras experienced sexually equal access, or a different but balanced access to power, authority, and autonomy. The author perceives that women on the Colville Reservation have not in the past, and do not now, have the secondary status in key realms of life experience which has been accorded women in mainstream society.

"Domestication and Americanization," by Janice Reiff, examines Scandinavian American women in Seattle during the years 1888–1900, particularly the young and single Swedes and Norwegians. She emphasizes the quickness of these late nineteenth-century Scandinavian American women to embrace mainstream American cultural patterns, rather than nurturing the cultures they brought to the United States. Reiff argues that Americanization was rapid, and efforts to maintain Old World culture slight, owing in part to particular circumstances in the growing and prosperous city of Seattle. In addition, most of the immigrants had already resided in the Midwest for about five years, in strong ethnic communities, where they had learned to read, write, and speak English, and had also mastered American customs and habits.

Seattle was a city that offered uncanny resemblances to the Scandinavian homeland in its climate, landscape, and natural resources. Seattle also offered the replication of many Scandinavian institutions, such as the Scandinavian Immigration and Aid Society, the Scandinavian-American Bank, the Lutheran Church, as well as Baptist and Methodist churches, the Baltic Lodge, the Swedish Club, the Norse Club, the Norwegian Workingman's Society, and various foreign-language newspapers. As at home, young women had to support themselves here, as domestics, dressmakers, or tailors if they did not labor within the family. In fact, a majority of them found employment in these areas in America. Ninety percent of Norwegian American and 59 percent of Swedish American young women worked in these familiar occupations, when three-quarters of Seattle's women workers, on average, sought other types of work. As in the old country, Scandinavian women in Seattle lived with their own families or with their employers until they married, generally in their mid-twenties.

Given the conditions, one might not expect a strong Scandinavian drive to adopt new American ways. Reiff argues, however, for a recognition of the ethnic forces that pushed acculturation rapidly. The absence of neighborhoods and the limited success of clubs to foster ethnic loyalties were contributing factors to the intermarriage of Seattle Scandinavian women. Almost half of them married outside their national groups. Only 57 percent of Swedish American women married Swedish American men, while 62 percent of Norwegian American women married Norwegian American men. Here, patterns broke with those of the Old World. Because good jobs and wages were common for men, these Scandinavian American brides did not work for wages. Their efforts were concentrated on supervision of their own households. They did not need to take in boarders. They had fewer children than their Scandinavian sisters in the old country, and their children were raised the American way—speaking English, interacting with non-Scandinavian neighbors, staying in school longer, living at home longer, and finally taking better jobs. Thus assimilation was hastened. Only later, at the beginning of this century, when Scandinavians entered Seattle as their initial city of embarcation in an era when a slower economy meant fewer jobs, did residential neighborhoods and a tighter ethnic culture arise.

There are great hazards in relying on sweeping generalizations about immigrants, as is well proven by the specific data collected and interpreted in Reiff's article. A multiplicity of forces shaped the experiences of various newcomers to this land. The individual's sex, age, nationality, religion and marital status, experiences abroad, migration patterns in America, societal tolerance for their upward mobility through schools, jobs, and neighborhoods, the level of prosperity in the adopted community, its rural or urban character, the time period of arrival—all exerted some influence. Our tired assumptions, that most immigrant women were housebound and dependent, that they functioned as preservers of Old World traditions and resisted change, and that rural transplants to urban centers continued to bear many children, more than they could support, clearly have a limited usefulness. Here, actually, they distract us from the facts. The broad lesson, then, is one of caution. Let us avoid a disregard for the ethnic diversity that was and remains as great as native heterogeneity.

Black Women in the Pacific Northwest: A Survey and Research Prospectus

Susan H. Armitage and Deborah Gallacci Wilbert

The black woman is truly the forgotten person in Pacific Northwest history. Regionally, black studies have mostly focused on black men; women's studies scholarship has been largely concerned with white and American Indian women. As a result, black women have been overlooked. This essay surveys the extent of our present knowledge and suggests fruitful areas for further research.

Our regional ignorance about black women is an extreme example of how remarkably little we know about black women in all of western history. From that larger history, however, we construct a useful general framework. Lawrence B. De Graaf's 1980 article, "Race, Sex and Region: Black Women in the American West, 1850–1920," provides the basic demographic information.[1] Until 1920 the total number of blacks in the West was small: black women never composed as much as 1 percent of the female population in the Mountain and Pacific states. However, in contrast to white women, black women from the very start were concentrated in urban rather than rural areas. This meant that isolation was to some extent offset by opportunities to create black communities, albeit small ones, in urban areas. There were very few single black women in the general western population. Although the proportion of black married women was high, western black women had a much lower child-bearing rate than black women in other regions. Nevertheless, like their black sisters elsewhere, black women were likely to be employed. De Graaf calculates that, in the West, "Married black women were twice as likely to be employed as married Indians or Asians; three times as likely as white women."[2] They were most likely to be employed as domestic servants.

Because the detailed demographic research has not yet been done for the Pacific Northwest, we cannot yet say how our regional picture may differ. But we know that the contours fit the general western picture: small numbers, concentration in urban areas, and a high incidence of paid employment. We also know that because of the paucity of sources, we are unlikely to learn as much about rural blacks, both male and female, as we would like. Furthermore, we have much richer sources for the twentieth century than we do for the nineteenth.

Ironically, one negative circumstance provides our best glimpse into the lives of black women in the earliest period of American settlement of the Pacific Northwest (1840–60). Early white settlers in Oregon not only outlawed slavery in the new territory but also outlawed settlement by black persons, whether slave or free. Outrageous as this "blaming the victim" approach seems today, it was only one of a number of tactics employed by early western states to avoid the slavery issue entirely.

In spite of the Oregon law, some early settlers brought their slaves with them. The legal efforts of some of those slaves to free themselves affords us a brief glimpse into the lives of black women in the early period of Pacific Northwest history.

Mommia Travers, a forty-five-year-old slave, was freed by her master, Captain Llewellyn Jones, at Fort Vancouver in 1851. No explanation is given on the brief country manumission record, but a commendation of her character was added to the document by Captain Llewellyn six years later, stating that she "is an honest and perfectly conscientious woman and deserves kind and good treatment at the hands of everyone."[3] This suggestion that Mommia Travers met with cruel treatment after being freed points up the special problems of free blacks, especially women, who were isolated in the sparsely settled, loosely governed West.

A county record gives a brief glimpse into the life of Jane Snowden Thomas, an ex-slave from Missouri. The document reveals that in 1852 she bought her eleven-year-old son Billy's freedom for $500 before emigrating to Oregon.[4]

The most famous slave case in Oregon was the 1852 legal suit of Robbin and Polly Holmes to gain custody of their children from their ex-master, Nathaniel Ford. Ford had brought the slave couple to Oregon from Missouri in 1844 and, according to the Holmeses, had promised them their freedom in return for helping him start a farm. In 1849, Robbin and Polly were freed but Ford kept their three children, two of whom had been born in Oregon. Ford maintained that Robbin and Polly had agreed to give him custody of their children until they reached legal age in return for Ford's having supported them during their "unproductive years." In 1853 Robbin brought suit by habeas corpus to get custody of the children. The judge ruled that since Ford voluntarily took them to a state where slavery was illegal, custody would be awarded to their father. Nevertheless, Ford's daughter kept one of the children, sixteen-year-old Mary Jane, who was sold for $700 in 1857 to a man who later married her. The suit was brought in Robbin's name and custody was awarded to him, so technically this is not a case of a black woman tackling the legal system. Yet Robbin and Polly are always mentioned as a unit, and the struggles with Ford were a joint effort.[5]

Some black slave women did bring suit in their own names, not only for their freedom but for back wages as well. In 1854 the *Oregon Statesman* ran a news item entitled "Luteshia Carson, Woman Slave in Missouri Brought to Oregon, Sues Estate of Master for Back Wages." The case was heard before the same judge that had tried the Robbin Holmes case, Judge Williams, but the jury could not reach a verdict.[6]

Oregon became involved in the slavery controversy because a large proportion of the early Willamette Valley settlers were southerners, mostly from the border states of Missouri, Tennessee, and Kentucky. Some brought their slaves with them, as was the case with Nathaniel Ford. Although by 1850 there were only 207 blacks in Oregon, the social and economic ramifications of this situation caused great agitation over the issue of slavery. As early as 1844 the antislavery forces in the provisional legislature passed an act that prohibited slavery in Oregon as well as excluding all blacks, slave or free, from emigrating to the territory. Yet slaves were kept in Oregon despite this act. The Territorial Legislature of 1849 passed a bill to prohibit blacks from settling in the territory, and the state constitutional convention of 1857 reaffirmed this exclusion law, although they struck down sections of the act that called for the whipping of blacks found in violation. Since Washington Territory had been separated from Oregon in 1853, Oregon's exclusion laws did not apply north of the Columbia River. After Oregon became a state (in 1859), the issue of slavery did not die down. During the Civil War, a paramilitary group called the Knights of the Golden Circle was organized in Oregon to fight the Union and propagate slavery. Blacks were still a subject of legislative action after the war when a special session of the legislature passed three resolutions: claiming that the issue of black suffrage belonged to the states; applauding blacks for loyal service to the Union; and declaring that Congress should colonize southern blacks in a new state. Throughout all the antislavery actions in Oregon there ran a fear of "negro equality" as well as resistance to southern dominance in the state. The successful exclusion of blacks from Oregon, though invalidated by the Thirteenth Amendment, helps account for the smaller number in the state today.[7]

Because of the Oregon Exclusion Law, several early black families settled north of the Columbia River in Washington Territory. One interracial couple, George and Isabella Bush, settled near Olympia in 1845. George Bush was referred to as a "mulatto"; his wife, Isabella, was white. One of their sons was a member of the state legislature in the 1890s, but there is no information about daughters of the family. Similarly, another black man, George Washington, is celebrated as the founder of Centralia, but there is apparently no information on his wife and daughters, if there were any.[8]

We know virtually nothing about rural black women in the early period of Pacific Northwest history. As a matter of fact, because until recently the historical view has been so exclusively focused on men, we don't know very much about white women in the early settlement of rural areas either. However, for this latter group, there is every reason to believe that research in diaries and county histories will fill out the picture. For black women in rural areas, however, the sources appear to be too scanty to repay the necessary research effort.

The picture is brighter when we turn to consideration of black women in mining towns. In fact, outside of the black communities in major cities, western mining towns are the best place to look for the nineteenth-century history of blacks in the West. The reason is obvious: gold does not discriminate. Blacks as well as whites saw opportunity in the mining towns, and those who could afford it came to try their luck.

From mining town histories and folklore has emerged the most widely known stereotype of the western black woman: the motherly but single former slave who gets rich doing laundry and investing the profits in mines and real estate. The West's best known black women—"Aunt" Clara Brown of Colorado, "Mammy" Pleasant, and "Grandmother" Mason of California—all fit this stereotype.[9] As we might expect, however, the reality is more complex.

Some black women came to mining areas with job-seeking husbands, and some came on their own. They usually provided much-demanded domestic services to miners and others—cooking, cleaning, laundry. Sometimes they owned their own boardinghouses, restaurants, laundries, and hotels. Some carried on their husband's business after his death, and there is evidence that many black women headed households with young children. The opportunities for black families to own property and obtain middle-class status in mining boom areas created another category of black woman—housewife. These women were often involved in establishing and maintaining black churches, clubs, and other community institutions. Black women were represented in each of the principal mining areas in the nineteenth century.

Company-owned coal mining activity in Washington in the 1880s helped created one of the few black towns in the Far West—Roslyn. A collection of taped interviews with former residents of Roslyn and nearby Cle Elum, housed in the Washington State University Archives, sheds some light on black women in that area.[10] Black laborers were brought into the region from the Midwest by the Northern Pacific Coal Company, a subsidiary of the railroad, as strikebreakers in 1888 and 1889. Many brought their families with them. An interview with Mrs. Ollie Rucker reveals that her family came to the area when her grandfather was recruited to work the mines. She was born in the mining town of Franklin and grew up in Cle Elum, where her father worked for the railroad. She remembers black social clubs and dances.

Two other descendants of the black strikebreakers who came to Roslyn are sisters, Leola Cravens Woffort and Beulah Cravens Hart. They recall that the black families first lived in nearby Jonesville on arrival because Roslyn residents would not allow strikebreakers in their town. As whites moved out, blacks became the majority in Roslyn. The sisters finished eighth grade in that town in the 1920s before attending a predominantly white high school in Cle Elum.

These interviews alone do not provide enough information to form conclusions about the nature of black women's roles in company mining towns such as Roslyn. More information can be found in the taped interviews of the Seattle Afro-American Project housed in the Manuscripts Section of the University of Washington Libraries. It contains interviews with Beulah Hart, LeEtta King, Eva Strong, and again, Leola Woffort—all early residents of Roslyn. In addition, Skip Ware of Central Washington University has conducted interviews with black residents of Roslyn. Examination of these materials will provide a more complete picture of black women in Washington mining regions.

The role black women played in mining communities in the West can be reconstructed through detailed investigation of manuscript censuses, newspapers, club records, and oral histories. Elmer Rusco's work on black Nevadans, *"Good Times Coming?" Black Nevadans in the Nineteenth Century*,[11] shows the value of the manuscript census in this regard. Documents rarely exist in the case of lower-class, dispossessed groups such as black women, making it imperative to sort painstakingly through the abundant material the census provides. The findings so far, though scanty, suggest that black women were indeed significant forces in local economies and community building through their jobs, businesses, and involvement in social institutions.

This picture of black women as important shapers of their communities is confirmed when we look at the Pacific Northwest's major cities, Seattle and Portland. Two recent studies, Elizabeth McLagan's *A Peculiar Paradise: A History of Blacks in Oregon, 1788–1940* and Esther Mumford's *Seattle's Black Victorians, 1852–1901*, and an

Calvary Baptist Church (*courtesy Ellensburg Public Library Local History Collection*)

earlier article, Quintard Taylor's "The Emergence of Black Communities in the Pacific Northwest, 1864–1910," provide much useful information.[12] Black communities were well established in Portland by 1870, in Seattle by 1890. In both cities, churches and clubs, newspapers and business served the black community. In all of these activities, black women played important but incompletely documented parts. The ideology of womanhood (both black and white) meant that the activities of many women were defined as simply "helping" her man run a business or a newspaper or establish a church. Even for single women, informal activity widely recognized within the community often went uncredited by later historians. For example, Mumford says that the nucleus of the Seattle A.M.E. Church had its first service in January 1890 at the restaurant of a widow, Mrs. Elizabeth Thorne. Subsequently, Mumford notes, the Ladies Social Circle raised the money to buy a church site.[13] Yet the official accounts of the enterprise list only the trustees of the early church—all men, as was the minister. Certainly a complete history of the church ought to name Mrs. Thorne and the Ladies Social Circle among its founding members. It is unlikely that the role played by black women in the founding of the Seattle A.M.E. Church was unique. Careful research will doubtless show that the support of women's societies for churches and church work was a basic element of community building.

One area exists, rich in documentation, which can tell us much more than we now know about black women and their communities in the Pacific Northwest. Black women's clubs, usually composed of middle-class women, played a special self-help and charitable role in black communities throughout the country. The cities of the remote Pacific Northwest were no exception. The rich club life of black women—church groups; literary, art, and musical groups; self-improvement societies; auxiliaries; sororities; and reform associations—was especially evident in the larger cities. Eliza McCabe recalled that when she moved to Tacoma in the 1930s she found a number of active clubs, among them the Cloverleaf Art Club, The Matrons, and the Mary McLeod Bethune Chapter of the Women's Christian Temperance Union. She went on to form the Irene McCoy Gaines Improvement Club (for community improvement) and the Stafford Study Club (for self-improvement). Later still she became president of the Washington Association of Colored Women's Clubs, as was Nettie Asberry, another Tacoma clubwoman, before her. Asberry was also the founder of the Tacoma chapter of the National Association for the Advancement of Colored People.[14] Local records of these clubs, and the national compilation of their histories, *Lifting As They Climb,*[15] can tell us much about the social organization and the role of women within black communities. The University of Washington's Black History Manuscript Collection is a particularly rich source for the history of black clubwomen in western Washington and Oregon.

By the early twentieth century, black professional women—especially teachers and social workers—had become more common. These were the women who were most likely to belong to black women's clubs, and much can be learned about their careers from the club sources. They are also the most likely subjects for magazine articles and compilations describing female black professionals as important "firsts." These articles are sometimes informative, although of limited usefulness. Most black women were not professional women. Historically and until very recently, black women have worked for white women as domestic servants.

Louella Cravens, graduation day
(courtesy Eastern Washington Historical Society)

The working life of the ordinary black woman is best learned through oral history interviews. Here again Seattle is fortunate to have several large and important oral history collections. In the following excerpt, Gussie Savage talks about her mother's work as a domestic servant:

> She did the housework and took care of kids, and everything, for 25¢ a week, can you beat it? She did everything, even cut the lawn outside . . . on her days off, she didn't have enough money to go anyplace, she'd sit in her room, . . . and the woman would have some fancy work for her to do—she had some beautiful linen napkins, and she wanted her to embroider the initial on them. . . .[16]

With the Second World War and the opening up of war industries to blacks, the black population in Seattle and Portland (as well as other West Coast cities) jumped.[17] Although the newcomers were welcome in the black communities, the external response was unfriendly. In both cities there was trouble over housing, schools, and public accommodations. The slumbering prejudices of whites, lulled because blacks were such a small part of the population, awoke as the numbers (still small) began to grow. Pacific Northwest blacks, like their brothers and sisters in other nonsouthern parts of the country, realized that they would have to insist on their civil rights.[18] This most recent phase of black Western history continues today and will last as long as discrimination in housing, schooling, and jobs persists. The changing history of the black communities of Seattle and Portland since 1940 and the role of black women in these struggles have hardly been studied. Here again oral histories are a major source.

Another major source is black newspapers. In the cities, there is rich newspaper documentation from the time of settlement into the 1970s. The coverage is provided by a series of newspapers, not by a continuous and steady single publication. This publishing record tells us of the desire of the black community for information and connection, and it also illustrates the difficulty of achieving that goal.

This brief survey has sketched the contours of life for black women in the Pacific Northwest. There is much that we do not know, but in most cases our ignorance is remediable. The sources are there: we simply need willing researchers.

As we learn more about the lives of black women in the Pacific Northwest, we will be able to answer some important questions. How different were the lives of western black women from their sisters in the Northeast and the Midwest? The answer to this question, which assesses the role of the environment, is of great significance for both black and western history. We also want to know in what ways the lives of western black women differed from those of their counterparts—white, Hispanic, and Asian. Answers to this question are of great interest to women's historians seeking to develop a consistently multicultural framework. Finally, what can we say about the black woman's search for community and continuity in the Pacific Northwest? This human question about life's satisfactions is of interest to us all, for it is the pioneer's question as well as our own.

Notes

1. Lawrence B. De Graaf, "Race, Sex and Region: Black Women in the American West, 1850–1920," *Pacific Historical Review* 49, no. 2 (May 1980): 285–313.

2. Ibid., pp. 286, 288, 296 (quotation).

3. D. G. Hill, "The Negro in Oregon: A Survey," M. A. thesis, University of Oregon, 1932, p. 18; Fred Lockley, "Some Documentary Records of Slavery in Oregon," *Oregon Historical Quarterly* 17 (June 1916): 108.

4. See Hill, "The Negro in Oregon," p. 19, and Lockley, "Some Documentary Records," p. 107.

5. For information on the Robbin and Polly Holmes case see Lockley, "Some Documentary Records," pp. 108–9; Fred Lockley, "Facts Pertaining to Ex-Slaves in Oregon, and Documentary Record of the Case of Robbin Holmes vs. Nathaniel Ford," *Oregon Historical Quarterly* 23 (June 1922): 114–17; Scott McArthur, "The Polk Country Slave Case," *Historically Speaking* 2 (Polk County, Oregon, Historical Society journal) (August 1970); *Oregon Statesman*, July 5, 1853; Hill, "The Negro in Oregon," p. 17.

6. *Oregon Statesman*, Oct. 17, 1854.

7. For information on the slavery controversy in Oregon see D. G. Hill, "The Negro in Oregon"; D. G. Hill, "The Negro as a Political and Social Issue in the Oregon Country," *Journal of Negro History* 33 (April 1948): 130–45; T. W. Davenport, "Slavery in Oregon," *Oregon Historical Quarterly* 9 (September 1908): 189–253; Helen Jean Poulton, "The Attitude of Oregon Toward Slavery and Secession, 1843–1865," M. A. thesis, University of Oregon, 1946; "History of Attempts to Legalize Slavery in Oregon," *Oregonian*, Feb. 14, 1899; and Robert W. Johannsen, *Frontier Politics and the Sectional Conflict: The Pacific Northwest on the Eve of the Civil War* (Seattle: University of Washington Press, 1955).

8. Lenwood G. Davis, "Sources for History of Blacks in Washington State," *Western Journal of Black Studies* 2, no. 1 (March 1978): 60–64.

9. Kathleen Bruyn, *"Aunt" Clara Brown* (Boulder, Colo.: Pruett Publishing Co., 1970), p. 61; Sherman W. Savage, "Mary Ellen Pleasant," in Edward T. James et al., eds., *Notable American Women*, 3 vols. (Cambridge, Mass.: Harvard University Press, 1971), 3: 75–76; Delilah Beasley, *The Negro Trail Blazers of California* (Los Angeles, 1919; reprinted, San Francisco: R and E Associates, 1969).

10. Black Oral History Interviews, Holland Library, Washington State University, Pullman.

11. Elmer Rusco, *"Good Times Coming?" Black Nevadans in the Nineteenth Century* (Westport, Conn.: Greenwood Press, 1975).

12. Elizabeth McLagan, *A Peculiar Paradise: A History of Blacks in Oregon, 1788–1940* (Portland: Georgian Press, 1980). Esther Hall Mumford, *Seattle's Black Victorians, 1852–1901* (Seattle: Ananse Press, 1980); see also her *Seven Stars and Orion: Reflections of the Past* (Seattle: Ananse Press, 1986). Quintard Taylor, "The Emergence of Black Communities in the Pacific Northwest, 1864–1910," *Journal of Negro History* 64 (Fall 1979): 346–51.

13. Mumford, *Seattle's Black Victorians*, pp. 78, 148.

14. Eliza Champ McCabe, oral history transcript, Schlesinger Collections, Black Women Oral History Project. Radcliffe College, Cambridge, Massachusetts, 1980 (copy at University of Washington Libraries, Manuscripts Section).

15. Elizabeth Lindsay Davis, *Lifting As They Climb* (Chicago: National Association of Colored Women, 1933).

16. Washington Women's Heritage Project Oral History Collection, University of Washington Libraries, Seattle.

17. There is a scattering of information on black women workers in the Portland shipyards. See Karen Skold, "The Job He Left Behind: American Women in the Shipyards During World War II" (in this volume), and "Good Work, Sister!," script and study guide by the Northwest Women's History Project, P.O. Box 5692, Portland, OR 97228.

18. Quintard Taylor, "Migration of Blacks and Resulting Discriminatory Practices in Washington State between 1940 and 1950," *Western Journal of Black Studies* 2:1 (March 1978): 65–71. Another, more recent part of the story is considered by Doris H. Pieroth, "Desegregating the Public Schools, Seattle, Washington, 1954–1968," Ph.D. diss., University of Washington, 1979.

Black Women in the Pacific Northwest: A Selected Bibliography

BACKGROUND INFORMATION AND STATISTICS

De Graaf, Lawrence B. "Race, Sex and Region: Black Women in the American West, 1850–1920." *Pacific Historical Review* 49, no. 2 (May 1980): 285–313.

Hogg, Thomas C. "Negroes and Their Institutions in Oregon." *Phylon* 30 (Fall 1969): 272.

Lerner, Gerda. *Black Women in White America.* New York: Pantheon Books, 1972.

McLeod, Don. "Factual Survey Made of Increase In Negro Population." *Oregonian*, October 4, 1942.

Taylor, Quintard. "Blacks in the West: An Overview." *Western Journal of Black Studies* 1 (March 1977): 4–10.

U.S. Department of Commerce. Bureau of the Census. *Negroes in the United States, 1920–1932*, 1935.

BIBLIOGRAPHIES AND INDEXES

Abajian, James de T. *Blacks and Their Contributions to the American West: A Bibliograhpy*. Boston: G. K. Hall, 1974.

Davis, Lenwood G. *Blacks in the American West: A Working Bibliography*. Council of Planning Librarians, Exchange Bibliography 582, 1974.

———. *Blacks in the Pacific Northwest, 1788–1972*. Council of Planning Librarians, Exchange Bibliography 335, 1972.

———. *Blacks in the State of Oregon, 1788–1974*. Council of Planning Librarians, Exchange Bibliography 616, 1974.

———. "Sources for History of Blacks in Oregon." *Oregon Historical Quarterly* 73 (September 1972): 196–211.

———. "Sources for History of Blacks in Washington State." *Western Journal of Black Studies* 2, no. 1 (March 1978): 60–64.

Mills, Hazel E., and Nancy B. Pryor. *The Negro in the State of Washington: 1788–1969*. Olympia: Washington State Library, 1970.

U.S. Department of Labor. Women's Bureau. *Guide to Sources of Data on Women Workers for the United States and for Regions, States, and Local Areas*. Washington, D.C.: U.S. Government Printing Office, 1972.

BLACK WOMEN AND SLAVERY IN THE PACIFIC NORTHWEST

Berwanger, Eugene H. *The Frontier Against Slavery: Western Anti-Negro Prejudice and the Slavery Extension Controversy*. Urbana: University of Illinois Press, 1967.

Davenport, T. W. "Slavery in Oregon." *Oregon Historical Quarterly* 9 (September 1908): 189–253.

"Habeas Corpus Proceedings in Oregon Supreme Court to Release Negroes at Dallas, Polk County, Who Were Once 'Held as Slaves in Missouri'." *Oregon Statesman*, July 5, 1853.

Henderson, Archie M. "Introduction of Negroes in the Pacific Northwest, 1788–1842." M.A. thesis, University of Washington, 1949.

Hill, D. G. "The Negro as a Political and Social Issue in the Oregon Country." *Journal of Negro History* 33 (April 1948): 130–45.

———. "The Negro in Oregon: A Survey." M. A. thesis, University of Oregon, 1932.

"History of Attempts to Legalize Slavery in Oregon." *Oregonian*, February 14, 1899.

Johannsen, Robert W. *Frontier Politics and the Sectional Conflict: The Pacific Northwest on the Eve of the Civil War*. Seattle: University of Washington Press, 1955.

Lockley, Fred. "Facts Pertaining to Ex-Slaves in Oregon, and Documentary Record of the Case of Robbin Holmes vs. Nathaniel Ford." *Oregon Historical Quarterly* 23 (June 1922): 111–37.

————. "Some Documentary Records of Slavery in Oregon." *Oregon Historical Quarterly* 17 (June 1916): 107–15.

"Luteshia Carson, Woman Slave in Missouri Brought to Oregon, Sues Estate of Master for Back Wages." *Oregon Statesman*, October 17, 1854.

McArthur, Scott. "The Polk County Slave Case." *Historically Speaking* 2 (Polk County, Oregon, Historical Society journal) (August 1970).

Poulton, Helen Jean. "The Attitude of Oregon Toward Slavery and Secession, 1843–1865." M. A. thesis, University of Oregon, 1946.

Thurman, Sue Bailey. *Pioneers of Negro Origin in California*. San Francisco: Acme Publishing Co., 1949; reprinted, San Francisco: R and E Associates, 1971.

BLACK WOMEN IN THE PACIFIC NORTHWEST: CLUBS AND CLUBWOMEN

Adams, Mary E. (1860–1947). Papers. Afro-American History Collection. Manuscripts Section, University of Washington Libraries, Seattle.

Asberry, Nettie J. Papers. Afro-American History Collection. Manuscripts Section, University of Washington Libraries, Seattle.

Bence, Erna. "101 Years of Living Fail to Dim Dr. Nettie's Love of Life, People." *Tacoma News Tribune*, July 17, 1966.

Davis, Elizabeth Lindsay. *Lifting As They Climb*. Chicago: National Association of Colored Women, 1933.

Farquarson, Mary. Papers. Afro-American History Collection. Manuscripts Section, University of Washington Libraries, Seattle.

Gage, Fern. Papers. Afro-American History Collection. Manuscripts Section, University of Washington Libraries, Seattle.

Lerner, Gerda. "Early Community Work of Black Club Women." *Journal of Negro History* 59, no. 2 (April 1974): 158–67.

Links (publication of a black women's organization). Documents Division, Eastern Washington State University Library, Cheney.

McCabe, Eliza Champ. Oral history transcript. Black Women Oral History Project. Schlesinger Collections, Radcliffe College, Cambridge, Massachusetts, 1980 (copy at University of Washington Libraries, Manuscripts Section).

Spokane Bethel African Methodist Episcopal Church. *50 Years of Progress.* 1940.

BLACK WOMEN IN THE PACIFIC NORTHWEST: COMMUNITIES

Anderson, Larry. "We Need Acceptance Where We Are: A Central Area Negro Leader Gives Her Views." *Seattle Times Magazine*, September 18, 1966.

"Clara Mae Peoples of Portland, Oregon." *Ebony*, December 1987, pp. 96–102.

Grimes, Leola. Oral history tape. Afro-American History Project, Manuscripts Section, University of Washington Libraries, Seattle, 1968.

McLagan, Elizabeth. *A Peculiar Paradise: A History of Blacks in Oregon, 1788–1940.* Portland: Georgian Press, 1980.

Mumford, Esther Hall. *Seattle's Black Victorians, 1852–1901.* Seattle: Ananse Press, 1980.

Northwood, Lawrence K., and Ernest A. Barth. *Urban Desegregation: Negro Pioneers and Their White Neighbors.* Seattle: University of Washington Press, 1965.

Taylor, Quintard. "The Emergence of Black Communities in the Pacific Northwest, 1864–1910." *Journal of Negro History* 64 (Fall 1979): pp. 346–51.

———. "Migration of Blacks and Resulting Discriminatory Practices in Washington State Between 1940 and 1950." *Western Journal of Black Studies* 2, no. 1 (March 1978): 65–71.

Woffort, Leola Cravens, and Mrs. Beulah Cravens Hart. Oral history tapes. Afro-American History Project. Manuscripts Section, University of Washington Libraries, Seattle, 1968.

BLACK WOMEN IN THE PACIFIC NORTHWEST: PROFESSIONAL WOMEN

Crowell, Evelyn. "Twentieth Century Black Woman in Oregon." *Northwest Journal of African and Black American Studies* 1 (Summer 1973): 13–15.

Sullivan, Ann. "Negro Woman Attorney Tries First Court Case." *Oregonian,* October 12, 1960.

Who's Who in Colored America. 7th ed. New York: Christian E. Burkel and Associates, 1950.

BLACK WOMEN IN THE PACIFIC NORTHWEST: WORK

Blood, Kathryn. *Negro Women War Workers.* U.S. Department of Labor, Women's Bureau, Bull. 205. Washington, D.C., 1945.

Brown, Jean. *The Negro Woman Worker.* U.S. Department of Labor, Women's Bureau, Bull. 165. Washington, D.C., 1938.

Hayes, Elizabeth Ross. "Negroes in Domestic Service in the United States." *Journal of Negro History* 8 (October 1923): 384–442.

Herzog, June. "A Study of the Negro Defense Worker in the Portland-Vancouver Area." B. A. thesis, Reed College, Portland, Oregon, 1944.

National Urban League Report. *Performance of Negro Workers in 300 War Plants.* New York: National Urban League, 1944.

"New Life in Seattle: In the Biggest, Fastest-Growing City in the Northwest, Negroes Have Found a New Frontier." *Our World* 6 (August 1951): 22–25.

U.S. Department of Labor. Women's Bureau. *Negro Women in Industry.* Bul. 20. Washington, D.C., 1922.

———. *Negro Women in the Population and the Labor Force.* Item 782. Washington, D.C., 1968.

————. *Negro Women Workers in 1960.* Bureau Publication 287. Washington, D.C., 1963.

————. *A Survey of Laundries and Their Women Workers in 23 Cities.* Bull. 78. Washington, D.C., 1930.

BLACK WOMEN IN THE PACIFIC NORTHWEST: ORAL HISTORY COLLECTIONS

Black Oral History Interviews. Fifty interviews by Quintard Taylor and his associates, 1972–74 (black pioneers and their descendants in Washington, Oregon, Idaho, and Montana). Holland Library, Washington State University, Pullman.

Inland Pacific Northwest Black History Collection. Eight interviews by Joseph Franklin, 1978. Library, Eastern Washington University, Cheney.

Afro-American Project. Eight interviews, 1968–70. Manuscripts Section, University of Washington Libraries, Seattle.

Black Women Oral History Project. Schlesinger Collections, Radcliffe College, Cambridge, Massachusetts. Two interviews transcribed for University of Washington Libraries, Manuscripts Section, Seattle.

Black Project Washington State Oral/Aural History Program. A Bicentennial Project. Oral History Index and microfiche copies of interviews are available in libraries throughout the state.

King County Black Oral History Project. Sixty-nine interviews by Esther Mumford. Part of the project described above.

Employment for Black Women in Seattle, 1915–1945. Metrocenter YMCA, Seattle.

Interviews. Washington Women's Heritage Project, Seattle office. Library, University of Washington, Seattle.

BLACK NEWSPAPERS (LISTED CHRONOLOGICALLY)

Portland:
  Advocate (1899–1902)
  New Age (1902–1907)
  People's Observer (1943–1948)
  Clarion Defender (1953–1970)
  The Newspaper (1967–1970)
  Portland Observer (1970–1974)
Seattle:
  Standard (1891–1902)
  Seattle Republican (1894–1915)
  Western Sun (1898–1900)
  World (1898–1903)
  Searchlight (1904–1927)
  Cayton's Weekly (1916–1921)
  Cayton's Monthly (1917–1921)
  Northwest Enterprise (1920–1962)
  Northwest Herald (1943–1946)

Puget Sound Observer (1957–1966)
Afro-American Journal (1967)
Spokane:
  Citizen (1908–1913)
  Forum (1908–1912)
Tacoma:
  Tacoma Forum (1903–1918)
  Searchlight (1904–1927)

Sexual Equality
on the Colville Indian Reservation
in Traditional and Contemporary Contexts

Lillian A. Ackerman

Many anthropologists consider it doubtful that sexual equality has occurred or might occur in any society, past or present.[1] Their opinion supports the idea that males are dominant over females in all societies.[2] The few studies demonstrating or suggesting the presence of sexual equality in certain groups have so far had little influence in changing such views.[3] Further examples of sexually egalitarian groups, then, are important to persuade social scientists and the lay public that such societies are not only possible but exist today. The culture of the Colville Indian Reservation in the recent past and in contemporary times presents just such an example of an egalitarian society.

The Colville Indian Reservation in the state of Washington is made up of eleven Plateau Indian groups. Sexual equality was reported for the traditional Plateau Indian societies over forty years ago,[4] but was insufficiently described. A study focusing on the relative status of men and women in Plateau culture seemed in order, and the Colville Indian Reservation was chosen for the locus of this research.

The research described here was conducted in 1979–80 on two levels. First, elders, age sixty to ninety (in 1979), were interviewed regarding the status of the sexes in their youth, a period dating from about 1910 to 1930 when the foraging economy was still predominant. This memory culture is called "traditional" here because, while many changes had been made from the "aboriginal" period, the foraging way of life was still a viable option, universally exercised. The memory culture recorded in 1979 may be compared with statements made to researchers around 1930 that sexual equality existed in Pla-

The research for this paper was made possible by fellowships from the Woodrow Wilson National Fellowship Foundation and the Educational Foundation of the American Association of University Women, and by grants from Sigma Xi and the Phillips Fund of the American Philosophical Society. Their support is gratefully acknowledged. I would also like to express gratitude to the many individuals on the Colville Reservation who helped me with their information, patience, and kindness, and also to the Colville Tribal Business Council who gave me permission to do the research on the reservation. My thanks to Robert E. Ackerman and Linda S. Stone for helpful comments on various drafts of this paper. They do not necessarily agree with the ideas presented.

teau culture.[5] The 1930 period is used as a baseline and then compared with contemporary sexual status, almost fifty years later.

Following interviews with elders, younger informants who work for wages or who have salaried employment were then asked to describe aspects of sexual status in the contemporary culture. Their information was cross-checked through observation.

Forty-five people from eleven tribes (Sanpoil, Nespelem, Colville, Lakes, Southern Okanogan, Methow, Chelan, Entiat, Columbia, Wenatchi, and one band of Nez Perces) were interviewed in depth during the research. While some details regarding sexual status varied within the political and religious spheres among these eleven groups, the variations were minor. In contrast, sexual status was identical in the domestic and economic spheres for all groups, probably because of the customary intermarriage among Plateau peoples.

The method for evaluating sexual status is based on Schlegel's definition of sexual equality. She defines sexual equality as the equal access, or the different but balanced access, of both sexes to power, authority, and autonomy in the economic, domestic, religious, and political spheres. Power is the ability to act effectively on persons or things, to secure desired decisions which are not of right allocated to the individual or to his or her role.[6] Political influence, widely used in Plateau society, falls into this category. Authority is the institutionalized right to make a decision and expect obedience. Autonomy is the right to take independent action without control by others.[7]

Using these definitions, tables were made for each of the four social spheres in both periods, and data gathered during fieldwork were classified and assigned to each sphere under the cells for power, authority, and autonomy for each sex. This process resulted in a summary statement of the degree of participation by each sex in each of the four social spheres in two periods (see Table 1 as an example).

THE ECONOMIC SPHERE: TRADITIONAL CULTURE

In the past, the Plateau Indians were fishers, hunters, and gatherers, living in small villages under the authority of a chief.[8] By the 1920s, people lived on reservations and were scattered on small allotments which they farmed, but chiefs continued to be elected and acknowledged. Along with maintaining their small farms, people pursued traditional economic activities as well: men continued to fish and hunt, and women continued to gather vegetal foods. The power, authority, and autonomy of each sex in the economic sphere during this period are outlined in Table 1. The power cell is blank, since no examples of what I could call economic power were recalled by informants,

TABLE 1
The Economic Sphere: Traditional Culture

Men	Women
POWER	

AUTHORITY

Each sex provided about half of diet

Flesh and vegetal foods equally valued and important in diet

Men	Women
Economic skill (hunt, fish) leads to political influence	Economic skill (gathering) leads to political influence

Work of both sexes considered equally important by both sexes

Men	Women
Only men made salmon weirs	Only women made lashings for weir tripods
Men fished	Women made nets
Men with Salmon Power built weirs	Women with Salmon Power ensured fish runs
Hunting leaders, Salmon Chiefs	Gathering leaders, salmon shamans
Men prohibited from proximity of root baking oven	Menstrual taboos
Men distributed meat	Women received meat
Boy's first kill ceremony	Girl's first gathering ceremony
Men own personal items and horses	Women own personal items and food

AUTONOMY

Men	Women
Traders in horses, weapons, hides, fishing implements	Traders in foods, handicrafts

Male and female trade equally important

Both sexes were interpreters

Both sexes gambled

Men	Women
Men made own weapons and tools	Women made own digging sticks for root gathering

although they may well have existed.

Table 1 shows that each sex provided approximately half the traditional diet, and both sexes valued both flesh and vegetal foods equally. All informants agreed that flesh foods were not considered more important than vegetal foods. This is an important point, for Friedl writes that all hunting and gathering societies esteem meat as the most valued food in the diet. She argues that since men distribute meat to other men, only they can accrue the prestige necessary for political power. Women cannot participate in political power because they do not have the means (meat) to accrue prestige. This situation, according to Friedl's argument, results in males achieving universal dominance over women.[9]

Friedl's theory fails to fit the hunting and gathering phase of Colville Reservation history. To illustrate the point, meat distribution in the Plateau will be described.

The important fall hunting was always done by a group of men and women working together for several days or weeks. The men hunted while the women cooked, made camp, and helped the men drive the animals. After the hunt, the meat was butchered and evenly divided among the families in the camp. This was done as follows: in the evening, all the women in camp sat in a circle. Each woman was presented with a portion of the kill by a man who was not necessarily the hunt leader or the successful hunter. Often an older man was selected to divide and distribute the meat.[10] If a man lived alone, he sat in the circle with the women. This procedure of distribution in the Plateau refutes Friedl's theory that men acquire power through the presentation of meat to other men in all foraging societies.[11] The successful Plateau hunter did not distribute the meat, and so he could not earn political power in this manner. Further, when a man hunted or fished independently, he gave all the food he obtained to his wife, who did what she wished with it. Her first responsibility was to keep the family well fed, but surpluses of food were hers to trade or give away as she pleased.

To explore this question further, informants were asked specifically if good hunters were more influential politically than other persons—that is, if their opinions during political discussions were more highly valued than those of others. The answer was negative. Both sexes said that men who were "good providers" of either meat or fish were influential with the chief and their peers, but women who were "good providers" of vegetal foods were equally influential, even though vegetal foods were rarely distributed outside the family. Nevertheless, the work of both sexes was equally valued, and the foods they obtained were equally valued. Thus political power was

Nancy Judge, Colville Reservation
(courtesy R. E. Ackerman)

not sex specific in the Plateau, since the economic skill of either sex qualified a person to have political influence.

It should be noted on Table 1 that few economic aspects of life as described by informants were identical (indicated by crossing the midline of the table) for men and women in the past. I judged that most items were balanced or equivalent (noted by being placed in opposition on the table). Thus only men built salmon weirs, but informants reported that only women provided the lashings or thongs for the weir tripods without which they could not be built, and without which salmon could not be captured. Only men fished for salmon, but women provided nets.[12] Men with magical Salmon Power directed the building of the weirs. Women were ordinarily prohibited from approaching the weir, because menstrual blood could frighten the fish away.[13] If the fish run failed, however, a woman with magical Salmon Power was asked to clear debris from the fish traps, a task usually performed by males. Her magical power exerted during this task effected the return of the salmon run. Thus, while fishing was a male monopoly, women had important roles in the task.

Men with superior hunting ability (and with the proper magical power by definition) were chosen as hunt leaders during the communal hunts. Men with superior fishing ability (and the magical power) were chosen to build the weirs and supervise the taking of the fish. Women, too, had such leadership roles. Those with the appropriate magical power were gathering leaders who led others in finding edible plants. It was not necessary to have magical power to find roots, hunt, or fish, but such power was seen as making these tasks easier, especially when the resource was scarce during a bad season.

Large quantities of roots, an extremely important component of the diet, were dried in earth ovens for winter use. Baking roots well was an exacting task, made easier by magical power. It was believed that roots did not bake properly in the proximity of men, particularly unmarried men. Their presence was prohibited in the area.[14]

It is possible that the prohibitions placed on men balanced the similar menstrual taboos placed on women. Since these prohibitions are no longer in effect today, it is difficult to judge whether they were comparable in emphasis for both sexes. The pattern of prohibitions for both sexes, however, suggests that the prohibitions somehow reenforced the sexual division of labor. The menstrual taboo, at least in this culture, was not an indication of low social status, but was only one of several taboos that confirmed the complementarity of the sexes.

The economic importance of both sexes was symbolized by ceremonies celebrating a boy's first kill or first catch of fish and a girl's first gathering of vegetal foods. A boy might get his first deer about age twelve; a girl's first independent gathering might occur about age eight. These ceremonies continue today.

A married couple did not own material goods jointly. Women owned all food coming into the household, including the meat and fish caught by her husband. She also owned the house poles, the tipi covering, housemats, baskets, all prepared skins, plus a few horses to transport herself and her goods. Men owned only their weapons, clothes, and a number of horses. In case of divorce, men had only these kinds of goods to take away.

Both sexes were involved in trade with Indians from other reservations. Women, as the sole proprietors of food, dealt mostly in that commodity, although they also traded handicrafts. Men traded horses, raw hides, and hunting and fishing implements, which they manufactured in earlier times. Informants of both sexes judged that the trade of both sexes was equally important.

In prereservation times, trading expeditions to the Pacific coast or to Montana required interpreters, and either sex filled this role, although women were said to learn languages more readily than men. Gambling was a prestigious economic activity in which large amounts of goods were redistributed. Both sexes participated in this activity, but only with opponents of the same sex. It was believed that menstruating women would destroy the magic on which successful gambling was based.

Men and women each made their own economic implements, thus accentuating their economic autonomy. Men manufactured their hunting and fishing implements. Women fabricated their digging sticks, used for collecting roots, and baskets used in gathering roots, berries, and greens.

The factors listed in Table 1 suggest that the sexes had not identical but equally balanced access to all aspects of the traditional economic sphere.

THE ECONOMIC SPHERE: CONTEMPORARY CULTURE

The foraging way of life became impossible for the Colville Reservation Indians around 1939. The building of Grand Coulee Dam destroyed many of the fish runs in the area. Hunting was curtailed by state law, and many of the gathering grounds were occupied by white farms. To survive, the Indians turned to the intensive working of their small farms and ranches, or to low-paid wage labor.

Half of the Colville Reservation lands were removed from Indian ownership in 1892 so they could be opened to white settlement.[15]

Commencing in the 1950s, moves were made by the federal government to force termination on the remaining reservation lands held communally. Only concerted action by many of the Indians defeated this move. In 1970, Congress decided against termination and awarded the tribal government more authority to run the reservation's affairs.

As a result of these and other changes, the economy of the reservation has altered from the past. In major respects, its economy is now similar to that of Euro-American society in that the tribal government staffs offices, manages forests, maintains roads, plans economic development, and administers health, education, and welfare programs. In other ways, the reservation economy remains a separate system. The tribal government does its own hiring by its own rules based on its indigenous cultural traditions. Since these rules differ from those of Euro-American society, the reservation cultural values become clear even in modern context. These values are evident in equal pay for equal work, the presence of female administrators, the ease with which female administrators work with either sex, and the equal importance given to work performed by both sexes. These are all legacies of the past. Further, those who need work get it—reflecting, I believe, the foraging ethos of sharing.

The contemporary economic sphere, as it operates within the reservation, is outlined in Table 2. It is immediately apparent that access of both sexes to the economic sphere is largely identical today instead of balanced as in the past. There are only two exceptions that may well be inequalities of access. One is that men outnumber women in the top three managerial positions on the reservation. This may be a result of acculturation—that is, copying the authority structure of Euro-Americans, either because of a change in culture or the need of Euro-American governmental structure to do business only with men. On the other hand, this may be an indigenous element, since Plateau men have always served as spokesmen for the group with outsiders, and these three officials often deal with outsiders.

The other possible inequality of the sexes in this sphere is that the quality of women's work is more highly valued than that of men's work today. Informants of both sexes say that women are more efficient and conscientious in completing a task and in working eight-hour days. The contemporary opinion is reminiscent of the phrase "Men don't work," which elders of both sexes use to describe the male economic role in the past. Of course men "worked," in the sense of providing fish and animal flesh for the diet; moreover, they risked their lives to defend the community. Their activities, however, occurred in strenuous spurts with leisurely periods in between, whereas women were more often occupied with tasks on a daily basis. Thus

TABLE 2
The Economic Sphere: The Contemporary Culture

Men	Women
POWER	
Influence exerted by both sexes	
Access to management positions by both sexes	
Top three managerial positions filled by men	

AUTHORITY	
First economic achievements of young people recognized	
Equally encouraged in training and employment	
Work considered equally important	
Jobs less sex typed than in Euro-American Society	
Equal pay for equal work	
Authority equally effective in management jobs	
	Women's work seen generally as more efficient

AUTONOMY	
The decision to work autonomous for both sexes	
	82% to 90% of women work
Trade proceeds owned individually	

it is likely that the traditional economic role of reservation women may have better prepared them for the eight-hour days required from workers in an industrial society. The traditional pattern, on the other hand, did not prepare men for this. Furthermore, the incentive to earn money for its own sake, which equals power and prestige in white society, has no attraction for Indian men.

The traditional male intermittent work pattern may account for the observation that women in many North American tribes acculturate more readily to modern society than men do. It is argued, for instance, that differential acculturation among the Oglala Sioux occurs because women are able to continue their homemaker roles in contemporary times, thus experiencing less disruption than men. In contrast, men are completely deprived of their former roles as warriors and hunters.[16]

While this explanation seems obvious at first, it cannot apply to the Plateau tribes of the Colville Reservation, for there has been little continuity in women's roles either. Child bearing and rearing continue, of course; but all else is changed. Office employment is as different from gathering and preserving wild foods as lumbering is different from hunting. What remains from the past is the ethic that women do what they must to support the family, and even provide the major share of support if needed, as they did in the traditional culture. It is suggested here that the better adjustment of Plateau Indian women in contemporary times may be due to their being accustomed to sustained rather than intermittent work.

Other than the two exceptions discussed above, Table 2 shows an identical access of the sexes to the economic sphere. Economic influence is exerted by both sexes, and access to management positions appears to be attainable by women on an equal basis. Ceremonies celebrating a young person's economic "firsts" continue to be performed for both sexes. Young men and women are equally encouraged to get higher education, and both expect to be employed when adult. Women's work and men's work continue to be equally important. While jobs are somewhat sex typed in the Euro-American manner on the reservation, women are also found in male types of employment. They are lumberjacks, they run Caterpillar tractors, and they work as night "watchmen." They were being trained as miners in 1979 when a molybdenum mine was planned on the reservation (the project was terminated by the mining company when mineral prices fell). For all tribally paid positions, men and women receive equal pay for equal work. Problems of sexual status in the workplace are not evident, and informants deny that there are any.

Today, both men and women make the decision to seek employment autonomously. Most women do not seek their husband's concurrence if they decide to work. Neither are they urged by their husbands to work. A woman's independence in making this decision is striking compared with a Euro-American woman's situation: she is expected to consult and negotiate with her husband before taking this step. Colville Reservation women expect to be employed unless they have preschool children and no child-care services are available. A recent survey shows that almost 82 percent of Colville women are employed.[17] The actual percentage may be higher, because some employment, such as providing child-care services to others, may not be reported in such a survey.

Today, trading among Plateau, Northwest Coast, and Plains tribes continues. Money from such trade is retained by the individual for personal use.

One may judge that, overall, the access of men and women to the economic sphere is equal in contemporary times. The fact that the access is identical rather than balanced, as in the past, is suggestive. It is possible that identical access of the sexes to the economic sphere is the only way to achieve sexual equality in an industrial society.

THE POLITICAL SPHERE: TRADITIONAL CULTURE

The political sphere as it existed around 1910–30 will be addressed next (see Table 3). Reservation tribes were still foraging during this period, but were also farming small allotments. They continued to elect chiefs and form assemblies made up of both sexes.

During this period, individual men and women with superior economic skills exerted equal influence on chiefs and their fellow band members, as described above. Although only men held the office of chief in most reservation tribes, it has been recorded that women could be chosen as chiefs or head political officers among the Southern Okanogan and Lakes tribes.[18] I discovered that a woman served as chief five generations ago among the Chelan as well. Another official, the "woman of great authority," shared power with a male chief in some groups, and is recorded among the Southern Okanogan, Methow, and Chelan.[19] All the above tribes reside on the Colville Reservation today.

Contemporary informants of these four tribes deny that women ever served as chiefs or head political officers. They confirmed, however, that a "woman of great authority" was elected to fill the office of judge and arbiter in criminal cases, notably feuds. Since the judicial function was reported by Ray to be the male chief's greatest prerogative,[20] the "women of great authority" were then at least as important as the chief in those groups in which both existed. Unfortunately, not much information regarding this role has survived today.

Chiefs were always advised in public affairs by their wives: this was an expected role. An indication of the importance of the wife's role is revealed by an incident occurring forty years ago when an otherwise suitable candidate for chief was rejected because his wife was considered unsuitable.

The chief's wife was influential in nominating the chief's successor after he died. In some groups, she served as chief until a successor was elected.

Lesser leadership roles were filled by women. One woman in con-

TABLE 3
The Political Sphere: Traditional Culture

Men	Women

POWER

Those with superior economic skills had equal political influence

Wives advised chief

AUTHORITY

Assemblies made up of both sexes

Men	Women
Male chief or head political officer	Female possible head political officer (chief) in past
	"Women of great authority" had judicial and advisory functions; called a "female chief"
Hunting and fishing leaders	Gathering leaders
	Chief's wife served as chief when husband away
	Chief's widow had right to nominate his successor; in some groups, she was temporary chief

Could serve as peacemaker for tribe

AUTONOMY

Both sexes spoke and voted in assembly

A married couple's votes did not need to coincide

Warriors of both sexes

tact times served as a peacemaker between her tribe and another. The gathering leaders mentioned above were influential politically as well as economically.

Both sexes spoke and voted in assembly when a communal decision was being debated. Husband and wife voted completely independently of each other. If there was disagreement between them in the way they spoke or voted, it was not a matter for discussion later.

In prereservation times, a woman had the option to become a warrior even if she was married and had children. It was an autonomous decision that no one could veto. Such women were rare, but numerous enough to be remembered today.

In the traditional political sphere, a more uneven access of the sexes appears. One may judge that there is a balanced access of the sexes to political life on the chief level, although the opposite opinion also has some validity. However, below the chief level, equal political access of the sexes is undeniable.

THE POLITICAL SPHERE: CONTEMPORARY CULTURE

In 1938 a tribal council took over the political functions formerly exercised by chiefs. Fourteen members sit on the tribal council today. Access to this political office is open to both sexes equally (see Table 4).

A number of women have occupied seats on the tribal council since 1938. Only two women were council members during the period of this study, but while they shared equal authority with the twelve male

TABLE 4
The Political Sphere: Contemporary Culture

Men	Women
POWER	
Access to political influence	
Age an advantage to either sex	
AUTHORITY	
Members of tribal council	
Men outnumber women on tribal council	
Both sexes orate on ceremonial occasions	
Active on boards	
AUTONOMY	
Both sexes speak publicly with equal frequency	
Married couples vote independently, do not know how spouse votes	
Equally active politically	

council members, their power or influence was greater. They earned this influence in the 1960s through their position as leaders in the fight against termination of the reservation. Even today, male council members seek their concurrence on solutions to problems, and they were seen to change their votes on important issues to coincide with those of the two women.

Women council members were more numerous in the past. In 1970, nine years before this study was made, six women and eight men sat on the council. Between 1963 and 1969, five women were council members. Informants said that women also served before those dates, and mentioned specific individuals.

Council women are usually assigned to the Health, Education, and Welfare Committee or the Enrollment Committee; subdivisions of the tribal council. These are seen as female concerns, although men sit on these committees as well. The work of these particular groups is perceived to be extremely important, for welfare concerns do not have the inferior status they have in Euro-American culture. The important Enrollment Committee determines the eligibility of a child for reservation membership, and consequently whether the child will participate in benefits such as per capita income. Women also serve on the council committees dealing with leases and timber sales—activities usually associated with males in Euro-American culture.

In the 1960s, the council met only once a month, for there was little business to be handled. Today, more work is needed to deal with problems coming before the council. Although the position of council member is full time and well paid, fewer women than before are willing to serve because extensive travel is now required for the job. Many women are reluctant to leave their children as frequently as the position requires.

The increased need for travel has come about since 1970, when greater autonomy was granted to the reservation. The extensive travel required today of council members seems to be a barrier to women— one that is perceived by both sexes. Consequently, while the sex of a candidate does not seem to be relevant in winning office, and personality and talent are the important criteria, the social structure is changing enough to handicap women who wish to serve on the council. They cannot take young children with them on business travels, and worry about adolescent children left alone at home. Only a few women can arrange for child care during long absences.

The polity loses more than the mere participation of women. Both male and female informants say that women are more suitable as council members because they generally do a better job and are more authoritative. They are seen as tougher, stronger, more outspoken, and more willing to challenge someone, whereas men as a group are more quiet and conservative. This is a generalization, of course, but one that was largely confirmed by observations made during tribal council meetings and conferences between Indians and whites.

Lesser political offices are filled by both sexes in approximately equal numbers.

All things being equal, reservation members tend to trust an older person over a younger one in a public role. Thus age in either sex is no handicap in running for office.

Elders of both sexes orate on ceremonial occasions, although in previous generations, men did so more frequently.

Autonomy in the political sphere today involves speaking publicly and voting autonomously. Husbands and wives never reveal how they cast their vote, either to each other or to anyone else before or after an election, whether the election is on the reservation or not. Someone married many years may guess how a spouse votes, but the matter is never discussed. This independence in voting is taken so seriously that one individual was incredulous when he learned that a Euro-American couple would discuss candidates with each other, and would probably influence each other's opinion and then vote identically.

In public meetings of a political nature, it was noted that both sexes spoke publicly with about equal frequency. Men and women appear to be equally interested in the political issues concerning the reservation.

The access of the sexes to the political sphere in the traditional period was a mixture of identical and complementary rights and privileges. The modern political arrangement displays an almost identical access of the sexes to this sphere (see Table 4).

THE DOMESTIC SPHERE: PAST AND PRESENT

Today, reservation women continue their roles as managers of the family's resources. The ultimate responsibility for the family's survival remains with her, as in the past. While foraging is still done on an occasional basis, employment provides the resources for the major economic needs of the family. If a man's wages are insufficient to meet family needs, his wife seeks employment, if she is not already employed. As noted above, her decision to do this is autonomous. She need not fear community disapproval, since employment is seen as the equivalent of gathering—that is, both activities sustain the family.

When divorce occurred in the past, the women who did not immediately remarry were able to support themselves completely through their gathering efforts. If they chose to live apart from parents or brothers, they traded surplus vegetal products for meat and fish. They received a certain amount of such foods in the communal distributions as well.

The same self-reliance is evident today. Most women do not expect long-term support for themselves and their children when divorce occurs, and are prepared to take complete responsibility. In fact, a female elder was heard to deride a young woman who was seeking support from her ex-husband. Because reservation women are self-reliant and confident, the loss of economic support is never an inhibiting factor when divorce is considered.

THE RELIGIOUS SPHERE: PAST AND PRESENT

The religious sphere in both periods is considered by informants to be the most important and valued aspect of the culture, and access to it by both sexes is almost identical. Women as well as men became shamans in the past and were equally powerful. Women shamans were outnumbered by the men in some groups, but equal in number in other groups. Everyone of both sexes sought and obtained guardian spirits.

Today, the native guardian spirit religion has persisted and is unchanged in terms of access by the sexes. However, several new religions have been added to the culture, with some consequent uneven access. For instance, in 1979, only men read the gospels and ushered in the Catholic Church. The native Indian Shaker Church, a combination of Christianity and the traditional guardian spirit religion, has a preponderance of female officials in the Colville Reservation branch of the church.

CONCLUSIONS

By examining the four sets of tables (only two sets have been presented here), it can be determined that, on the Colville Reservation, the access of both sexes to the economic, political, domestic, and religious spheres is identical, or balanced, resulting in a condition of sexual equality.

One of the implications of the study of sexual status on the Colville Reservation in the past and present is that there is no automatic correlation between the level of socioeconomic integration and sexual equality. Leacock writes that sexual egalitarianism, like all equality, can exist only among hunting and gathering groups, but that it is destroyed in industrial societies.[21] Modern Colville Reservation culture indicates, however, that modern economic conditions are not incompatible with sexual equality. On the contrary, sexual equality has persisted as a legacy from the past despite erosion of the traditional culture in other areas. Where the Colville Reservation Indians have the power to control their society, they have not reduced women's status, but have adapted modern economic conditions to their ideology of sexual equality.

Notes

1. Sherry B. Ortner, "Is Female to Male as Nature Is to Culture?" in Michelle Zimbalist Rosaldo and Louise Lamphere, eds., *Woman, Culture and Society* (Stanford: Stanford University Press, 1974), pp. 67–87; Michelle Zimbalist Rosaldo, "Woman, Culture and Society: A Theoretical Overview," in *Woman, Culture and Society,* pp. 17–42.

2. William Tulio Divale and Marvin Harris, "Population, Warfare, and the Male Supremacist Complex," *American Anthropologist* 78, no. 3 (1976): 521–38.

3. Albert S. Bacdayan, "Mechanistic Cooperation and Sexual Equality among the Western Bontoc," in Alice Schlegel, ed., *Sexual Stratification: A Cross-Cultural View* (New York: Columbia University Press, 1977), pp. 270–91; Patricia Draper, "!Kung Women: Contrasts in Sexual Egalitarianism in Foraging and Sedentary Contexts," in Rayna R. Reiter, ed., *Toward an Anthropology of Women* (New York: Monthly Review Press, 1975), pp. 77–109; Eleanor Leacock, "Women's Status in Egalitarian Society: Implications for Social Evolution," *Current Anthropology* 19, no. 2 (1978): 247–75; and Alice Schlegel, "Male and Female in Hopi Thought and Action," in Schlegel, ed., *Sexual Stratification,* pp. 245–69.

4. Verne F. Ray, *Cultural Relations in the Plateau off Northwestern America* (Los Angeles: Publication of the Frederick Webb Hodge Anniversary Publication Fund, Southwest Museum, 1939), p. 24; L. V. W. Walters, "Social Structure," in Leslie Spier, ed., *The Sinkaietk or Southern Okanagon of Washington* (Menasha, Wisc.: George Banta Publishing Company, 1938), p. 96.

5. Ray, *Cultural Relations,* p. 24; Walters, "Social Structure," p. 96.

6. M. G. Smith, *Government in Zazzau, 1800–1950* (London: Oxford University Press, 1960), pp. 18–19.

7. Alice Schlegel, "Toward a Theory of Sexual Stratification," in Schlegel, ed., *Sexual Stratification,* pp. 8–9.

8. Ray, *Cultural Relations,* pp. 11–12.

9. Ernestine Friedl, *Women and Men: An Anthropologist's View* (New York: Holt, Rinehart and Winston, 1975), pp. 8–9, 13.

10. Richard H. Post, "The Subsistence Quest," in Spier, ed., *The Sinkaietk,* p. 22.

11. Friedl, *Women and Men,* p. 22.

12. Post, "The Subsistence Quest, p. 14.

13. Ibid., p. 17.

14. James A. Teit, *The Salishan Tribes of the Western Plateaus,* Bureau of American Ethnology, 45th Annual Report (Washington, D.C.: U.S. Government Printing Office, 1930), p. 185.

15. M. Gidley, *With One Sky Above Us* (New York: G. P. Putnam's Sons, 1979; paperback ed., Seattle: University of Washington Press, 1985), p. 31.

16. Eileen Maynard, "Changing Sex-Roles and Family Structure among the Oglala Sioux," in Ann McElroy and Carolyn Matthiasson, eds., *Sex Roles in Changing Cultures,* Occasional Papers in Anthropology, State University of New York, Buffalo, 1:12–13.

17. Colville Confederated Tribes Health Plan, Nespelem, Washington, 1979.

18. Ray, *Cultural Relations,* p. 24.

19. Walters, "Social Structure," pp. 95–96.

20. Ray, *Cultural Relations,* p. 22.

21. Leacock, "Women's Status," p. 255.

Scandinavian Women in Seattle, 1888–1900: Domestication and Americanization

Janice L. Reiff

One theory currently popular among historians of American immigration holds that, insofar as possible, immigrants tried to recreate their old familiar society within the new American context. For evidence, some scholars have pointed to institutional continuities between Europe and the United States.[1] Others have looked to the maintenance of traditional family roles.[2] Whatever their approach, most have concluded that all immigrant groups, whether Swedes, Germans, Jews, Poles, or Italians, have made similar attempts to preserve their identities.[3]

To be sure, this new emphasis is a useful corrective to the idea of rapid, unimpeded Americanization. However, the model of persistence has difficulty accounting for change, especially in the second generation, and the emphasis on values has tended to neglect the differential impact of specific economic and ecological environments on immigrants. Diversity, not uniformity, characterizes the history of American immigrants.

The study of a polar case, the experience of Scandinavian women in Seattle, Washington, at the turn of the century, helps to clarify the relationship between traditional values and a particular urban environment. Two major factors, the dynamics of the city itself and the migration patterns of Scandinavians on their way to Seattle, led these women to discard their traditional roles and responsibilities and embrace those of the city's native-born white women. For them and their male counterparts, the preservation of their European past was far less important than their American future.

Seattle in 1900 was a boomtown. The boom had begun in the 1880s when the Northern Pacific Railroad completed its transcontinental line to Puget Sound and transformed the small port town of 3,500 into a major urban center of 42,000. Growth slowed as a result of the 1893 depression but returned with even greater vigor three years later when prospectors discovered gold in Alaska. Profits from outfitting miners for the gold fields, shipping lumber to the East, and construction of new buildings for the growing city created thousands

Janice L. Reiff, "Domestication and Americanization: Scandinavian Women in Seattle, 1888–1900," *Journal of Urban History* 4 (1978): 275–90. Copyright © 1978 by the *Journal of Urban History*. Reprinted by permission of Sage Publications, Inc.

of new jobs, which in turn attracted ever more residents. By 1900 over 80,000 persons lived in Seattle.

Of these new residents, a large proportion were Norwegians and Swedes. Over 12 percent of the city's total population in 1900 came from the Scandinavian peninsula or were children of Scandinavians.[4] Most had come to the United States as part of the massive wave of emigration from Sweden and Norway during the last quarter of the nineteenth century, and they exhibited the demographic and social characteristics of that migration. A large majority were daughters and sons of peasants, pushed from the land by the rapid increase in population in both countries.[5] About half were women and half left Europe while between the ages of sixteen and twenty-five.[6] Single emigrants outnumbered married emigrants. By the decade 1891 to 1900, fewer than 30 percent of the Swedish emigrants traveled as a part of their nuclear families.[7]

Like the Scandinavian men and women who had come before them, these Swedes and Norwegians went first to the Midwest.[8] They settled in Illinois, Iowa, Wisconsin, Minnesota, or the Dakotas, primarily in rural areas but also in the cities of Chicago and Minneapolis. There they learned the basics of American life: the English language, the political and educational systems, and the importance of getting ahead. Yet, after some time in the Midwest, thousands of Scandinanvians, both male and female, chose to leave the ethnic communities there and settle in the Pacific Northwest.

Seattle, during the years from 1880 to 1900, seemed a particularly propitious spot for Scandianvian immigrants. It bore a striking physical resemblance to the land in Sweden and Norway. As one homesick Norwegian explained, "the fjords of Norway are sublime, and Puget Sound is equally so."[9] Physical similarities also meant economic similarities: fishermen, loggers, farmers, and woodworkers could anticipate employment in the fields already familiar to them.[10] The general prosperity of the city and its hinterland ensured the availability of those and other jobs.

In addition, the town was receptive to Scandinavian immigration. As early as 1876 a Scandinavian Immigration and Aid Society had been formed to encourage migration to Seattle.[11] One of the city's earliest Swedish settlers, Andrew Chilberg, arrived in Seattle in 1875 and, with his two brothers, opened a grocery store. By 1878 he had gained enough prominence to be elected to the city council. In the next year he was appointed vice-consul for Sweden, and three years later he became the county assessor. His wealth increased with his prestige. He was able, in 1892, to found the Scandinavian-American Bank and actively support his fellow immigrants.[12]

By the late 1880s enough Scandinavians had been attracted to Seattle to make Swedish and Norwegian communities within the city possible. Churches provided the first institutional proof of the Scandinavian presence. In 1888 the Swedes organized a Lutheran church. The next year the Norwegians and Danes opened their own Lutheran church. Other Scandinavian organizations appeared soon after. Some achieved a great deal of success. The all-Scandinavian Baltic Lodge, International Order of Good Templars, founded in 1888, claimed 140 members by the mid-1890s.[13] The Swedish Club attracted 200 members in the eight years after its organization in 1892.[14] A Norwegian Workingman's Society grew to 200 members before it dissolved in the mid-1890s. In its place the Norwegians established a Norse Club, organized appropriately on Norwegian Independence Day. Several other churches were congregated. By 1900 the Norwegians supported two different Lutheran churches, a Baptist church, and a Methodist church. The Swedes attended either a Lutheran, Methodist, Baptist, or Swedish Mission church. Some residential concentration of Scandinavians also emerged as Swedish and Norwegian households located in the broad region north and east of the downtown and south of Lake Union. At the turn of the century, then, it seemed as if well-defined Scandinavian communities existed in Seattle.

To a large extent, however, that impression was deceptive. Both the Swedish and Norwegian newspapers decried the divided nature of the ethnic communities. When the editor of the *Washington Posten* surveyed Norwegian membership in ethnic clubs and churches in the mid-1890s, he could count only 915 persons—even when he included all members of the joint Scandinavian clubs and did not adjust for duplication of membership. His only consolation for this fact came in the discovery that the more numerous Swedes could claim only 430 joiners.[15] Upon closer inspection, the residential clustering resulted more from occupational and marital status than ethnic affiliation. Swedish and Norwegian neighborhoods as such did not exist. Instead, the families of Scandinavian skilled workers lived with the families of other skilled workers around Lake Union. Domestics and the most successful Scandinavian businessmen lived on the hills east of downtown overlooking the waterfront.[16]

In reality, the Swedish and Norwegian communities were loosely held together by a relatively small group of people. Their single most important function, as indicated by institutional activities, was to assist Scandinavians in becoming good Americans. The two largest Norwegian organizations were the Fremad, a young people's society providing free instruction in English, and the Workingman's Society, seeking better jobs and wages for its members.[17] The Scandinavian newspapers captured the essence of both Seattle communities when they repeatedly reported that Scandinavians in Washington were anxious to speed their acculturation into American life.[18]

This was the context in which Seattle's Swedish and Norwegian women lived their lives. Their experiences mirrored the nature of their ethnic communities. In fact, the life stages of Scandinavian women reflected the different stages of the communities of which they were a part. Single women, younger and more recently arrived in America, resembled their Scandinavian counterparts in their behavior and style of life. Once they married, their lives took on new patterns fundamentally different from those they would have followed in Europe and more consistent with those that prevailed in Seattle. By the second generation of immigrant women, assimilation had been virtually completed. The sense of Swedish or Norwegian heritage remained, but the reality was American.

The fundamental problem confronting the unmarried Scandinavian women in Seattle was the same problem they had faced in Sweden and Norway—supporting themselves. Because most had come alone, first to America and then to Seattle, few had any relatives or friends to whom they could look for financial support. Less than 10 percent of the single women in the sample examined for this study had any identifiable relatives in the city.[19] Therefore, they had no alternative but to find some sort of employment. Numerous job opportunities should have been available to them. Seattle's working women enjoyed a wide variety of occupations, and the characteristics of the single Scandinavians ought to have qualified them for many of those positions. Fifty-five percent were in their twenties (n = 53). Eighty percent had lived in America for at least five years. As a result, all could speak English (n = 50; census literacy tabulations confirm this knowledge of English). They were also, according to the census manuscripts, able to read and write. Yet, 59 percent of the Swedes and 90 percent of the Norwegians worked as domestics, proportions in sharp contrast with the 25 percent figure for all working women in the city.[20]

A part of the explanation for this concentration of Scandinavian women in domestic service might lie in the long-established pattern of Nordic maids in the city. As early as 1888, K. G. Faegre advised the Norwegian readers of *Norden* and *Amerika* that women without means ought to avoid Seattle unless they were willing to work as house servants, because few other jobs existed for them.[21] Far more important, however, was the Scandinavian tradition behind the women workers. When daughters left their father's farms in both Norway and Sweden in search of work, the job most easily obtainable was domestic service. When these same young women heard that maids in America earned more money and were treated with greater respect than in Europe, they came to the United States and took positions with which they were familiar. The women who came on to Seattle were no exception.

Those few who took other employment worked in jobs they also could have had at home. Most were dressmakers or tailors. Only two Swedes and two Norwegians in the sample of fifty-three unmarried women could be classified as white collar workers. Two of these taught school, another worked as a nurse, and the fourth clerked in a store.

If the jobs held by the single Scandinavian women illustrate their reliance on traditional roles and positions, so, too, did their living arrangements. In both Sweden and Norway, teenage sons and daughters lived in household situations until the time of their marriages. When their parents needed their labor, they remained in their familial homes. More often, the children went to live in the households of other peasants for whom they worked as domestics or farm laborers.[22] In Seattle as well, Scandinavian women hired as domestics usually lived with their employers. Less than a fourth of the Swedish maids resided elsewhere; only two of the twenty Norwegians did so. Those who roomed elsewhere, as well as the nondomestic single women, lived as boarders or lodgers in other persons' homes. Swedish women were far more likely to room than Norwegians were. Only five of the twenty-one single Norwegian women lived in a boarding or lodging situation, and two of those five lived with relatives. Fourteen of the thirty-three single Swedes, on the other hand, were boarders or lodgers.

Despite this discrepancy between the Norwegians and Swedes, one fact is clear. Single Scandinavian women lived in household situations. Whereas single Scandinavian males in a majority of cases lived in hotels and large boardinghouses, the women stayed either with their employers or in private homes that let rooms.[23] Only two of the more than 300 Scandinavian women who appeared in the sample lived in a hotel, and the two of them lived together. Thus the prescribed and practiced behavior for virtually all of Seattle's single Scandinavian women followed the Scandinavian practice of living in a homelike situation until the time came when one could marry and start one's own home.

For most of the women, marriage came when they were in their mid-twenties; the average age for Swedish women was 27.0 years, and for Norwegians 26.5 years.[24] As might be expected, those ages correspond quite closely to the ages at marriage in Scandinavia.[25] Once again, the single women conformed to the patterns they brought with them from Europe. Yet in marrying they took their first major step toward abandoning their traditional Scandinavian roles.

The Scandinavian women of Seattle found their husbands and established their households in a variety of ways. Some of the women who married in Seattle had met their husbands during an initial residence period in the Midwest.[26] Others came directly to Seattle from Scandinavia to marry men who had preceded them to America.[27] Some of these marriages involved earlier engagements made in Europe, and a few were marriages of convenience between old acquaintances, but the bulk of Seattle's single Scandinavians met and married their husbands in Seattle.

Fortunately for those who married in Seattle, there was a seemingly inexhaustible supply of single men. In 1900, single men outnumbered single women by a ratio of 2.3 to 1.[28] As can be seen in Table 1, the surplus of males over females was greatest in the most marriageable age categories. The major problem facing unmarried Scandinavian women, therefore, was where to meet eligible men.

Recognizing the difficulties facing young Scandinavians who wanted to meet members of the opposite sex, the ethnic communities organized a variety of social occasions. The Swedish Club held dances for

TABLE 1
Sex Distribution by Age Group, Seattle, 1900

	Sex	
Age Category	Male	Female
Under 1	538	505
1–4	2,043	2,087
5–9	3,022	2,971
10–14	2,441	2,542
15–19	3,008	2,651
20–24	5,029	3,095
25–29	6,791	3,148
30–34	6,451	3,045
35–44	10,857	4,539
45–54	4,797	2,213
55–64	1,887	1,126
65+	887	667
Unknown	3,770	551
Total	51,521	29,140

SOURCE: U.S. Bureau of the Census, *Twelfth Census of the United States* (1900), vol. 2: *Population 2*, p. 144, Table 9.

young Swedes.[29] Churches organized young people's leagues. More directly, a group of anxious Swedish men formed the Jolly Bachelors Club to ensure meeting eligible young women. To the extent that the ethnic communities attempted to foster intragroup marriages, their efforts met with limited success. Only 57 percent of the Swedish women married Swedish men, and 62 percent of the Norwegian women married Norwegian men.[30]

Intuition suggests that the 40 percent of the women marrying outside their ethnic group would have experiences vastly different from the women who married within it. Actually, their experiences varied little. It appears that the act of marriage itself and the resultant change in status were more important in causing a break from Scandinavian patterns than the act of marrying outside the group.

For both groups of women, marriage entailed a definite change in economic status in the household. The traditional status in Scandinavia was for women to continue working after marriage.[31] If her husband farmed, the wife worked in his fields with him. When he supplemented the family income by mining, fishing, or logging, she oversaw the farm. In addition, she cared for the large household of farm laborers, domestic servants, and children of other peasants common throughout Scandinavia.[32]

Unlike their Old World Scandinavian sisters, Seattle's married women, whether they married in or out of their ethnic group, neither worked outside the home nor played any particular economic role within the household. Only one of the 162 married Scandinavians in the sample held a job outside the home. A cook, she was doubly unique because she was also the only married woman living with her husband who boarded in another family's home instead of having her own. For the remainder, marriage meant a chance to give up their work, usually as domestics, in exchange for caring for their own households.

Relatively few of those households contained outsiders. Whereas over 60 percent of the households in Norway included boarders or servants, less than 20 percent of the Swedish and Norwegian households in Seattle did.[33] Once again, the city pattern predominated over the European pattern, leaving the women with the tasks of what one of their daughters described as "taking care of their husbands' houses and raising their children."[34]

Several factors explain this shift. First, the women did not want to work. Domestic service was not a particularly desirable job in either Scandinavia or Seattle. The demands of married life also precluded working as a live-in servant. And, as noted earlier, few other options existed. Second, Seattle's labor pool was so full of young single men that there was little call for women workers. Only 20 percent of all women over age ten in the city worked.[35] By not working, the married Scandinavians followed the Seattle norm.

Finally, Seattle's prosperity also made it unnecessary to work or to bring in boarders. Jobs as skilled workers were held by 43.5 percent of the husbands of Swedish wives and 35.1 percent of the husbands of Norwegian wives. As such, they enjoyed steady jobs with regular pay. In addition, 21 percent of the households with Swedish wives and 25 percent of the Norwegian households had heads with white collar jobs. Because of the city's constant demand for steady workers not tempted by the Alaskan gold fields, even those who worked in less skilled positions experienced little unemployment.[36] Also, the need for the women to work as a buffer against future setbacks seemed unnecessary in light of the improving economic status of their husbands. Between 1892 and 1900, Scandinavians enjoyed one of the highest rates of upward mobility in the entire city.[37] As a result, Scandinavian women could and did stay out of the work force and in their own homes.

Although the Scandinavian women willingly relinquished their customary economic roles, they did adhere to traditional maternal patterns. For them, marriage was quickly followed by the birth of a child. Forty-seven percent of the Norwegian women and 61 percent of the Swedes had given birth by the year following their marriage (n = 112, Swedes; n = 90, Norwegians). Significantly, this did not establish a pattern of frequent pregnancies. Rather, the already low Scandinavian fertility rates were further reduced in Seattle. However, the child-bearing patterns of these women continued to conform more closely to the Scandinavian norm than to that of Seattle. Thus, while the child-to-woman ratio for Seattle in 1900 was 81 per hundred, those for Seattle Swedes and Norwegians in the same year were, respectively, 106 and 126 per hundred. By way of comparison, the ratios for Norway (1865) and Sweden (1902) were both 131.[38]

With few children and no explicit economic role to fulfill, Seattle's Scandinavian women were left with much free time. The use of part of this time to socialize with friends and neighbors worked, at least in Seattle, to initiate the women into the city's way of life.

There were, to be sure, opportunities for contact with other Scandinavian women, but the lack of organizational affiliation apparent in the Swedish and Norwegian communities was even more noticeable among the women. Of all the ethnic clubs, only the Good Templars admitted women. There was one club especialy for women, the Daughters of Norway, but it was not founded until 1907. For those women who sought organized ethnic fellowship, the churches, with their circle meetings and congregational dinners, were the only significant option. However, probably no more than one-fourth of the women belonged.[39] The only other large-scale ethnic activities came at events like Norwegian Independence Day celebrations or Swedish Club dances.

Certainly informal exchanges with other Scandinavians existed. The common practice of sharing one's home with more recently arrived relatives encouraged these associations among members of the ethnic groups.[40] In most instances the relatives stayed just long enough to find a job and secure a home of their own. Yet their continued presence in the city expanded the ethnic circle for the older residents.

Despite the presence of opportunities for interaction among Swedes and among Norwegians, the dynamics of the city worked to discourage ethnic isolation, even for the women who stayed at home. Most important in this respect was the near absence of residential segregation. Even when Scandinavians lived in the same broad areas of the city, their immediate neighbors, the people on the same block, and the neighborhood businessmen were most often non-Scandinavians.[41] For these women whose sphere of activities centered in the home, this neighborhood configuration helped speed acceptance of the American way of doing things by repeatedly and frequently putting them into contact with their native neighbors. It also led to an intimacy with American patterns, as neighbors also became friends. Not atypical was the Norwegian woman who, upon finding few Norwegians in her immediate vicinity, shared coffee and fellowship with her non-Norwegian neighbors.[42]

To a large extent, these married Scandinavian women had exchanged their traditional life-style for one more consistent with that of Seattle's other women. The weakness of the two ethnic communities contributed to this shift, as did the economic and social structure of Seattle in the last decades of the twentieth century. Insofar as they maintained a Scandinavian tradition in childbearing, it in no way conflicted with their Americanization. Their families were still small enough that they could help to ensure their children's complete assimilation into American life by providing economic and educational opportunities that had not been available to them.

This, in fact, appears to have been what happened. The way in which the women raised their children suggests that they wanted to preserve very little of what they had known in Scandinavia. Use of their native language was one of the first cultural traditions to be abandoned. Parents taught their children English, and it was frequently spoken within the home.[43] The children increased their familiarity with it by playing with English-speaking neighbors. By the time the children started school, they were already fluent in English.

Attendance at the public schools was an almost universal experience for Scandinavian children. A survey of the three oldest children in each Scandinavian home showed that, in the entire sample, a total of only four children between the ages of seven and fifteen worked instead of going to school. Of these, three were sons (n = 40). Between the ages of sixteen and eighteen the children began to enter the job market, but a large proportion continued on to graduation.[44] Not until their later teens and early twenties were the second-generation Scandinavians integrated into Seattle's work force.

This represented several significant changes from their parents' experiences. First, it provided a new definition of the time of adulthood. No longer was the Scandinavian practice of tying adulthood to confirmation at age fourteen or fifteen appropriate.[45] Instead, completion of school began to be a more common indicator of the best time to begin working.

Another departure came in the children's tendencies to remain at home beyond confirmation and the completion of school into their early twenties. Whereas Scandinavian children consistently left home in their mid-teens, their children in Seattle prolonged the familial affiliation for five to seven additional years. Several facts suggest that this continued residence at home was not primarily to ensure the family's economic well-being. The age at which children entered the job market implies that their wages were not necessary to maintain the family financially. The presence of older daughters who provided no census occupation other than "helps mother" also leads to the same conclusion. Once again the Scandinavian pattern, the family as an economic unit, was replaced by the Seattle and middle-class American norm of the family as an emotional support and convenience unit.

The occupations of daughters also suggest that a fundamental change had taken place in the expectations of single women. Although the small number of Scandinavian daughters sixteen and over prevents drawing any broad conclusions as to the second-generation experience, their experiences are, nonetheless, indicative of a major change. Of the twenty-three women for whom information exists, only three entered the traditional Scandinavian profession of domestic service.[46] Two others worked in related positions as cooks. Unlike their Scandinavian-born counterparts, two of the women did not work at all. Instead, they helped at home, relying on their fathers to support them. Three women worked as store clerks and two worked as school teachers. Nine more remained in school. Clearly, a shift had been made away from domestic service into more varied and higher status jobs. Equally important, many second-generation Scandinavian women had been freed from the need to work before marriage. For these women the break from Scandinavian practices and culture was almost complete.

Seattle's Scandinavian women illustrate how easily two ethnic groups gave up their European origins. As indicated by this research, two main factors hastened this process. The first was the initial residence in the Midwest before moving west to Seattle. There the strongest confrontation between the Scandinavian and American cultures occurred. By the time the immigrants reached Seattle, they had learned the basics of American life. They could speak English and negotiate with American businessmen and employers, and knew what "good" Americans ought to do. They had made a break from the ethnic communities of the Midwest. They no longer needed a strong ethnic community to serve as a buffer against their unfamiliarity with American life. The weakness of Seattle's Swedish and Norwegian communities testifies to this fact.

The second factor was that upon arriving in Seattle, they found a society in a state of flux. Numerous and varied jobs were open to the Scandinavians. The city's prosperity worked to guarantee that there would be steady jobs that paid a living wage. Good housing was available throughout the city. The Scandinavians could choose the options they thought best. Their earlier experiences and Seattle's opportunities made the transition from Swede or Norwegian to American an easy one.

The effect of these two forces working in tandem made Seattle's Scandinavian experience unique. This can be seen even in the city's later history. By the 1910s Seattle's Scandinavian community had begun to change significantly. By that time, Seattle had become a port of entry for Scandinavians. Initial acculturation for large numbers of Scandinavians now had to take place within the city itself. Seattle's slowing rate of growth and its economic fluctuations no longer provided the kinds of opportunities the earlier Scandinavian settlers enjoyed. As a result, a greater ethnic consciousness emerged, and with it a distinctly Scandinavian settlement within the city, complete with Scandinavian organizations and institutions.

Despite the changing nature of the community, the Scandinavians willingly worked toward becoming Americans at the expense of their European heritage. The spirit that had guided the Swedish and Norwegian women in the decades before 1900 continued twenty years later. Perhaps it is best characterized by the editor of a history of

Scandinavians in Seattle's neighboring city, Tacoma, when he explained that his informants agreed that "the sooner the Scandinavian people forget about their mother country, mother language, and ancestry, the better."[47]

Notes

1. Perhaps the best example of this approach is Josef J. Barton, *Peasants and Strangers* (Cambridge, Mass.: Harvard University Press, 1975).

2. See Virginia Yans McLaughlin, "A Flexible Tradition: South Italian Immigrants Confront a New Work Experience," *Journal of Social History* 8 (Summer 1974): 429–45.

3. The choice of the particular immigrant groups belongs to Alice Kessler-Harris, "Comments on the Yans-McLaughlin and Davidoff Papers," *Journal of Social History* 8 (Summer 1974): 449.

4. The breakdown was Sweden-born (2,510), children of Swedes (3,248), Norway-born (1,642), and children of Norwegians (2,577).

5. The Swedish population grew from 2,347,303 (1800) to 4,565,668 (1880). The Norwegian population grew from 881,449 (1800) to 1,689,786 (1865). See Florence E. Janson, *The Background of Swedish Immigration* (Chicago: University of Chicago Press, 1971), p. 39, and Michael Drake, *Population and Society in Norway, 1735–1865* (Cambridge: Cambridge University Press, 1969), pp. 164–67.

6. The decadal percentages of women immigrants from Sweden were as follows: 1861–70, 41.95 percent; 1871–80, 43.17 percent; 1881–90, 43.7 percent; 1891–1900, 47.73 percent. Corresponding figures for all immigrants sixteen to twenty-five were 31.5 percent, 44.2 percent, and 49.6 percent. Janson, *Background,* p. 500, Table 4.

7. As a rough indicator of proportion of persons emigrating with their nuclear families, the following formula was used: two times the number of married men or women (whichever was lower), plus the total number of children under age fifteen, divided by the total number of Swedish emigrants to the U.S. Ibid., p. 500, Table 3.

8. One source for migration patterns was the birthplace of children born to women in the sample (see note 19). Scandinavian biographies provided another source. See Ernest Skarstedt, *Washington och Dess Svenska Befolknung* (Seattle: Washington Printing Company, 1908), and Hans Bergman, *History of Scandinavians in Tacoma and Pierce County* (Tacoma: H. Bergman, 1926).

9. Thomas Ostenson Stine, *Scandinavians on the Pacific, Puget Sound* (Seattle[?], 1900), p. 24.

10. Drake, *Population,* chap. 5. John S. Lindberg, *The Background of Swedish Emigration to the United States* (Minneapolis: University of Min-

nesota Press, 1930), p. 66, Table 3, provides the occupational categories of the Swedish immigrants.

11. Jorgen Dahlie, "A Social History of Scandinavian Immigration, Washington State, 1895–1910," Ph.D. diss., Washington State University, 1967, p. 13.

12. Clarence B. Bagley, *History of Seattle,* 3 vols. (Chicago: S. J. Clarke, 1916), 3:14.

13. Kenneth Bjork, *West of the Great Divide, Norwegian Migration to the Pacific Coast* (Northfield, Minn.: Norwegian-American Historical Association, 1958), pp. 620–21.

14. Dahlie, "Social History," p. 165. See also John Nordeen, *Svenska Klubbens Historia, 1892–1944* (Seattle: Consolidated Press, 1944).

15. Bjork, *West of the Great Divide,* pp. 620–21.

16. Indexes of segregation were computed for Seattle in 1910 when the city was more segregated than in 1900. Segregation was measured against statistics for native-born whites.

17. Bjork, *West of the Great Divide,* pp. 620–21.

18. Dahlie, "Social History," p. 5.

19. The sample used for this study was drawn as follows: every fourth household containing a Swede or Norwegian in the 1900 U.S. Census manuscripts was included in the sample. There were two exceptions to this rule. Construction work camps were excluded. So, too, were Seattle's two downtown wards. The downtown wards were excluded because their populations were artificially inflated by Alaska-bound boats in the harbor and because virtually no Scandinavian women lived in them. A sample of half of the first ward produced only one Scandinavian woman. Given that this particular study focuses on women, the study of the downtown wards proved unnecessary. Information on the men derives in part from the much larger sample taken for my dissertation of five censuses for the entire city of Seattle.

20. U.S. Bureau of the Census, *Twelfth Census of the United States* (1900), vol. 2, *Population 2* (Washington, D.C.: U.S. Government Printing Office, 1901), Table 94, pp. 591–93. Of Seattle's 4,774 working women, 1,217 were domestics.

21. Bjork, *West of the Great Divide,* p. 453.

22. Janson, *Background,* p. 56; Orvar Lofgren, "Family and Household among Scandinavian Peasants: An Exploratory Essay," *Ethnologia Scandinavica* (1974), pp. 28–30.

23. Residence samples for males are based on larger, citywide samples.

24. The age-at-marriage figure is based on the age at marriage of those married women in the household sample who neither emigrated with their husbands nor had children born outside Washington State.

25. See Drake, *Population,* chap. 6: "Determinants of Marital Age Patterns."

26. Marriage licenses provide many examples of one Scandinavian spouse giving a Seattle address and the other giving a Midwestern address. The parents of one of the women interviewed followed this pattern; RH interview, April 18, 1977, Seattle, Washington.

27. King County marriage licenses also revealed this pattern.

28. U.S. Census (1900), p. 309, Table 31.

29. A detailed account of Swedish Club activities can be found in Nordeen and in the Swedish Church Archives, Swedish Club file, University of Washington Libraries, Seattle.

30. Because of problems in using the marriage licenses themselves, these figures are based on married Scandinavians in the household sample excluding persons who had either children born in the United States outside Washington or who had children born in Scandinavia.

31. Janson, *Background,* p. 56; Drake, *Population,* p. 145.

32. Lofgren, "Family and Household," pp. 28–30.

33. Drake, *Population,* pp. 222–23. For a comparison with other American cities see John Modell and Tamara Hareven, "Urbanization and the Malleable Household: An Examination of Boarding and Lodging in American Families," *Journal of Marriage and the Family* 35 (August 1973): 467–68.

34. This particular respondent also suggested that Scandinavian women were, in her term, "chattel." RH interview cited.

35. U.S. Census (1900), p. 591, Table 94. Of Seattle's 23,587 women, 4,774 worked.

36. The lure of Alaska was great. Even Seattle's mayor gave up his post to seek his fortune in the gold fields.

37. See J. Reiff, "Urbanization and the Social Structure: Seattle, 1851–1910," Ph.D. diss., University of Washington, 1981.

38. See Drake, *Population,* p. 227; Nathan Keyfitz and Wilhelm Flieger, *World Population* (Chicago: University of Chicago Press, 1968), p. 461; and U.S. Census (1900), p. 144, Table 9. In each case except Seattle the measure is children 1 to 10 per 100, women 21 to 50. For Seattle, the measure is children 1 to 9 per 100, women 21 to 44.

39. Membership estimate is from Bjork, *West of the Great Divide,* pp. 620–21. Also, Gethsemane Lutheran Church file, Swedish Church Archives, University of Washington, Seattle, and Immanuel Lutheran Church Archives, Immanuel Lutheran Church (Norwegian), Seattle.

40. 8.2 percent of the Swedish households and 8.5 percent of the Norwegian households contained a relative on June 1, 1900. These were not always the same as households containing boarders.

41. Neighborhood reconstructions were made from the 1900 manuscript census.

42. RH interview cited (see note 26); JW interview, April 15, 1977, Seattle, Washington.

43. RH and JW interviews cited.

44. The sample of sixteen- to eighteen-year-olds is so small that it is best seen as suggestive. A record of Ballard High School's graduating class in 1904 that contains several Scandinavians confirms the impression gleaned from the sample.

45. Janson, *Background,* p. 56.

46. All were Swedes. The significance of this move away from domestic

service is even more apparent when compared with the experience of second-generation immigrants in Pittsburgh, where they continued to work as domestics. See Susan J. Kleinberg, *Urban Women, Industrial Families* (forthcoming), chap. 5: "Education and Work."

47. Bergman, *History of Scandinavians*, p. 4.

Part 4

THE ARTS

No matter how many responsibilities and hardships may have arisen in family life, work experience, or political struggles, women have seldom failed to search for some touch of beauty in their lives. If it has oftentimes been difficult for them to obtain the training and patronage necessary to become acclaimed professional artists, they have sought to create and delight in accessible art forms that could reflect their needs for self-expression. Women's interest in color, texture, and design, through utilitarian objects like clothing, and in imagery, language, and rhythm, through poetry, are the two domains we will explore in this section.

Blanche Payne devoted her life to the study and documentation of European folk costume, meticulously researching and recording the construction, fabrics, and ornamentation of the garments of ordinary citizens in remote villages of the world, especially in the Balkan countries. Her intrepid and thorough examination of taste and craftsmanship in clothing, both for daily life and special celebrations, lends scholarly weight to concerns women have held through time. Although Payne's writings and classes at the University of Washington illuminated for students of home economics the complexities of costume's role in women's domestic realm throughout history, her own career embodies an impressive range of nondomestic talents too rarely honed in women of her era. Not only did Payne travel widely throughout the mid-twentieth century, to research folk costume in libraries, museums, world capitals, and tailors' shops in quiet European villages, she studied clothing construction with French designers and documented her knowledge in several ambitious scholarly manuscripts. She also won accolades from the professionals in her field of expertise and from colleagues at the University of Washington. She created institutions to facilitate study in her field and she supervised student internships in apparel design in Seattle. Her legacy of scholarships, funded by royalties from her acclaimed textbook, testifies to her lifelong commitment to translate her primary research for students who would carry on the serious study of costume. Her forty-year career as a university professor, collector of costumes, and expert in clothing through history remains a noble example of the use of impressive professional skills and credentials in the service of subject matter heretofore neglected, trivialized, or consigned to the world of the unheralded homemaker in America.

"Tsugiki, A Grafting," by Gail Nomura, narrates the story of an individual artist, Teiko Tomita, a Japanese-born woman pioneer in Washington State. Much of the account would fit appropriately in the section on racial and ethnic diversity. Yet Tomita's extraordinary poetry compels us also to recognize the difficulties of producing art without the support of a group. No nourishment, criticism, or camaraderie from like-minded poets assisted Tomita during most of her artistic life. Instead, interruptions, injustices, and hard farm labor were the rule. Her creative drive and growth were self-generated, against all odds.

Tomita's parents arranged her marriage in Japan in 1920, to a countryman who farmed in Wapato, Washington, on land leased from the Yakima Indian Reservation. The *issei* (first generation) couple resembled a great many immigrants to America. They expected to earn enough from a few years of work in the New World to return to the homeland with sufficient profits for a comfortable life. They discovered, however, that their new lives were hard, profits scarce, and return impossible. Teiko Tomita's story, in other ways as well, represents that of other *issei* women in the region. She left behind her family and country during the years when the United States government still permitted entry of Japanese brides for male Japanese settlers here (1908–24). She raised her children and farmed difficult land under spare conditions. Adversely affected by tightening American laws forbidding Japanese Americans to own, rent, lease, or sharecrop the land, the Tomita family moved to the isolated town of Satus, where Teiko's husband supervised a white-owned nursery while she cooked for the laborers.

World War II tested the Tomitas' efforts to balance their ties to the United States and Japan. In an effort to demonstrate loyalty to the United States, they destroyed their mementos of the homeland. Unlike the Scandinavian immigrants described by Reiff, it was only under duress that the *issei* parted with reminders of their cultural heritage. Relocation and incarceration—in Tule Lake, California for the Tomitas—uprooted the family, forced the closing of their Sunnydale nursery business, and taxed their spirits by demanding that life be carried on behind barbed wire. Unable to reassemble the pieces after the war, Teiko Tomita moved to an urban environment where, alongside women of every nationality, she became a worker in a garment factory.

Teiko Tomita's biography lends special insight into the Japanese American woman's experience, because of the poetry she wrote, in the manner of a journal, steadily recording her observations about life in America. Her *tanka* poems are translated here by Nomura to demonstrate the history of a woman whose strength and creativity did not falter despite numerous obstacles. For Tomita, the poetry provided private solace. For her many readers in Japan, it described both her family life in America and her broader societal concerns, including her postwar interest in the movement for nuclear disarmament. For us, the poetry reveals her own "grafting"—in her life, as in her art—representing neither Old World nor New, but a unique blend of both.

Blanche Payne, Scholar of Costume History and University Professor

Diana Ryesky

A University of Washington faculty member from 1927 to 1966, Blanche Payne capped many years of research and teaching in costume history and apparel design with her book, *History of Costume*. Today, twenty years after its publication, the book is still the most widely used text for university courses in the field. Its author and her other work, however, remain little known. This study, based on her papers, research materials, and artifact collection and on interviews with her former students and colleagues, illuminates the career of Blanche Payne, a scholar of costume history.

She was born October 2, 1896, in Thayer, Kansas, to John Everett Payne, a farmer, and Virginia Rosalie Mitchell Payne, a housewife. The youngest of several children, Blanche Payne was closest to her sister Helen, who early encouraged her curiosity and inspired her lifelong admiration for beauty. She obtained her bachelor of science degree in home economics in 1916 from Kansas State Teachers College in Pittsburg, Kansas, and afterward taught high school English and home economics, first in Kiowa, Kansas, and then in Lewiston, Idaho. In the fall of 1918, she joined the war effort, becoming a student nurse at Camp Lewis, in Washington, with the rank of private. In 1919 she took a job at Arizona State Teachers College in Flagstaff, where she taught textiles and clothing, coached the girls' basketball team, and sponsored the girls' hiking club. Her quiet, shy ways, great intelligence, and conscientiousness made her an excellent role model for the students, with whom she was popular. She also impressed the college president, who "recognized that she was fitted for a larger place than we could offer her so [he] constantly pushed her toward higher education." After four years there, Payne joined Helen in New York and enrolled in Columbia University, which granted her a master of arts degree in clothing in 1924.[1]

Between 1924 and 1926, Blanche Payne taught clothing at high schools in New York City, studied draping as a private pupil of the French designer Madame Geo (and much later, in the early 1940s, with Madame Lyolene), and started her own commercial designing

This chapter was published in *Pacific Northwest Quarterly* 77, no. 1 (1986): 21–31.

business. In 1927 she took a position with the Department of Home Economics at the University of Washington in Seattle. Granted a leave in 1929, she returned to New York to study flat pattern at the Mitchell School of Design and went on to investigate costume in several European countries. She resumed her teaching career at the University of Washington in 1931, advancing to the rank of associate professor in 1936 and to professor in 1942. During summer breaks and sabbaticals, she traveled to Europe and cities in the United States to conduct research.[2]

As a university faculty member, Payne participated in several organizations related to her professional interests. She served as president, trustee, and secretary of the Faculty Women's Club, a group that promoted "social and professional interest in all the women of the institution." Not until 1960 did she receive an invitation to join the prestigious University of Washington Research Society. Composed of scholars with national reputations "for productive scholarship through ten years of investigation along lines of original research of high quality," the society only began admitting women in 1958. Payne also belonged to the American Home Economics Association, the American Association of University Professors, and the Fashion Group (a national organization for professionals in the fashion industry), and she held honorary membership in Omicron Nu, the home economics honorary society.[3]

A small exhibit of Rumanian embroideries and material at the Metropolitan Museum of Art initially stirred Payne's interest in folk costume. She also studied with Madame Geo at a time when Russian émigrés were influencing apparel design. Through this experience, Payne came to realize the significance of folk costume and textiles as source material for silhouette, cut, construction, and adornment of modern clothing. Extending her unpaid leave from the University of Washington in 1929–30, she and her sister Helen traveled through Central Europe and the Balkans, surveying folk costume in Czechoslovakia, Hungary, Rumania, Bulgaria, Turkey, Greece, Albania, and Yugoslavia. Six years later, in 1936 and 1937, she returned to Europe to conduct an extended study in Yugoslavia, where a large percentage of the population still wore folk costume.[4]

Payne believed that Americans had lost both the ability and the desire to create good things and, further, that taste had degenerated. In contrast, people in traditional societies continued to produce objects of fine craftsmanship and lasting beauty in folk embroidery, perhaps because of their daily contact with such artifacts over generations. Payne wanted to bring to her students "an appreciation for such craftsmanship, raise their standard of taste and possibly arouse in them the desire to create for themselves household embroideries and costumes as harmonious with their mode of life as the peasants' are with theirs" (intro., p. 4).

She spent her first two and one-half months in Yugoslavia studying the collections of the ethnographic museums in Belgrade and Zagreb. Once spring came, using passes provided by the government, she began to travel throughout the country, where she visited regional museums "to learn the standard of excellence set by the museum and to compare the costumes of various localities before deciding which ones to study in detail" (intro., p. 3). In her ethnographic research, she sought out inaccessible villages, sparing no effort to reach them. She frequented markets and festivals where people often appeared in folk costume. She analyzed her role as a fieldworker: "I all but removed the shirts from the peasants' backs or brazenly invaded local tailor shops and begged for permission to measure and draw their haberdashery. When you realize that the Turkish women still veil themselves and that in many of those places no decent woman is ever seen alone, you may have some conception of the problem I was to these people" (intro., pp. 3–4).

As part of her field study, Payne photographed avidly. Sometimes she requested that people pose for her in their best attire, which they donned just for the photograph. An example is a man from the region near Lake Bohinj; his outfit shows the influence of eighteenth-century urban dress and of that area's long identification with Austria (chap. 11, p. 5) in the leather pants, high boots, elegant waistcoat, cravat, and beaver hat. She also took candid photographs in markets and plazas. She often captured a side or rear view, as important to her for study purposes as a front view.

To augment her data on costume, Payne studied cut and decoration of garments by drafting patterns from clothing she encountered in homes, shops, museums, and private collections. For example, in Dubrovnik, she sought out a well-known tailor:

Having observed the curtness with which he dismissed some of his customers, I felt highly honored when he answered my innumerable questions. It was with almost breathless respect that I watched him direct his assistant in the drafting and cutting of the patterns [I] reproduced in the scale drawings [dr. 77a–d]. He, himself, though well past seventy, took the pencil in his still steady fingers and sketched in the braiding design on the outer jacket. And when he said, "If you will return to Ragusa . . . and spend a month in my shop, I shall teach you the construction and decoration of the garments." I felt as if I had been knighted. It was, perhaps, the greatest disappointment in my year's study that I could not accept his generous offer. (chap. 7, p. 20)

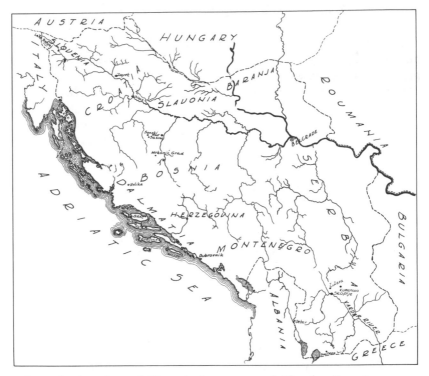

Lake Bohinj region of Yugoslavia, source of Blanche Payne's costume research *(courtesy University of Washington Archives)*

Payne recorded some garments with unique cuts, including a coat from the vicinity of Sisak, in which the front, back, and flared skirt are cut in one piece (dr. 93). She carefully noted detail of the placement of design elements, such as cording, as illustrated by the pattern she drew of a sleeveless coat from Smilevo.

She also made an extensive collection of folk costume and textiles while there. Among the artifacts she brought back were complete costumes; garments; and fragments, such as sleeves and chemise fronts, specifically selected to show embroidery.

Her research centered on the regions known, prior to World War I, as South Serbia (Macedonia), Croatia, Bosnia, North Serbia, and Dalmatia, although she made brief visits to Baranja, Slavonia, Slovenia, Montenegro, and Herzegovina. She focused conceptually on the relationship between costume and custom, the historic antecedents of costumes, and the analysis of design.

Payne visited the region of Skopska Crna Gora during Easter time when people wore their finest attire. In the town of Čučera, she observed the elders watching the young people as they danced the *kolo*

Man from Lake Bohinj region *(courtesy John Sweet)*

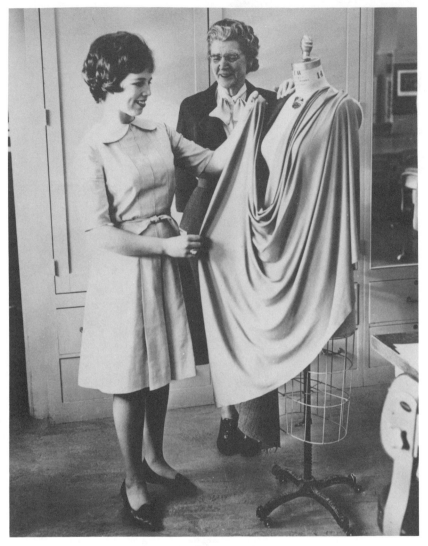

Blanche Payne with student
(courtesy Museum of History and Industry)

and commented: "It is on such occasions that the qualifications of el[i]gible maids and men are weighed by match-making parents. Hence, the display of costume and coins denoting social and financial standing is a definite asset to the wearer" (chap. 3, pt. 1, p. 4). Particular items of clothing caught her eye. For example, a chemise held special interest because she saw in it the cut and decoration of the Roman tunic complete with stripes (*clavi*). Bringing in historical data on population movements in Yugoslavia, she wrote: "[S]ince the town of Skoplje is the successor of the old Roman town of Scupi and since this region was exposed to Byzantine culture, it seems plausible to me that we may have in the košulja of Skopska Crna Gora the lineal descendant of the Roman tunic. At least the resemblance is provocative of thought. The fact that since the fall of the Byzanti[n]e empire these mountain people have been subjected to slight outside influence other than Turkish strengthens my belief" (chap. 3, pt. 1, p. 5).

Payne carefully analyzed the black-and-white costumes of the local women, noting that even though the overall design exhibits sharp contrast of color, when the whole outfit is worn, a clever transition exists between one part of the ensemble and another. She photographed and took patterns of the women's sleeveless fringed jacket. She collected two costumes, including an old-style wedding apron seldom seen, even then, outside museums. The apron consists of wool fabric covered with a layer of white cotton decorated with embroidered circle motifs of silver thread and sequins.

The costume of Kumanovo, near Skoplje, intrigued Payne with the design concepts it embodied. She acquired a woman's outfit dating from about 1920. By 1937 it was worn only for festivals, and she was unable to photograph anyone wearing it. She commented on the "large solid surfaces of embroidery, the boldness of the design, the intensity of the color and the sharp contrast of dark and light" (chap. 3, pt. 1, pp. 15–16) and noted that the designs on the jackets were daintier than the bold motifs adorning the chemise and apron.[5]

Headdresses especially fascinated Payne. She included detailed explanations of their assembly in many of her descriptions of costume. For example, near Sanski Most, she searched out a specific type seen often in Durer's sixteenth-century drawings. In fact, immigrants from Saxony had settled in this area in the sixteenth century. Finally, in Sasina, she was presented to a *baba* (grandmother) who appeared "in all the splendor and regality of her headdress. . . . Not until the baba was sure that all the men and boys were gone and the door securely fastened would she remove her crowning glory and let me examine its construction. The foundation of it consists of a thin wooden band one to one and one-fourth inch wide, curved to fit the top of the head from ear to ear. To this is mounted the halo-like frame made basketry fashion of thick strands of hemp" (chap. 6, p. 26). Towels drape over the frame, Payne noted, then pass under the chin like a wimple.

In Croatia, as in some other places, it distressed Payne to see some of the modern adaptations of folk costumes: "The modern costumes of Sisak are quite hideous with their bombastic floral designs done in rayon of harsh coloring with long shaggy overshots" (chap. 8, p. 19). Since she was unable to obtain an older Sisak outfit, she had one copied from a woven costume from about 1850 in the Zagreb museum. Peasants, hired to weave the fabric for the costume, copied the color and proportion of the designs exactly. She also had an embroidered Sisak costume, representing a somewhat later style, made for her under similar conditions.[6]

Payne returned from the Yugoslavian experience with an appreciation of peoples the world over. In spite of economic hardships inherent in their lives, the Yugoslavians she met showed her "kindness, generosity and hospitality [that] moved me deeply. Their invincible courage, endurance and loyalty set an exampl[e] for all men. Would that we could exchange some of our super abundance of material riches for some of their wealth of spirit."[7]

Although her aim in undertaking this trip to Yugoslavia had not been to write a book, she did, in fact, produce a book-length manuscript that presents her research findings, provides data not readily available in English, and holds a wealth of information for designers. This manuscript has more than 400 photographs; line drawings of over 100 costumes and embroidery designs; and 24 hand-painted color plates of costumes done by Olga Benson, staff artist with the Skoplje museum. Payne felt strongly that the illustrative material brought the manuscript to life. When World War II was declared, most of the material was with the Studio, Limited, a London publisher, for final consideration. But the war eliminated the European market for this book, and a 1941 air raid destroyed the plates for the color prints. Payne then tried U.S. publishers, but the cost of producing a book with many color illustrations proved prohibitive. Though she moved on to other projects, Payne still had hopes for her Yugoslavian manuscript. In 1958, the University of Washington Press reviewed and declined it. Five years later, in Payne's words, the book was "still in storage awaiting an angel." Even after her death, the attorney for her estate encountered the same problems when he attempted to have it published.[8]

Payne published a single brief article on her Yugoslavian research; it appeared in the *Bulletin of the Needle and Bobbin Club* in 1957.

Illustrated with eleven photographs, it gives but an inkling of the material and insights she accumulated.[9]

Payne's interest in historic Western costume, which began early in her career, eventually culminated in the publication of her book, *History of Costume*. She made several trips to Europe to visit museums and architectural monuments in search of subject matter. In conjunction with her 1936–37 stay in Yugoslavia, she had spent another nine months touring museums in various West European countries. In 1950, she took sabbatical leave to study collections of the Victoria and Albert Museum, London; the Royal Armory, Stockholm; Rosenborg Palace, Copenhagen; Musée Carnavalet, Paris; and others. During this trip, she drew many pattern drafts from costumes she had the privilege of examining at first hand. In 1961, she visited Europe on an assignment from the Brooklyn Museum to study garments designed by the nineteenth-century couturier Charles Worth for an exhibit of his work in 1962. She spent another sabbatical year, 1958–59, examining costume collections and related objects at museums in the eastern United States. Many of her summers were devoted to study at American museums and libraries as well. A testimony to her good working relations was the Brooklyn Museum's lending her valuable costumes from which to take patterns. Indeed, one shipment of four nineteenth-century gowns, sent by rail to Seattle in 1957, had a value at that time of $1,000.[10]

In the course of her travels, Payne examined the original of nearly every illustration used in her book. In her words: "I made a pilgrimage to St. Gall to see the Golden Psalter; to Bayeux to see the Bayeux Tapestry; to Sakkara to see the reliefs in place in the tombs of the Old Kingdom. . . . I explored Norman towers, mediaeval castles and outstanding Manor Houses to see and absorb the background of the people who had lived there. I think it important in teaching for the student to be able to visualize the costume he is studying in its native setting."

She purchased at least two thousand black-and-white photographs of works of art. On the backs, she wrote notes on colors, fabrics, and other details. She collected other materials for her study of costume: postcards, art prints, magazine clippings, fashion plates, and artifacts. All in all, she accumulated a tremendous archive of resources from which to work.[11]

By 1960, Payne had completed a rough draft of *History of Costume*. The inadequacy of the available textbooks on the subject compelled her to write. Specifically, she thought Carolyn G. Bradley's *Western World Costume* (1954) had inaccurate illustrations and that the text overemphasized the nineteenth and twentieth centuries. Mary

Evans's very brief *Costume Throughout the Ages* (rev. ed., 1950) short-changed topics Payne considered crucial. She did, however, recommend Millia Davenport's *Book of Costume* (1948) to her students, even though it was not written primarily as a text.[12]

Payne's own text emphasized one of her aims in teaching: to awaken appreciation by bringing the student as close to the real record as possible. With this aim in mind, Payne originally wanted to include 699 illustrations, including line drawings and photographs. Elizabeth Curtis, of the University of Washington School of Art, made all the line drawings. She used line and shading sparingly in order to reinterpret the original source material as little as possible, and she maintained a uniform style throughout. Since Harper and Row, the publisher, could not publish so many illustrations and still sell the book as a text, Payne's editor at the college department there asked her to eliminate 135 photographs but retain all the line drawings. Payne's correspondence shows the anguish she felt as she undertook this task.[13]

Particularly expendable, according to Harper and Row, were photographs of live models in historic clothing. These pictures, made under Payne's direction at the university, clearly showed the cut and detail of the dresses; the models posed in a straightforward manner. Payne's editor felt that there was little *"atmosphere"* in the photographs, but a colleague of Payne's from the Brooklyn Museum convinced her of the value of the information they contained. He then helped arrange for some garments to be shipped to the Brooklyn Museum for rephotographing on live models in architectural or interior settings. Although the resulting photographs are perhaps more aesthetically appealing than those Payne submitted, they lack her keen presentation of design elements in costume.[14]

In March 1964, once the final selection of illustrations was made, Harper asked Payne to obtain permissions to publish all the illustrative material. Besides reading and correcting galley proof of the text, Payne spent the summer of that year in a letter-writing campaign, sometimes writing two or three times to a museum before receiving an answer. Finally, in 1965, the book appeared in print.[15]

The published text, with overview, summary, and background information, was much revised from an undated earlier draft that discussed historic costume almost entirely through reference to illustrations. Even though Payne had to eliminate many photographs, references to these works of art remained in the book because the textual descriptions alone satisifed the editor and because deleting them would have required major rewriting.[16]

Payne felt that her most original contribution to the book was "the scale drawings of the actual cut of the costumes which I have had the privilege of studying in the famous collections here and abroad." In drawing the scale patterns, she set very thin pins upright in the garment to mark grids of grain lines from which she took measurements. "There was no guesswork involved. Each line was determined by detailed measurements (sometimes only $1/2''$ apart when a subtle curve was involved) and reproduced with the greatest accuracy we could devise." Of approximately 140 of these pattern drafts preserved at the University of Washington, only 43 appeared in her book. Since that time, other authors have published accurate pattern drafts of historic garments.[17]

Payne limited her study to the clothing of Western civilization between 5000 B.C. and A.D. 1900, a herculean task in itself. She left out twentieth-century costume because of time constraints, because other studies already existed, and because she felt that the period offered little original source material. Nor did she attempt a systematic treatment of folk costume; her Yugoslavian research experience had convinced her of "the impossibility of mastering the subject of national costumes within one incarnation." Yet the relationship between European folk costumes and elite dress intrigued her. In her book she notes superficial resemblances between present-day folk costumes and earlier styles. For example, she points out a similarity in form between seventeenth-century men's petticoat breeches and folk costumes from Mezőkövesd, Hungary, and a continuity between medieval headdresses and those of Vrlika in Yugoslavia. Her perspective on folk dress, derived from knowledge of both history and historic Western costume, offers insights into the original fashion. Although scholars have since explored in greater depth the evolution of folk costume from elite antecedents, the topic remains relatively unresearched.[18]

Reviews in periodicals aimed at libraries called *History of Costume* "superior," "a handy one-volume reference for small libraries," and they praised Payne's "awareness of documentation" and her extensive use of illustrations that "brilliantly elucidate what the text can only barely describe." For the general reader, reviewers faulted the book for its lack of a glossary and its somewhat mechanical presentation of facts.[19]

Scholarly reviews stressed Payne's thorough and well-researched descriptions and the useful pattern drafts and illustrations. The reviewer for the *Journal of Home Economics* praised the text highly and considered it appropriate for the stage designer as well as the advanced student of textile and costume history. The ideas presented in the book stimulated Bernadine Morris of the *New York Times* to write a review essay based on the concept of the evolution of clothing. She observed, however, that Payne did not go "too deeply into the philosophy or psychology of fashion." A review in the *Quarterly Journal of Speech* lauded the book for its scholarly descriptions and detailed analyses but suggested that Payne had missed the relationship of dress to the environment, especially to architecture. The *Times Literary Supplement* review, the most critical one, declared that the text was not well organized, that it did not emphasize the main developments of fashion, and that it failed to differentiate clearly between major styles and minor variations.[20]

History of Costume, then, emerged as the product of Payne's own research and experience rather than as a recapitulation of older sources. Just two years after it appeared, François Boucher, a well-known French costume historian, published *20,000 Years of Fashion* (1967). Payne feared that his book, with its lavish illustrations (many in color, which hers lacked), would eclipse her work. In many respects, however, the books complement each other.

Over the years, Payne became an influential member of the university's home economics faculty. As head of the clothing area, she helped shape school policy. She also had a reputation among her colleagues as a first-rate teacher because of her high standards and her immense dedication to integrating research with teaching.

Payne played an instrumental role in the founding of two mainstays of the textiles program: the Costume and Textile Study Center and the Apparel Design Internship Program. Although the establishment of the study center through a private donation to purchase the Elizabeth Bayley Willis field collection of Indian textiles occurred in 1958 while Payne was on sabbatical leave, she quickly took charge on her return. Grants from the Graduate Research Council and from the Asia Society enabled the school to hire a curator, set aside a room, and build storage facilities. Payne had her way on the naming of the center, made decisions on acquisitions and policy, researched and planned the storage system, and set strict, protective rules for use of the collection. Eventually, the facility accessioned the personal teaching collections of various professors. It also included donations and pieces purchased with school funds, such as those Payne had bought in Yugoslavia.[21]

While in New York in 1959, through her contacts at Columbia Teachers College, Payne received an offer of material from the school's teaching collection, which was being disbanded. Unable to pass up such a windfall, she accepted and then wrote home, telling the director of home economics that she had just "packed and wrapped the loot. . . . Railway Express [will] pick it up and it should be deposited by them in the Raitt Hall office—and here comes the blow—

transportation collect. I know it is the end of the biennium but I'm hoping there will be enough left in the piggy bank to cover the charge." This acquisition included a valuable Worth dolman from the 1880s and an early nineteenth-century brown satin dress, among other items.[22]

Payne's second major project was the Apparel Design Internship Program, started in 1948 in conjunction with the School of Art and the College of Economics and Business. Students completed course work in the various disciplines, then became interns at local apparel factories. Payne carefully chose students for the internships; in the early years, she supervised them herself. When the program began, only four other schools in the country had industrial internship programs in apparel design.[23]

Payne taught a variety of courses and demanded much of her students. The needlework course she developed combined historical information and design analysis with practical application. Students analyzed ethnic and Western needlework, including items from Payne's collection, to learn what constituted good design and good craftsmanship. Then they designed items based on their research. Payne discussed some of these concepts in a series of articles on needlecraft published in the *Seattle Post-Intelligencer*. Drawing on her Yugoslavian experience, she stressed planning and designing as fundamental to creating fine needlework. In conjunction with the articles, a series of exhibits at the Seattle Art Museum, the Seattle Public Library, Frederick and Nelson department store, and the university showed examples of well-designed needlework. The *Post-Intelligencer*, along with Frederick and Nelson, sponsored a contest for hand embroidery.[24]

In Payne's draping class, students learned that the fabric "speaks" to the designer. She frequently said, "Let the fabric talk to you," and asked, "What is the fabric telling you?" As she did in her other classes, she tried to instill the skills of observation.

Students in the history of costume courses compiled notebooks of clippings, art prints, and other examples of dress from each period they studied. They haunted secondhand book and magazine stores to purchase items for their growing notebooks. Some subscribed to *National Geographic,* and others purchased prints and postcards as budgets allowed. Payne further enlivened this class with tales of her travels to various museums and historical sites, bringing enthusiasm to her teaching and excitement to the subject matter.[25]

Clothing selection and family clothing were among the courses Payne taught. She used concepts from them in "The Clothing of Seattle Citizens in 1951, A.D.," a record she prepared for inclusion in a time capsule at Alki Point, where the founders of Seattle first landed in

1851. This document surveys clothing use and attitudes by age, income, and occupational strata. It includes sketches of garments as well as swatches of fabric. Suits and coats of the time, observes Payne, featured fabrics with tactile surfaces. For the rapidly dwindling number of women in the leisure class, Seattle stores stocked designer clothing, the most popular being Balenciaga, Fath, Irene, Adrian, and Milgrim.

Payne comments on the use of the images of current stars to sell clothing for children: "For the past year, backyards, alleys and playgrounds have been peopled with minor Hopalongs, complete with cowboy boots, broad brimmed hats, blue jeans, jackets, studded belts, holsters and shootin'-irons." Then, as now, Seattle's teenagers had clothing fads. In 1951, girls insisted on wearing Joyce platform shoes. And how they wore a head scarf expressed group membership; wearing it, according to Payne, "far back on the head (exposing the bristling bobby-pinned curls) may prevail at one school; lifted and tied over the chin may indicate another."[26]

Payne, a strict teacher who expected high standards of her students, demanded perfection of herself. Many of her students went on to teach home economics or to careers in the apparel industry. One of them recalled that "a 'nice' from Miss Payne was worth ten superlatives from another instructor." Payne's formal demeanor, like that of many influential woman academics of that time, led some to characterize her as a Victorian lady. Students respected her highly, although some found her distant or possibly shy. Almost everyone addressed her as Miss Payne. Students with whom she became close knew her to be kind, warm, sincere, understanding, and concerned. She appreciated humor and fun. A tall woman, she dressed simply but elegantly in tailored clothes with a feminine touch that expressed her interest in design. She favored muted grays and rusty browns. Lacking family obligations, she spent long hours in her office and studio. For relaxation, she enjoyed nature. In one of the annual newsletters that the home economics faculty sent to its graduates, she wrote: "Highlights of the summer include a picnic among the avalanche lilies at Paradise [Mount Rainier]; . . . Glacier National Park with the sheer slopes of the Rockies banded and sprayed with grayed red purple and blue green argillite."[27]

After her retirement in 1966, she traveled and also built a close relationship with the Museum of History and Industry as a volunteer with the costume collection. Becoming ill, she moved in 1972 to Quincy, California, where she died on July 30 at the age of 75. Her private collection of textiles, clothing, other artifacts, furniture, and knickknacks she left to the museum; this collection included predominantly Yugoslavian, Central European, and Balkan textiles and clothing as well as period costume and some of her own clothing. For many years, her furniture and hooked rugs were displayed in a special room to commemorate her generosity.[28]

Payne's will also provided for the establishment of a fund in the name of her sister Helen, to be used for scholarships for apparel design students of outstanding ability. Its principal came from stocks she held; earnings from this and royalties from *History of Costume* provided eight annual scholarships of $1,650 each in 1983, the year the university terminated the textiles program. Book royalties totaled $1,500 to $2,000 annually at the time of her death; by 1984, they amounted to more than $6,000, and the book continues to be the most frequently used text for courses in costume history.[29]

The words of the dean of the College of Arts and Sciences, in a letter to her at the time of her retirement, summarize the professional esteem felt for her: "I should like you to know that your work with textiles and costume has been a source of great satisfaction to the College. As you well know, your contributions cannot be measured in terms of the present; they will continue to be an influence for many years to come. The continuing regard of your students, as well as of your colleagues, has been well and truly earned."[30]

Blanche Payne's book made an important and lasting contribution to scholarship in costume history. Her legacy as a teacher still influences students through *History of Costume* and through the professionals she trained. Payne accumulated extensive information on Yugoslavian costumes and customs, many of which have disappeared since World War II. Her carefully selected collection of costumes and textiles and the research materials she gathered, now part of public collections, broaden the cultural and educational heritage of the Pacific Northwest. The achievements of Blanche Payne throughout her long and fruitful career continue with us today.

Notes

1. Blanche Payne Papers, offices of John Sweet, attorney, Seattle (hereafter, Payne Papers–JS); "Blanche Payne: October 2, 1896–July 30, 1972"; "University of Washington Biography" sheet, April 23, 1956; personal history sheet; and L. B. McMullen to Effie Raitt, April 24, 1927 (quotation), all in Faculty, Past, file on Blanche Payne, Interdisciplinary Degree Program in Nutritional Sciences (IDPNS) Records, University of Washington. *Alumnae Newsletter* (University of Washington School of Home Economics),

Dec. 3, 1941, p. 5, Nutritional Sciences and Textiles School (NSTS) Records, University of Washington Libraries.

2. "UW Biography"; personal history sheet; and McMullen to Raitt, April 24, 1927; Payne's responses to questionnaire requesting information for advertising for her book (n.d.), Blanche Payne Papers, UW Library (hereafter, Payne Papers—UW).

3. *University of Washington Daily*, May 26, 1915 (women); Membership Committee to Walter G. Johnson, Feb. 24, 1960, and "The Research Society, 1958–59, University of Washington, Seattle" (investigation), University of Washington Research Society Records, UW Libraries; "UW Biography."

4. Blanche Payne, untitled, undated, hand-corrected typescript of "Some Costumes of Jugoslavia," Payne Papers—UW. Most of the information for this essay comes from the UW manuscript, which lacks complete front matter and, save for the introduction (of which there is a retyped copy incorporating the hand emendations), is an earlier version of what appears to be a final draft of the book in Payne Papers—JS. Page references to, and scale drawing numbers from, the former will be incorporated parenthetically in the text. Also see "UW Biography."

5. This costume is housed at Seattle's Museum of History and Industry (MOHAI) and is illustrated in Diana Ryesky, "The Blanche Payne Collection at the Museum of History and Industry," *Portage* 5 (Summer 1984): 28–29.

6. These costumes are at MOHAI and at the Henry Art Gallery Textile Collection, University of Washington. Also see Ryesky, "Blanche Payne Collection," p. 30.

7. *Alumnae Newsletter*, Dec. 10, 1942, p. 5.

8. Payne, "Some Costumes of Jugoslavia" (n.d.), front matter, Payne Papers—JS; Payne to Faculty Study and Research Committee, April 10, 1958, and F. A. Mercer to Payne, July 29, 1941, Payne Papers—UW; Payne to Paul Cross, March 13, 1958, in Faculty, Past, file; questionnaire responses (quotation).

9. Blanche Payne, "Some Costumes of Yugoslavia," *Bulletin of the Needle and Bobbin Club* 41 (1957): 3–21.

10. Questionnaire responses; memo reporting on activities of sabbatical year 1958–59, Jan. 13, 1960, and "University Research Society Guide Sheet for Prospective Members—1960 Election," Faculty, Past, file; Dassah Saulpaugh to Payne, Aug. 6, 1957, Payne Papers—UW.

11. Questionnaire responses. The University of Washington Libraries system has much of Payne's material: the Rare Book Collection, Special Collections Division, houses the postcards, photographs, and fashion plates; the Archives and Manuscripts Division has the pattern drafts, illustrations, papers, correspondence, and manuscripts; the Drama Library holds the clippings and other ephemera she gathered (however, this material has now been integrated with similar items from other sources). The artifacts she collected with School of Home Economics funds are housed in the Henry Art Gallery

Textile Collection. MOHAI holds most of her private collection (for more information, see Ryesky, "Blanche Payne Collection," pp. 27–31). The Payne Papers–JS include a manuscript, photographs, books, and papers.

12. "University Research Society Guide Sheet." In 1960, Payne had just completed the evaluation of all the articles on costume and fashion in the 1959 edition of the *Encyclopedia Americana;* Payne to Georgette Preston, Feb. 18, 1963, Payne Papers–UW.

13. Questionnaire responses; Payne to Preston, Feb. 18, 1963, and Preston to Payne, Jan. 31 and March 11, 1963, Payne Papers–UW. Blanche Payne, *History of Costume: From the Ancient Egyptians to the Twentieth Century* (New York: Harper and Row, 1965), xiii.

14. Preston to Payne, March 11 and April 4, 1963, and Robert Riley to Payne, March 25, 1963, Payne Papers–UW. The published photographs follow the trend set by Doris L. Moore's *Woman in Fashion* (London: B. T. Batsford, Ltd., 1949), in which English entertainers and members of the peerage posed in period dress in interior settings. Owing to increased knowledge about the nature of fabrics and factors causing their degradation, museums today do not permit the display of their costumes on live models. Instead, they use dress forms or mannequins.

15. Fran Lohman to Payne, March 20, 1964, Payne Papers–UW.

16. "Women's Costume of the Eighteenth Century" (typescript, n.d.), Blanche Payne Photograph File, UW Rare Books; Preston to Payne, April 4, 1963.

17. Payne to Faculty Study and Research Committee, April 10, 1958 (privilege); questionnaire responses (guesswork). Lois Keeler prepared the pattern drafts for publication (Payne, *History of Costume,* p. xiii). For example, Janet Arnold's *Patterns of Fashion,* new ed. (New York: Drama Book Specialists, 1977; London: Macmillan London Limited), includes more descriptive text with each pattern.

18. Payne to George D. McCune, Jan. 27, 1958, Faculty, Past, file; Payne, *History of Costume,* pp. xii (quotation), 340, 247; Veronika Gervers, "The Historical Components of Regional Costume in South-Eastern Europe," *Textile Museum Journal* 4, no. 2 (1975): 61–78; Linda Welters, "Greek Women's Chemises," *Dress* 8 (1982): 10–21.

19. See reviews of *History of Costume: From the Ancient Egyptians to the Twentieth Century* by Blanche Payne, in *Choice* 3 (1966): 45 (handy); *Virginia Kirkus' Service* 33 (Aug. 1, 1965): 816 (superior, awareness); and, by Henry Halpern, *Library Journal* 90 (Sept. 1, 1965): 3440 (brilliantly).

20. See reviews of Payne's book by Lavinia M. Franck in *Journal of Home Economics* 58 (1966): 318; by Bernadine Morris, "The Greeks Had the Best of It," in *New York Times Book Review* 70 (Aug. 29, 1965): 7; by Annette Geber-Garceau, in *Quarterly Journal of Speech* 52 (1966): 92; and "Italian Dressing," in *Times Literary Supplement* 64 (Dec. 16, 1965): 1175.

21. Mary Louise Johnson to Solomon Katz, Jan. 10, 1966, Faculty, Past, file; Blanche Payne Donor File, Old Accessions records, Henry Art Gallery Textile Collection. The Costume and Textile Study Center's collection and

the School of Drama's Historic Costume Collection both came under the administration of the Henry Art Gallery in 1982, at the time the university was in the process of terminating the textiles program.

22. Payne to Johnson, April 27, 1959, Faculty, Past, file.

23. Memorandum, Oct. 12, 1948, "School's Cooperation with the Apparel Industry," NSTS Records; Johnson to Katz, Jan. 10, 1966.

24. Blanche Payne, "Needlecraft" (a weekly series of ten articles), *Seattle Post-Intelligencer*, beginning Oct. 10, 1941 (reprints bound together in Payne Papers—UW).

25. See the 1943 notebooks of Agnes Read for Home Economics 133, 4 vols., Payne Papers—UW.

26. Blanche Payne, "The Clothing of Seattle Citizens in 1951, A.D." (copy of survey enclosed in a time capsule at Alki Point, 1951), pp. 20–21, 26 (Hopalongs), 30 (bobby-pinned), Payne Papers—UW. See also Mary Petoff, "Blanche Payne" (typescript, 1981), p. 6, Women Studies Program (WS) Library, University of Washington.

27. Margaret E. Terrell to Ryesky, June 16, 1981, and Carolyn Fix Blount to Ryesky, July 15, 1984 (nice); "UW Biography"; Payne to graduates, Department of Home Economics newsletter, Dec. 10, 1935 (highlights), 3, NSTS Records. See also D. A. Sager, "The Life of Miss Payne" (typescript, 1980), p. 8, and accompanying tape, WS Library.

28. Charles Odegaard to Payne, May 23, 1966, Faculty, Past, file; *Seattle Times*, Aug. 3, 1972. Regarding the disposition of her collection, see accession records, MOHAI. (Some items from her collection were lent to the museum before her death.)

29. Personal communication, John Sweet, July 2, 1984.

30. Katz to Payne, June 10, 1966, Faculty, Past, file.

Tsugiki, a Grafting:
A History of a Japanese Pioneer Woman
in Washington State

Gail M. Nomura

In the imagination of most of us, the pioneer woman is represented by a sunbonneted Caucasian traveling westward on the American plain. Few are aware of the pioneer women who crossed the Pacific Ocean east to America from Japan. Among these Japanese pioneer women were some whose destinies lay in the Pacific Northwest.

In Washington State, pioneer women from Japan, the *issei* or first (immigrant) generation, and their *nisei*, second generation, U.S.-born daughters, made up the largest group of nonwhite ethnic women in the state for most of the first half of the twentieth century.[1] These issei women contributed their labor in agriculture and small businesses to help develop the state's economy. Moreover, they were essential to the establishment of a viable Japanese American community in Washington. Yet little is known of the history of these women.[2] This essay examines the life of one Japanese pioneer woman, Teiko Tomita, as a method of exploring the historical experience of Japanese pioneer women in Washington State.

Through interviewing Teiko Tomita, I have been able to gather certain facts about her life. But beyond this oral history, Tomita's experience is illumined by the rich written legacy of *tanka* poems she has written since she was a high school girl in Japan. The tanka written by Tomita served as a form of journal for her, a way of expressing her innermost thoughts as she became part of America. Tomita's poems give us insight into how she viewed her life in America and captured the essence of the Japanese pioneer woman's experience in Washington State. Indeed, *tsugiki,* the title Tomita gave to her section of a poetry anthology, meaning a grafting or a grafted tree, reflects her vision of a Japanese American grafted community rooting itself in Washington State through the pioneering experiences of women like herself.

The tanka provided a natural and common vehicle of expression for Japanese immigrants like Tomita. Coming from a country that had instituted compulsory education in the late nineteenth century, issei were often highly literate. But one did not have to be highly educated or uniquely gifted to compose tanka. Although the *haiku,* which is the Japanese short poem of seventeen syllables arranged in

207

three lines of five, seven, and five syllables, is better known in the United States, the tanka is the more traditional poetic form. The tanka is a Japanese short poem consisting of thirty-one syllables arranged in five lines of five, seven, five, seven, and seven syllables successively. Japanese have from ancient times used the tanka to express their deepest emotions. Lyrical verse of the earliest collections of Japanese poetry used the brevity of the tanka form to speak of life, love, and grief of separation. Commoners as well as aristocrats wrote tanka, which for centuries remained the most popular means of poetic expression for men and women of all classes. Concentration and compression are the essence of the tanka, and in its brief thirty-one syllables Japanese were able to convey what might otherwise have required many pages, or even volumes.

Japanese immigrants like Tomita brought this poetic form with them to America and recorded their new lives through it. Issei-composed tanka in America reflected the imagery, feelings, and sensibilities of an immigrant generation taking root in a new land. Teiko Tomita used a traditional Japanese image, the cherry tree, in many of her tsugiki tanka to speak metaphorically of the grafting process of the Japanese immigrants to the root stock of America. Thus using the traditional poetic form and traditional metaphors, Tomita created new meanings expressing the issei immigrant experience. In writing of this immigrant experience so different from life in Japan, issei poets also created new metaphors and images and added new vocabulary. Tomita's early tanka in eastern Washington mention sagebrush and deserts unknown in Japan, and some of her tanka contain English words. The issei-written tanka was itself adapted to the new land, the poet adapting its content and language while maintaining its ancient form. Together with oral histories and other prose accounts, the tanka poems of Tomita give us a better understanding of the Japanese immigrant woman's experience in Washington State.

In an interview, Tomita recounted that she was born December 1, 1896, in Osaka Prefecture, Japan, the second of nine children born to the Matsui family.[3] She graduated from girls' high school, and while there learned to write tanka. Her teacher gave her the pen name "Yukari," which she used even in America. She went on to take a one and a half years' course at a normal school, which earned her a certificate to teach at the elementary school level. She taught until her marriage in 1920.

Most women in Japan at that time married before they were twenty-five, and as Tomita approached her mid-twenties she was urged to marry. Family-arranged marriages were the norm in Japan, rather than love marriages, since marriages were more of a contract between families than between individuals. Through a go-between, she was matched with her husband, Masakazu Tomita, who was farming near Wapato, Washington. She was shown his picture and told of his background and character. She met with his family in Japan, in the neighboring prefecture, and was impressed by them. Tomita and her husband-to-be exchanged letters for two years before their marriage, as a get-acquainted period. In late 1920, Masakazu Tomita returned to Japan for the marriage ceremony. The newlyweds then traveled in Japan for a couple of months before going to Wapato, in February 1921, to farm on the Yakima Indian Reservation.

Tomita's husband had promised her grandparents, who headed the extended family, that they would return in three years; and the grandparents consented, expecting her to work in America for three to five years at most. No one knew that the three-year stay would turn into more than six decades, though Tomita says that when she got to Washington and saw the poor conditions there, she knew they would not be able to return to Japan in so short a time. Indeed she would never again see her parents.

Tomita's poems indicate the feelings of issei women toward the families and life they left behind in Japan. Although starting a new life in America, the women still had solid roots in their homeland. Ties with their families were strong. In one poem Tomita recalls the parting words of her parents:

> "Live happily,"
> Said my parents
> Holding my hands,
> Their touch
> Even now in my hands[4]

Tomita always remembered her parents' words of hope for her happiness in the new land. The warmth of her parents' love as expressed in their parting words and touch would sustain her through the years of separation. Tomita herself would pass this hope of happiness on to her own children in America.

Separation from her family gave Tomita new insights into the depths of family ties. This is apparent in a poem about her father which grew out of an incident that Tomita likes to recount over and over again. Marriage meant for her that her husband and children became the focus of her life and thoughts, and that work left little time to feel any longing to return home. She claims that she had no thoughts of returning to Japan, no sadness over her life in America. But her husband once saw her in the fields, shedding tears. He thought that she had become homesick after receiving a letter from her father. At dinner that night, he sympathized with her, saying he understood that she longed for her home, far away from the harsh land of Yakima. To his surprise, Tomita replied that she had no thoughts of returning to Japan. Rather, she had cried upon reading the letter, because it revealed a gentle, caring father she had not understood (*Hokubei hyakunen zakura,* p. 325):

> The father I thought so strict
> Where did he conceal
> Such tender feelings
> Revealed in those gentle letters
> Many days I cried

"Those gentle letters" inquired after her well-being and happiness in the new land. Tomita came to have a fuller picture of her father than the severe figure of her childhood. She came to understand the love of father for child. The tears were tears of understanding.

The strength of ties with family and homeland over the thousands of miles separating them is apparent in another tanka by Tomita, encapsulating her emotions upon receiving a package from her family (p. 490):

> When I think
> It is from Japan
> Even wrapping paper
> Seems so close to me
> It's hard to throw it away

Issei women had settled in the Yakima Valley since the 1890s, but even in 1921, when Tomita came to Wapato, the valley was still a raw frontier. Instead of moving from Japan to a richer life, Tomita embarked on a primitive pioneer life. In Kazuo Ito's book *Issei: A History of Japanese Immigrants in North America* (pp. 428–29), Tomita wrote that her Wapato house "was only a little better than a shack, being a two-room cabin hastily put together." Although everyone she knew in Japan had electricity, in Wapato "there was no electric light, so I had to polish oil lamps every morning. We had one small stove in there which took wood or coal, and from time to time I picked up roots of sagebrush and used it as fuel, too." There was no running water. Water had to be drawn from the well outside. The weather, too, was not gentle. Tomita remembers that in deepest winter it was so cold in the house that "you could hear the eggs in the cupboard in the kitchen cracking" and "the place where the sheet was turned down under our chins at night got covered with frost from our breath." When summer came roaring in, "it was scorching hot with a temperature of more than 100 degrees," and at night the Tomitas would have to "spread a blanket under the peach tree" to sleep on.

Tomita helped her husband with the farming on the Yakima Indian Reservation, where he had leased land to grow hay. But in 1921, the year she arrived, and again in 1923, Washington passed stricter anti-alien land laws, which anti-Japanese agitators pressured the Department of Interior to apply to the Yakima Indian Reservation. The Yakima Indian Agency thus was forced to stop issuing leases to Japanese issei, since the new antialien land laws prohibited not only the ownership of land but the renting, sharecropping, and issuance of leases to those who had not in good faith registered their intent to become citizens. Inasmuch as the Japanese were denied naturalization rights by U.S. law strictly on a racial basis, they could not in good faith register their intent to become citizens. Thus they were ineligible to lease land either in Washington or on the reservation. The Tomitas lost their lease rights to their farm on the Yakima Indian Reservation.

Luckily, Tomita's husband was an accomplished agriculturist, and a white nursery owner quickly hired him as a foreman for his nursery in Satus. Tomita served as cook for the laborers working under her husband. She remembers having to cook in shifts in her small house, first serving the work crew, then her own family. It was in Satus that her first child was born.

For Tomita, Satus was an even more remote, isolated area of Washington than Wapato had been. She had to walk five miles to see another Japanese face. Isolated as she was she took solace by writing tanka for herself, recording her life and thoughts.

Issei pioneer women often lived in very isolated regions of Washington. Tomita conveyed in a poem the loneliness and monotony of this life, in which the only way to distinguish one day from another might be the sun's rising and setting (*Hokubei hyakunen zakura,* p. 519):

> Neighbors are five miles far away
> Many days without seeing anyone
> Today, too, without seeing anyone
> The sun sets

This isolated life was common to most pioneer women of the West, as was exposure to the harshness of nature. The houses built by the pioneers with their own hands were not proof against the elements. Tomita's poems speak eloquently of this ceaseless intrusion of nature (p. 519):

Tei Tomita holding her first-born daughter, Kiku, Satus, Washington, 1924
(courtesy Kay Hashimoto)

> Yakima Valley
> The spring storm raging
> Even in the house
> A cloud of sand
> Sifts in

The Yakima Valley was a desert that with water and sweat could be made to bloom. They worked the land, transforming desert and sagebrush into fertile fields of alfalfa, onions, tomatoes, beans, and melons. But hard work did not ensure success. In another poem, Tomita expresses her realistic assessment of the immigrants' struggle to cultivate the land (p. 519):

> Sagebrush desert to fertile plain
> A transformation, I hear,
> But when the windy season comes
> There's no transforming the sandstorm

The persistent sand was a constant reminder of the desert that could reclaim the newly fertile land at any moment, and of the tenuous hold on success that the Japanese as aliens had on the leased land. At any moment the whirling sandstorm could engulf them and return the fertile plain to sagebrush desert.

Tomita's poems evoke not only the grit of desert sand in the newly developed Yakima Valley, but also the severe desert heat (p. 539):

> As we busily pick beans
> Even the breeze stirring
> The weeds at our feet
> Feels hot

Perseverance in the face of adversity characterized the early issei women. This spirit was taught to the children, who worked in the fields with their parents. Tomita writes (p. 539):

> "Soon the heat will be gone"
> While picking beans
> I encourage my children
> And myself

In encouraging her children to persevere in adversity, Tomita strengthened herself to persevere for her children.

Tomita's poems offer a key to her motivations for enduring and continuing to tame and cultivate the burning frontier. Her use of the symbolism of grafted cherry trees, particularly, makes clear the way she viewed her place in this new land (p. 539):

> Carefully grafting
> Young cherry trees
> I believe in the certainty
> They will bud
> In the coming spring

The cherry blossom is a Japanese symbol not only of spring but of Japan and the Japanese people themselves. In the grafting of cherry trees, Tomita sees the grafting of the Japanese immigrant onto the root stock of America, where the graft will continue to grow and become a permanent part. The importance of this symbolism is again underscored in her choice of the title "Tsugiki" (a graft or grafted tree) for her section of the issei poetry anthology *Renia no yuki*. She views not only her past work in the nursery as grafting but perhaps also her own self.

In the poem above she expresses her belief in a coming spring when the grafted tree will bud and grow, just as the hopes and dreams of the immigrant Japanese will be fulfilled. The centrality of this hope of a coming spring is expressed in another poem (*Hokubei hyakunen zakura,* p. 539):

> Whirls of storming winter
> I tolerate
> Believing in spring
> To come again

By believing in the certainty that the grafted tree will bloom in its new environment, the winter of travails can be endured. Perhaps, though, the blossoms will be the next generation, not Tomita's own. Meanwhile the grafting process is an arduous one, as another poem indicates (*Renia no yuki,* p. 248):

> Grafting cherry saplings
> Along long furrows
> The August sun
> Burns on our back

In 1929 the Tomitas moved to Sunnydale, near Seattle, where Seattle-Tacoma International Airport (Sea-Tac) now sprawls. There, they started their own nursery. Moving to more populous Sunnydale meant that Tomita was able to have many Japanese families as neighbors for the first time in America. It also meant the further development of her poetry writing, for she heard of a tanka club in Seattle, and joined the group in 1939. Although she was not able to attend the monthly meetings, she would each month send new poems for criticism. Many of her poems were sent on to Japan for publication. But

The Tomita family, Seattle, 1941. The family lived in Sunnydale at that time. *Left to right:* Masakazu Tomita, Kiku, Joe, Jun, Tei Tomita, Kay *(courtesy Kay Hashimoto)*

in Sunnydale, misfortunes and hardships continued, with the loss of the youngest daughter of the Tomitas' five children and the impact of the Great Depression. Tomita became a Christian during the Sunnydale years, and many of her later poems reflect her new faith.

The small economic gains made by the Tomitas were wiped out by the outbreak of war between the motherland and the adopted land in December 1941. Since they were denied naturalization rights, all Japanese immigrants were aliens, now enemy aliens. Furthermore, even their U.S.-born children were considered suspect. The old anti-Japanese agitation was rekindled, and this time succeeded in perpetrating one of the most massive violations of civil rights in American legal history. With no formal charges of any wrongdoing, more than 110,000 issei and their U.S. citizen-children were removed from their homes on the west coast to incarceration in concentration camps. They were not to be allowed to return to their homes until 1945. Although most Seattle Japanese were interned in Minidoka in Idaho,

those in the outlying areas of Seattle, like the Tomitas, were interned
in Tule Lake, California, in 1942. In late 1943 they were moved to
Heart Mountain in Wyoming, where, ironically, Tomita was reunited
with Japanese from the Yakima Valley, her first home in America.[5]

Immediately after the bombing of Pearl Harbor, many rumors circulated in the Japanese community that military men were searching
all Japanese homes for any incriminating evidence that would link
them with Japan. Later, there was talk about something fearsome
called "camp." Under this pressure, Tomita gathered up her precious
poetry manuscripts, took them to the fields, and burned them all,
fearing that the private thoughts recorded in her tanka might be twisted
into something harmful to her family. Being forced to burn her poems
remains one of the most painful memories of the war for Tomita.
Much of the poetic record of her life was wiped out.

But despite the destruction of the manuscripts, not all the poems
were lost. Many of the burned tanka remained etched in Tomita's
mind, to be recalled in later years. Easily committed to memory, poetry has often been the device of oral tradition's preservation of pre-
literate history, passed on from one generation to the next.

When war broke out between Japan and the United States in December 1941, it looked as though spring would not come, even for
the next generation. The war years were difficult ones for the issei
women. After years of struggling, the little they had gained was
wrenched from them overnight. Forced by the government to leave
the land they had pioneered, they were imprisoned in even more isolated and desolate regions of America than they could ever have
imagined. The internment camps were located in remote desert lands.
Yet even here, surrounded by barbed wire, the creative spirit of the
issei inmates persisted. The creative arts in the camps found expression in forms ranging from polished sagebrush roots to accomplished
poetry. Many issei learned to write Japanese poetry for the first time
in camp, and continued to write even after they had left the camps.[6]

At Heart Mountain, Tomita, with other issei, attended lectures and
classes in poetry to while away the seemingly endless years of internment. Tomita began to keep a journal of her class lectures, as
well as of her poems—a fresh book to replace the volumes she had
burned. Her book of poems shows the changes she made from one
draft to another, to final form. In poetry many issei found the solace
Tomita noted in a poem written in 1943, at Tule Lake internment
camp (*Renia no yuki*, p. 243):

> Within the iron stockade
> Always composing poems

> From the sorrows of war
> A little consolation

As she had done in the desert of Yakima, Tomita turned to poetry to comfort herself in her troubles. But, as always, her poems also reflected hope. In the midst of the sorrow and uncertainty of imprisonment in Tule Lake, in January 1943 she could still write (p. 243):

> In the war concentration camp
> The New Year's Day's sun rises
> Look up at the light
> Which breaks up the darkness of night

New Year's Day meant the hope of a new start, the hope that the darkness of the past year might be pierced by the light of freedom. But freedom did not come quickly. The war continued. Tomita's poems written in 1944 reflect the inner turmoil experienced by the issei caught by a war between the country of birth and the adopted country which had not accepted them as its own (p. 243):

> I read the war news
> Today again
> My heart clouds
> And my thoughts are frozen

When the war finally ended, in 1945, the Tomitas were living in Minnesota, having secured a work release earlier in the year. The war that had torn them from their homes and made prisoners of them had ended, but the war's end was bittersweet news (p. 243):

> Among whites jubilantly shouting
> "The war is over"
> My husband and I
> Cried throughout the night

Japan was defeated, horrifying atomic bombs had been dropped, and Japanese Americans had at last been released from the camps in which they had been held for years without any justification. Joy and relief at the end of the grief and hardships of the war combined with the sadness of war's aftermath and destruction and the uncertain future. Tomita worried over the fate of her family in Japan and their mutual concern over her fate in America (p. 243):

> For the first time in five years
> Letters are permitted to the home country

> Today I only write
> "We're safe"

The link with family in the home country was reestablished. The silence brought by war ended with the simple message, "We're safe."

They were safe. They had survived another hardship, but now they once again had to start from scratch. She wrote (p. 244):

> Returning home from the iron stockade
> Five years ago
> Reconstructing our lives
> Is no small thing even now

Her poem reflects the cold reality for Japanese Americans that even after returning from the concentration camps they still faced a long struggle to rebuild their lives. But although it was indeed not a "small thing," Tomita did reconstruct her life. Because of the internment, the Tomitas had not only lost their nursery business but had no capital to invest in another venture. Tomita took the only wage job available to her. She became a garment worker in Seattle. This job opened new worlds for her.

Sewing alongside other immigrant women in Seattle, Tomita gained closer contact and better understanding of women from other ethnic groups. The poems written while she was a seamstress reflect a growing awareness of the commonality of experience and emotions she shared with her co-workers. In one poem she writes (p. 243):

> A German woman and I
> Sewing together
> Sharing the same feelings
> Speaking of the war destruction
> In each of our home countries

Although they came from two countries separated by thousands of miles and by different cultural traditions, here in the workplace the two women shared their wartime experiences and became one.

While her prewar poems dealt mainly with herself or her family, Tomita's poems were now enlivened with observations of other people. In contrast to the isolation of her former rural life, her urban workplace offered a microcosm of the multiethnic, multicultural American society of which she was a part. In a series of more narrative poems, Tomita observed some conflict between white and black workers, but in general her poems suggest a sisterhood among the women workers that cut across ethnic lines.

Tomita's poems bring to life the variety of women she worked with, among them a black woman who had such a fine voice that when she sang, her voice rose clear and strong above the roar of the sewing machines, and a Filipino woman who seemed very cheerful and carefree, and who had learned a little Japanese that helped her communicate with Tomita. Tomita savored and valued these experiences (p. 245):

> For many years
> Mixed among the workers of different races
> I sew
> I'm used to it
> Such life is enjoyable

Tomita's growing appreciation of interaction with other ethnic groups is further demonstrated in a series of poems about her Italian neighbors. The first in the series notes the presence in her neighborhood of many Italians, most of them farmers who worked very diligently. She admired their industry, which made her feel an affinity with them. In the next poem she again took up this theme (p. 246):

> In their hard work
> Italians are like we Japanese
> Daughters and wives, too
> Work all day in the fields

It was in their shared history of the hard work of farming that Tomita found a commonality of experience with these European immigrants. And the feelings were mutual, it seems, for in the next poems we see that at least one of the Italian neighbors had become a friend. Beyond sharing hard work and vegetables with his Japanese neighbors, he shared the immigrant experience of separation from the land of one's birth (p. 247):

> Mutually shared feelings
> This Italian
> Speaking fervently about
> His homeland

In the postwar period we see Tomita's poems reflecting not only a more urban, multiethnic awareness but also a more global viewpoint. Fully understanding the terrible costs of war, Tomita is well aware of the world events that may lead to a war for which her children would have to pay the high price (p. 250):

> My son is still young
> I daily pray

For eternal peace
In this violent world

In particular, she has become ardently opposed to the nuclear arms
race, devoting a whole series of poems to this subject. News of the
Bikini Island nuclear test victims moves her to write (p. 251):

Reading of the condition
Of Bikini patients
Incurable disease
The power of science
Is rather a curse

She notes that Japan is a leader in the nuclear disarmament movement (p. 252):

A country that experienced
The death ash
Japan's accusing voice
Voice of desperation

In another poem in the series, Tomita observes that a ban on nuclear
bombs has already been written with the blood of Japan, the only
country to suffer an atomic bombing. But she notes, sadly (p. 252):

Regardless of the earnest prayers
Of the suffering country
Nuclear bombs
Are steadily produced

After decades of hard work, Tomita was finally able to realize her
dream of owning a home. Her joy in the fulfillment of the dream is
recorded in a series of poems (p. 249):

I enjoyed drawing pictures
Of my desired house
The long held dream
Became a reality

The dream became a reality just when they had virtually given up
hope of achieving it in their generation (p. 249):

The dream I passed
On to my children
How many years!
The house is finished

But this joy at a dream finally fulfilled in America was also to be
dashed. Her Sunnydale home was directly north of Seattle-Tacoma

International Airport. Soon the roar of the airplanes shook her house (p. 245):

> The runways are to be expanded,
> I hear,
> The roaring sound
> Is drawing closer to me

The airport expanded, she wrote, despite the complaints and puzzlement of the surrounding people. Its expansion changed the environment (p. 246):

> Farms and houses, too
> Before I'm aware
> I see their shadows no more
> The runways are being built expansively

As houses and farms disappeared, the people disappeared. The Port of Seattle responded to the complaints of noise and low-flying jets by removing the people who complained. It acquired by eminent domain the property of people like Tomita to form a buffer zone around Seattle-Tacoma International. In 1967, Tomita was once again forced to relocate. More fortunate than some, she and her husband were able to move in with her daughter's family in Seattle.

The realization of the passing of time is very much part of the later writings of Tomita. Reflecting on the decades of pioneering that have flown past, she writes (p. 251):

> Long ago are the days
> I helped my husband
> Cultivate the raw land
> And raised our children
> We two have grown old

Another poem continues the theme of old age (p. 251):

> My husband
> Reading with bifocals
> So many decades of struggles
> Engraved deeply
> In the wrinkles on his face

Thoughts rise of the unfulfilled aspirations of youth. For Tomita those memories are of dashed hopes of continuing her studies. In a series of poems she recalls these hopes of scholarship, symbolized in a treasured box given to her as a graduation prize (p. 247):

As a lifetime memory
Placed in a suitcase with love and care
For thirty years
A lacquer calligraphy box

She remembers the words that accompanied the prize—words admonishing her to continue to train her mind and soul. But since coming to America (p. 247):

Too busy were
Thirty years of life
In a foreign country
Never used the brush and ink

There had never been time for her formal studies. She had written her tanka in isolation in the fields of Yakima. Even after moving to the Seattle area, though she had been able to join a tanka club, she had not been able to attend the monthly meetings, because the nursery had required her constant care.

Her life, she said in an interview, could be summed up in one word, *isogashii*—busy, a life filled always with things she had to do.[7] As for thoughts of the luxury of studies (p. 247):

Never to return are the days
When I put my heart and soul
In my studies only
I grow old in a foreign country

Although her aspirations may have had to be set aside in the grafting process of settling in America, there was always the belief in the fulfillment of dreams for the next generation, when the grafted tree would bloom and bear fruit. The struggles were well worth the pain for Tomita, if her children could fulfill their own dreams and aspirations. Tomita reveled in the fact that her children had not been adversely affected by the family's hard life (p. 246):

My daughter has
A rainbow-like dream
Cheerful as she is
The poverty of me her mother
Hasn't stained her life.

Memories of the poverty of much of her life in America, with repeated setbacks, led her to write (*Hokubei hyakunen zakura*, p. 173):

When winter comes
I wonder what it was

> That enabled me to endure
> Heartrending sorrows

It had been for her children that she worked, and it was the hope of their spring that sustained her through her winter of struggles and sorrows. In her poems, she celebrates the triumphs of her children as they go off to college, get married, and start new, exciting jobs. Her poems reveal a conviction on her part that her children will not suffer the trials and tribulations she endured (*Renia no yuki,* p. 250):

> My son's start in life
> Like a clear morning
> Without a single cloud
> Limitless blue sky of hope

Her struggles have not adversely affected the lives of her children, but rather seem to have ensured their future. She could write hopefully in 1968:

> The centennial of
> The Japanese immigrants in America
> Our next generation
> With a great future before them[8]

Fifteen years later Tomita looks back on her more than six decades of life experiences in America and concludes:

> The bitter ordeals I have suffered
> One after another
> As I remember
> Now without sorrow
> Filled with grace[9]

Tomita's most recent poems reflect a continuation of her thanksgiving that her grandchildren, too, are enjoying the spring out of the travails of her winters. In a series of poems in the summer of 1983 she writes of her trip to the East Coast to attend her granddaughter's graduation from Sarah Lawrence. With commencement comes a new flowering for the third-generation tsugiki, and a celebration uniting the generations. The ties that bind the generations together appear strong, as her grandchildren make efforts to communicate with their grandmother in Japanese:

> From my granddaughter in New York
> A letter in Japanese
> As I read it
> Tears of joy overflow[10]

Whatever their literary merits, the poems presented in this essay provide valuable information and insight into the life of Teiko Tomita. Each poem is a diary entry relating a significant event or thought in her life. Often a series of poems gives a full account of a particular incident in her life. Even more than a diary, the poems reveal the inner thoughts and emotions of the author. Tanka critic Hideko Matsui, in an article in *Cho-on*, the Japanese poetry magazine to which the Seattle tanka club sent their selected poetry for publication, believes that although poems such as Tomita's in *Renia no yuki* have a simple, classical moving quality about them, their importance is mainly that they relate the immigrants' history in the traditional form of the Japanese tanka.[11] In fact, both the historical value and the literary merit of issei poetry deserve a great deal of further discussion.[12]

Recognition of the value of issei poetry as a vehicle for understanding the Japanese American experience in America has led to the publication of anthologies of translated poems written by the issei. One such anthology is *Poets Behind Barbed Wire*,[13] which contains Japanese short poems, haiku and tanka, written by Hawaii issei interned during World War II. The editors of the anthology note that "in view of the scarcity of writing paper, these short poems, being less cumbersome than long diaries, were ideal forms for the internees' expression of their pent-up emotions." They further point out that "it also perpetuates the Japanese tradition of expressing their innermost emotions through short poems instead of prose." The editors believe that the short poems express the issei internment experience far better and more explicitly than prose written on the experience.[14] Indeed, one of these poets behind barbed wire scribbled hundreds of poems on the only two sheets of paper he was able to take with him from detention to internment camps.

For Tomita and a great many issei, poetry was a means of recording their lives for posterity, as well as an artistic release of their emotions. They wrote their tanka as poetic expressions of their lives and thoughts. In writing their tanka they were conscious of their role in recording their history—a history they believed would not be included in general histories about American immigrants. Another issei woman poet, Keiko Teshirogi, wrote:

> Not recorded in immigrant history
> Your struggles are inscribed
> In the depths of my heart alone[15]

As it was for Tomita, the cherry tree was a common issei symbol of Japan and the Japanese. Teshirogi also composed a tanka similar to those of Tomita, speaking of the issei as cherry trees making the adaptation to the American continent from their roots in the island environment of Japan:

> A cherry tree
> That cannot adapt itself to a continent
> Is small
> And without taking on autumn colors
> Its leaves fall[16]

Despite great hardships, the issei immigrants did indeed adapt to their new environment. For some, like Tomita, poetic expression helped to make that adaptation more endurable. Their poetry, in turn, helps us to grasp the history of that adaptation and survival.

Teiko Tomita's life as presented in this essay provides an outline generally representative of the issei woman's rather harsh life in Washington State. Although the early Japanese immigrants to Washington were predominantly young, single men, women began to enter the state in large numbers after the so-called gentlemen's agreement in 1907–8 which restricted the further immigration of Japanese male laborers to the United States. Like Tomita, most women who came were wives of settled immigrants. Many were "picture brides" whose marriages had been arranged by their families through the exchange of pictures with Japanese male immigrants living in Washington. After 1921, because the Japanese government did not issue passports to picture brides, most grooms, like Tomita's husband, traveled to Japan to marry, and brought their wives back with them. In 1924, Congress passed a new immigration and naturalization act which prohibited the immigration of "aliens ineligible to citizenship," a category the U.S. Supreme Court had created in its 1922 *Ozawa* decision and 1923 *Thind* decision, ruling that Mongolians as a racial group and people from India were not eligible for naturalization. Thus no new immigrants from Japan, male or female, arrived after 1924. Still, because the Japanese males had been able to send for wives from 1908 to 1924, there occurred a dramatic increase in the numbers of women of Japanese ethnicity in Washington.[17]

The Japanese women who came between 1910 and 1924 played a crucial role in the growth of a Japanese American community in Washington. The summoning of wives like Tomita reinforced the commitment to permanent residency in America more than economic stakes in farms and businesses. There was a settled family life with the coming of wives, and an emergence of Japanese American family units with the dramatic increase in American-born children between 1900 and 1930. With the birth of the second generation, there was a transformation from immigrant society to permanent settlers, as issei began to focus and identify their own futures in terms of the future of their children in America. Entry of women into Japanese immigrant society was an integral part of the process by which Japanese immigrant society sank its roots into American soil. The arrival of women guaranteed that a community with a family life could be established in America. The Japanese community developed a family orientation around schools, churches, clubs, and associations. The women brought both community and Japanese culture with them. Often highly educated, like Tomita, they preserved such values as love of learning and an appreciation of the arts.

Tomita's lifetime of work in the Yakima Valley, Sunnydale, and Seattle underscores the fact that Japanese pioneer women were not only wives and mothers but also workers. Their labor was indispensable in the operation of farms, small businesses, and labor camps, as well as in family enterprises, such as small shops and tiny farms. Japanese women played a vital economic role in the new land.

The majority of Japanese women initially lived in rural areas, helping their husbands till the soil as farmers. Japanese agriculturalists were especially prominent in Washington. In urban areas, women entered small businesses operated by their husbands, such as laundries, markets, restaurants, and boardinghouses, or they became domestic servants, seamstresses, and cannery workers. Labor camps that provided laborers for railroads, lumber camps, and mills were often run by issei men. Many issei women worked in these labor camps. As Tomita did in her Yakima years, the women cooked for the large group of workers employed by their husbands.

Japanese women performed tasks essential to the maintenance of the family by earning income, rearing children, preparing meals, shopping, and tending the sick. Because of their essential role in running the family and their valuable economic role, the women enjoyed greater power in decision making for the family than did their counterparts in Japan. Moreover, in the pioneer setting the issei women were free of the traditional control of the mother-in-law, another factor that greatly enlarged their influence in the family.

In the 1930s the power of issei wives in the family increased, as the men aged. Many of the issei men in the 1930s were over fifty-five. As the men aged, their wives—on the average ten years younger— took on increased economic responsibilities, and made more of the important decisions. The women thus became increasingly the focal point of the Japanese American family.

Issei women did not have an easy time making a home in Washington. The most sustained and serious difficulty they faced was anti-

Japanese sentiment. As we have seen, Japanese were denied natural-ization on the basis of race, and so were condemned to remain aliens in their adopted land. In Washington, their status as "aliens ineligible to citizenship" made it possible to restrict their economic opportu-nities severely through a series of antialien land laws. The culmina-tion of these anti-Japanese policies came with World War II, when thousands of Washington Japanese—aliens and U.S. citizens alike—were removed to concentration camps.

After the war, the issei pioneers, now nearing retirement age, had to begin their lives over again. Like Tomita, many issei women, whose assets and capital had been taken from them by the internment, went to work in garment factories or into domestic service. Tomita's post-war urban life also reflects a general shift of Japanese Americans after the war to urban residences and occupations.

In the postwar years, hard work once more bore fruit—though not as great a harvest as might have been possible, given more hospitable conditions. The children of the pioneers, the nisei, married and had children of their own. A third generation was born. The issei women looked back on their years of struggle, and saw in their grandchildren the fulfillment of their young hopes when they first came to America. They believed the tsugiki to be strong and firmly rooted in its adopted land. The children and the grandchildren, the second and third gen-eration branches of the tsugiki, are blooming in the spring that has finally come. Tomita can write in May 1983:

> The seeds I planted
> Sprout and grow up
> Even in this very old body
> Joy overflows[18]

Through the struggles of Tomita and other issei pioneer women, the history of Washington State has been enriched.

Notes

1. In the 1920, 1930, and 1940 censuses, women of Japanese ethnicity were the most numerous nonwhite women in Washington State, making up almost half of the nonwhite female population, including Native American women. See U.S. Bureau of the Census, *Sixteenth Census of the United States* (**1940**), *vol. 2: Population 2: Characteristics of the Population* (Washington, D.C.: U.S. Government Printing Office, 1943), pt. 7, Utah-Wyoming, p. 304.

2. The best English source of information on issei women in Washington

is Kazuo Ito, *Issei: A History of Japanese Immigrants in North America,* trans. Shinichiro Nakamura and Jean S. Gerard (Seattle: Executive Committee for Publication, Japanese Community Service, 1973). This is a translation of Ito's *Hokubei hyakunen zakura* (North American Hundred Years Cherries) (Tokyo: Hokubei hyakunen zakura jikko iinkai, 1969), which contains written statements and poetry by issei women recalling their lives in the Pacific Northwest.

3. The biographical information is drawn from an interview with Tomita, Seattle, Washington, July 26, 1983.

4. Mihara Senryu et al., *Renia no yuki* (Snow of Rainier) (Kamakura, Japan: Cho-onsha, 1956), p. 249. This anthology contains the best published collection of Tomita's poems. Some of the earlier poems have annotations that give the date of writing. Other poems can be dated by their content, since Tomita wrote her poems contemporaneously with the events about which she wrote. The best source of her more recent poems is the Seattle newspaper *Hokubei Hochi,* in which her poems appeared monthly.

The English translations of Tomita's tanka that appear in this chapter do not fully convey, of course, the poetic beauty, rhythm, and nuances of the original. I have made an attempt to remain as close to the original Japanese meaning of the tanka as possible, though I was not able at this time to render the translation into an English poetic equivalent, if that is ever possible. It is hoped that in the near future better translations will be forthcoming to allow the reader to understand and appreciate more fully the poetic beauty of these poems.

5. See Frank F. Chuman, *The Bamboo People: The Law and Japanese-Americans* (Del Mar, California: Publisher's Inc., 1976), for information on restrictive laws, and for information on the internment of Japanese Americans see such works as Commission on Wartime Relocation and Internment of Civilians, *Personal Justice Denied* (Washington, D.C., 1983); Roger Daniels, *Concentration Camps: North America* (Malabar, Fla.: Robert E. Krieger Publishing Company, 1981); Peter Irons, *Justice at War* (New York: Oxford University Press, 1983); and Michi Weglyn, *Years of Infamy* (New York: William Morrow, 1976).

6. Interview with Toshiko Toku, Seattle, Washington, July 25, 1983. Toku learned to write *senryu,* Japanese satirical poems, in an internment camp during World War II and continues to write to the present.

7. Interview with Teiko Tomita, Seattle, Washington, July 26, 1983.

8. Kazuo Ito, *Zoku hokubei hyakunen zakura* (North American Hundred Years Cherries, Supplement) (Tokyo: Hokubei hyakunen zakura jikko iinkai, 1972).

9. "Shiatoru tankakai," *Hokubei Hochi* (Seattle), May 25, 1983, p. 7.

10. Ibid., Oct. 12, 1983, p. 5.

11. Hideko Matsui, "Renia no yuki no igi" (Significance of *Renia no yuki*) *Cho-on* 42, no. 6 (1956): 27–28.

12. For a discussion of how local American settings, history, and culture have affected the creation of an issei poetry see Stephen H. Sumida, "Localism in Asian American Literature and Culture of Hawaii and the West

Coast," *Hawaii Literary Arts Council Newsletter* 71 (August-September 1983): n.p. The essay was originally delivered in this form at the Asian Studies on the Pacific Coast Conference, University of Alaska at Fairbanks, June 1983. Issei poetry calls for literary evaluation in terms of the poetry's own issei contexts.

13. Keiho Soga, Taisanboku Mori, Sojin Takei, and Muin Ozaki, *Poets Behind Barbed Wire,* ed. and trans. Jiro Nakano and Kay Nakano (Honolulu: Bamboo Ridge Press, 1983).

14. Ibid., p. vii.

15. Mihara, *Renia no yuki,* p. 239.

16. Ibid., p. 240.

17. U.S. Census (1940), p. 304. In 1900 there were 185 Japanese women in Washington, including 21 born in the United States; in 1910 there were 1,688, with 347 being U.S. born. But in 1920, after a decade of immigration of wives and picture brides, there were 6,065 women of Japanese ethnicity, with 2,117 U.S. born. From 1920 until 1940, women of Japanese ethnicity composed the largest group of nonwhite women in Washington State. In 1920, women of Japanese ethnicity numbered 6,065 out of 13,836 nonwhite women in Washington. In 1930, out of 16,744 nonwhite women in Washington there were 7,637 women of Japanese ethnicity, including 4,308 U.S. born. And in 1940, out of 15,975 nonwhite women, there were 6,532 women of Japanese ethnicity, including 4,234 U.S. born. The numbers of issei women actually fell between 1920 and 1940 because of increasing legal restrictions which greatly limited the issei's economic opportunities, forcing them to seek better opportunities in other states.

18. "Shiatoru tankakai," *Hokubei Hochi,* June 8, 1983, p. 7.

Part 5

NEW DIRECTIONS
FOR RESEARCH

Having amassed considerable information about Pacific
Northwest women and varied interpretations of their history, Susan Armitage asks what we gain by engaging in
the activity. She asserts that by explaining the significance
of the daily lives, pursuits, and values of the ordinary
woman, we will discover behavior, problems, and perspectives heretofore ignored. We have begun to build the
biographies of "woman worthies" from the past, and to
describe some of the contributions women have made to
standard areas already respected by historians. Now we
are establishing a "transitional" woman-centered study
which assumes that woman's experience may well be different from man's, but just as valuable, in any given era.
The necessary material to sustain this type of inquiry will
be gleaned from neglected documents, such as household
accounts, diaries, club minutes, and records of women's
wage-earning experiences in service work or local industry. The effort should yield extraordinary results. It will
correct serious omissions, challenge earlier interpretations
of historical events, build a more complex synthesis of the
past, and teach a truer portrait of Northwest growth and
development.

We have here, then, a beginning. There is considerable
investigation yet to be undertaken. Yet these initial studies
already offer significant implications for Northwest his-

tory. Our women, of every class, race, and age, were neither sheltered nor passive. With the strength from their
own networks, they operated in ingenious ways to make
a considerable impact on public life as well as within the
domestic sphere. As the Washington State Centennial of
1989 approaches, women can look back on a heritage of
which they should be proud, and take inspiration to build
further.

The Challenge of Women's History

Susan H. Armitage

What is women's history? The occasional mention of an extraordinary woman is not enough; nor is a sentimental paragraph eulogizing the woman in the sunbonnet as the true pioneer. Women's history seeks to explain the significance of the daily lives, activities, and values of ordinary women. This explanation is not easily achieved. The idea of seriously and comprehensively treating women as historical subjects is still novel and requires detailed research in unfamiliar topics. This, then, is the first challenge, and for the researcher, a new perspective is required. Then, too, findings in women's history inevitably challenge earlier interpretations of historical events. This second challenge affects all historians whatever their own research specialties, for it concerns how they teach history to their students.

Viewed from the perspective of women's history, present Pacific Northwest history is incomplete. The history of the women of the region is largely unexplored. In this respect, the Pacific Northwest is not unique: in all regions of the country, women's history has been neglected. Furthermore, state and regional historians are generally ill-informed about women's history at both the theoretical and the national levels because it has not seemed relevant to their interests. This essay provides information on those aspects of women's history that are relevant to the history of the Pacific Northwest, points out some omissions in regional studies, and suggests some insights that may prove useful in future investigations.[1]

Women's history is generally considered to have begun as a contemporary specialty with the publication in 1968 of Gerda Lerner's article "New Approaches to the Study of Women in American History."[2] Since then, there has been an explosion of historical research on women and a rapid refining of insights. Like all developing academic specialities, women's history has changed as it has grown. Yet Lerner's categorization of the stages in that development provides us with a useful framework within which to consider Pacific Northwest studies of women.[3]

The first works were biographical studies of "women worthies"— those unusual women whose extraordinary achievements could not be ignored. Clifford Drury's accounts of the "First White Women

This chapter is included in David Stratton and George Frykman, eds., *A Changing Pacific Northwest* (Pullman: Washington State University Press, 1987).

Over the Rockies"—Narcissa Whitman, Eliza Spalding, and the other missionary women who followed shortly after—fall into this category.[4] Other regional "women worthies" have not been ignored. The best known are Abigail Scott Duniway, journalist and leader of the suffrage movement in Oregon; Jeanette Rankin of Montana, the first U.S. Congresswoman; and suffragist May Arkwright Hutton of Spokane.[5] Bethinia Owens-Adair, M.D., historian Frances Fuller Victor, suffragists Eva Emery Dye and Emma DeVoe, and more recent figures such as Bertha Landes and Anna Louise Strong of Seattle have also received some attention.[6]

Lerner termed the second stage of historical writing about women as "contribution history." What have women done that can be considered significant by the accepted historical criteria? Apparently the answer for the Pacific Northwest is Sacajawea and suffrage. About Sacajawea there is embarrassingly little to say. Rarely has such a large heroine been created out of so little historical fact.[7] For all practical purposes Sacajawea has passed into American folklore and beyond the reach of historians. She should be consigned to American mythology, henceforth to keep company with Paul Bunyan, Mike Fink, Pecos Bill, and friends.

Suffrage is a different story. T. A. Larson's articles on suffrage in the western states have made a good start, and recent studies of politically active regional women are adding detail. However, there is as yet no link between studies of western suffrage and the most recent interpretations of the eastern suffrage movement.[8]

Lerner's third stage, which she terms "transitional" history, incorporates the current scholarship. Historians in this third stage share a perspective that is openly and honestly woman centered. A serious effort has been made by these historians to view women's historical experience through women's eyes. Some of the results of this reinterpretation are controversial. Two articles in particular (Faragher and Stanstell, "Women and Their Families on the Overland Trail,"[9] and Lillian Schlissel, "Women's Diaries on the Western Frontier,"[10]) aroused the wrath of historians who did not share their feminist perspective. One critic accused the authors of taking women's experience out of context; furthermore, they were accused of creating a dreadful new stereotype, that of the "downtrodden drudge."[11] In fact, the initial portrait was too limited in those two early articles, as the authors themselves implicitly admit in their subsequent monographs.[12] But their final conclusion is even more radical than that of the earlier articles. Faragher concludes that there were *two* Overland Trail experiences—a male one and a female one:

For men the trip west was an active test of competition, strength, and manliness. It meant measuring themselves against the already romanticized images of their heroic fathers and grandfathers traversing the Wilderness Road and the Cumberland Gap. For women the trip west was a test of their inner strength. They did their part and more; they were comforting wives and attentive mothers, to the many single men of the trail as well as their husbands. They did all this, because of, not in spite of, their not wanting to leave home in the first place.[13]

This point is important. The evidence that men and women experienced the Overland Trail differently is fully in accord with recent research in eastern nineteenth-century women's and family history. The two sexes inhabited separate spheres; what women did was dramatically different from what men did, and their perceptions were shaped accordingly. David Potter saw all this years ago, and he also saw clearly the implications for historical interpretation. As he said, an explanation that does not apply to women cannot be considered comprehensive. Looking at the West, Potter observed, "in cold fact, the opportunities offered by the West were opportunities for men and not, in any direct sense, opportunities for women."[14] This is serious, indeed, for it means that Frederick Jackson Turner was, at best, half right.

Turner's thesis—that the frontier liberated the individual from social, class, and psychological restraints—is apparently not true for women (and perhaps not true for all men). We are so accustomed to thinking of the frontier as an area of freedom and of choice that this conclusion is unwelcome. Yet the most substantial book so far published on women in the West, Julie Roy Jeffrey's *Frontier Women,* argues convincingly that most women did not view the frontier as an opportunity to liberate themselves from conventional sex roles. Indeed, they resisted changes that would have caused them to deviate from traditional woman's work and a womanly role.[15]

How shall historians respond to the challenge that female frontier experience poses to the traditional norm? The rationalization that because the West was largely settled by men, the prevailing culture was masculine in tone, does not fit the Northwest reality. The initial Willamette Valley settlement was made largely by families. A recent study shows that in rural areas (although not in towns) the sex ratio was roughly equal from the beginning of the settlement.[16]

There is another very simple way to justify the historical omission of women, and that is to say that whatever women did, their activities were never as important as those of men. As T. A. Larson has said, "Women, after all, did not lead expeditions, command troops, build railroads, drive cattle, or ride Pony Express."[17] But some women did indeed participate in these events. For example, the writings of Elizabeth Custer and other military wives are a valuable source of information on many aspects of western army life. A Pacific Northwest example, Emily Fitzgerald's letters, in *An Army Doctor's Wife on the Frontier,* conveys a vivid sense of the tension and confusion at Fort Lapwai in the days before and during the Nez Perce war of 1877.[18]

Yet another, and better, explanation is that earlier historians simply did not ask the basic women's history question: "What were women doing while men were doing the things that they deemed important?"[19] This is the question that can and must now be answered. Historians can indeed discover the actual, historical roles that women played in the development of the Pacific Northwest. Information to document women's activities exists. Much of it is readily available in archival collections; much has recently been catalogued. Sometimes more persistence is required; information about women must be pieced together or "teased out" of the documents.[20] More frequently, it is simply a matter of not taking women's activities for granted.

The following example illustrates how taken-for-grantedness has affected the writing of history. Among the early settlers in Thurston County were the Bush family, who have attracted attention because George Bush was black. Their presence is frequently mentioned in Washington histories, usually as the "George Bush family." A careful search in sources such as county histories provides valuable information for this case. One report on the Bush family, which is largely based on an oral history with Lewis Bush, the youngest son, describes the active role of his mother, Isabella Bush, in the family's survival.

Hudson's Bay Company officials were not pleased when a pioneer group of thirty Americans, including the Bushes, settled a part of Thurston County in 1845. The local factor at Fort Nisqually, Dr. William Fraser Tolmie, had orders not to sell food to American settlers. Consequently, life for the new arrivals was hard, indeed frightening, for the first few years. Lewis Bush recounted how his family found a solution:

> Mother made friends with Dr. Tolmie and it was through him that she got her first start in poultry and sheep. She had traded for a few hens from a French family who were connected with the Hudsons Bay Company, and when one of these hens showed her willingness to set, mother got a setting of turkey eggs from Dr. Tolmie. She was very successful with this hatching and by coddling those young turks soon

had a nice flock. Dr. Tolmie had not been so lucky with his turkeys so he told mother he would trade her a fine ewe for every turkey she would let him have. She was glad to do so and in that way she got the first start of the large flock of sheep which was one of the greatest sources of profit in a few years. From Dr. Tolmie also, we got the first start of hogs. Well, so we lived for years, always getting ahead a little and I am glad to say, always having a little to share with our poorer neighbors. Neither father nor mother could bear to deny anyone who applied to them for assistance.[21]

Isabella Bush provided food for her family at a difficult time; most other women in the Pacific Northwest did the same as a matter of course, but in less dramatic circumstances. Throughout the region, whenever possible, women grew and preserved the family food supply; and the lower the family's cash income, the more important this female provider role became. Accumulating evidence tells us that this provider role was the basic female responsibility throughout the West, even after eastern urban women had been fully incorporated into a cash and consumer economy. The domestic activity of women made a direct contribution to the household economy. To overlook this role, or to take it for granted, falsifies the reality of how early settler families survived and functioned as economic units.[22]

Unfortunately, evidence to document the economic contributions of women within the household is often difficult to find. Census records contain only those parts of women's work that fall within the wage economy. Even such a widespread female economic activity as taking in boarders escapes specific mention, and its existence in each particular case has to be a supposition based on household size and the number of unrelated persons recorded by the manuscript census. Furthermore, census data are unavailable for the period after 1910. Historians have turned, therefore, to two other sources for documentation of women's household activities: personal documents (diaries and letters) and personal testimony (oral history).

A recent book, Mary Beth Norton's *Liberty's Daughters,* is a useful model. Based mainly on women's personal documents, the study links changes in the attitudes and household activities of women with ideological and economic changes in the revolutionary and early national periods.[23]

We need regional studies that will do the same. For instance, women's wage work is still a neglected topic in Pacific Northwest history. The one exception is research on women shipyard workers in World War II, which has produced two excellent recent studies.[24] However, it may be that the very novelty of wartime employment has distracted attention from the ways in which more traditional women's labor, particularly as service workers, has contributed to regional industries such as agriculture, logging, mining, and fishing.[25]

Moving from the family to the community level, the same pattern of omission of women's activities persists. Most community histories mention only men; it often seems that women had only a minor part in the founding and shaping of community institutions. In this case, appearances are deceiving. All over the country, historians of women are now documenting a forgotten range of female community activities.[26] Recent research shows a strong pattern of informal female activities in which many community projects are begun, lobbied, and arranged. But when the moment of formal organization comes, the women seem to step back. Men are elected as officials, and often given public credit for the entire enterprise.[27] Newspapers report this final, formal stage and thus overlook women's activities. To fill out the record, other, less customary sources must be consulted as well as newspapers. In many areas of the West, women's clubs were deeply involved in community affairs.[28] Where club records exist, they should be examined. Oral history is another important tool in community history, when used to explore the "unofficial" story of the founding and development of community organizations. Often there are family stories about the mother's role in community building. In this recently settled region, interviews with (now aged) children of pioneers can frequently carry us back nearly to the point of white arrival.[29]

These few brief examples illustrate the ways in which women's history challenges earlier interpretations. Women's history means more than adding a few female names to existing history. New kinds of evidence, new issues, and new perspectives inevitably arise. Consideration of the historical activities of women in the Pacific Northwest will change our regional history. The challenge for historians of women in the Pacific Northwest is to put together a coherent narrative that is simultaneously true to the personal and emotional experience of women and integrally connected to the developing social and political realities of the region.

Some examples will illustrate the possibility of illuminations and connections. The lives of the missionary women have yet to be explored on their own terms. What do their diaries and letters tell us that we cannot learn from the writings of their husbands? Myra Eells, shocked at the grime and discomfort of the Overland Trail, wrote emphatically to her female relatives that *only* dark-colored undergarments could be considered suitable for the trip. Mary Walker, overwhelmed by child rearing and housekeeping, repeatedly filled her diary with her sense of failure because of the frustration of her own missionary activities. With increasing urgency, Narcissa Whitman's letters express her longings to be reunited with her parents.[30] These three examples are not trivial. They are some of the clues we need to reimagine the missionary experience through women's eyes. There are many other unasked questions about the first women missionaries and about the lesser-known female missionaries who followed them west. What was the relationship of the pioneer missionary women to the newly founded Mount Holyoke College and other institutions intended to train women for Christian teaching in the West? Hundreds, perhaps thousands, of single eastern women traveled west to teach school. Some of the best known of these women were motivated by missionary zeal.[31] What can we discover about the more numerous teachers who ventured to the Pacific Northwest?

Once in the West, on what resources did the pioneer women draw for their psychological survival? Narcissa Whitman and Eliza Spalding formed a Maternal Association almost as soon as they arrived in the Oregon country. In the East, maternal associations provided important emotional support to mothers in the early nineteenth century.[32] The Oregon organization was therefore an effort to recreate eastern conditions on the frontier. But what kinds of supportive bonds did single women create among themselves in the West? These and other questions about female companionship and support networks have been asked about eastern women. Research in western sources is needed to fill out the picture.

The same kinds of questions need to be asked about our regional "women worthies." Why was Abigail Scott Duniway, for example, such as radical? To answer that question fully, we need to know about the lives of ordinary women of her time and place, about the support that women derived from remaining within the conventional female sphere, and the possible rewards for breaking out of that sphere. Duniway herself answers some, but not all, of these questions.[33] As an undergraduate at the University of Washington, Montana's Jeanette Rankin was active in the women's suffrage movement, and then in its culminating drive in Washington. Many women originally found their own voice within supportive women's political groups, subsequently moving into mainstream politics. Was Rankin's Washington activity such an experience for her?

There are other questions to ask about women's groups and clubs. Historians of women are interested in understanding the formation, development, and growth of women's groups. A clear pattern has emerged in national research: from conventionally social beginnings, many women's groups evolved into vehemently activist reform groups.[34] The strong support that the General Federation of Wom-

Harvest cook and crew in Eastern Washington wheat fields, 1916 *(courtesy Washington State University Archives)*

Ella Diedrich Potter, operator in old Chewelah Telephone Company Exchange, n.d. *(courtesy Chewelah Museum)*

en's Clubs gave to the suffrage movement is just one example of this trend. How did women's clubs develop in the Pacific Northwest? What role did women play in local reform movements? How and why did women join the suffrage struggle, and what did work within that movement mean to them? These questions, which seek to understand the activism of women's groups within the context of women's lives, have not yet been explored in our region.[35]

Beyond these topics are some other, more personal questions. Sexual behavior and attitudes, marriage and divorce, birth control, childbirth, child rearing, and widowhood are among the personal items that historians of women have helped us to view as historical questions. These questions are not gender specific; the answers can shed new light on the lives of men as well as women. Nevertheless, historians ought not to overlook that some or all of these matters have been central, overriding concerns in the lives of women. Yet in some recently published women's primary sources, the editors *do* overlook these concerns. Commentary focusing only on landmarks and political events does not adequately illuminate the lives of women. Sensitive reading, alert to personal concerns, is essential.[36]

The considerable agenda outlined in the preceding pages is far from being achieved. Regional historians of women are still deeply engaged in discovering what women actually did and how they felt about it. We are beginning to make strong connections between our materials and the wider social context. Finally, however, the challenge of developing good women's history for our region is everyone's. If women's history is regarded as a narrow subspecialty, of interest only to women, then the connections between women's activities and regional political and economic history will be slow to develop. If, on the other hand, historians work together to consider sources in the light of the concerns mentioned above, our regional history will change quite dramatically.[37] Pacific Northwest history will be larger, more complete, and more representative than it could be when the women were missing.

Notes

1. Karen Blair of Central Washington University has recently completed her manuscript for a comprehensive bibliography of women's sources for the Pacific Northwest. Tentatively titled *Northwest Women: An Annotated Bibliography,* it is under consideration by a publisher. The best general bibliography is Joan Jensen and Darlis Miller, "Gentle Tamers Revisited: New

Approaches to the History of Women in the American West," *Pacific Historical Review* 49 (May 1980): 173–213.

2. Gerda Lerner, "New Approaches to the Study of Women in American History," *Journal of Social History* 3 (Fall 1969): 53–62.

3. Gerda Lerner, "Placing Women in History: A 1975 Perspective," *Feminist Studies* 3 (1975): 5–15.

4. Clifford Drury, *First White Women Over the Rockies*, 3 vols. (Glendale, Calif.: A. H. Clark Co., 1963–66).

5. Duniway's uneven autobiography *Path Breaking* was reprinted by Schocken in 1971. Biographers of Rankin have faced difficulties because of scattered and inaccessible papers. Hannah Josephson's *Jeanette Rankin, First Lady in Congress* (New York: Bobbs-Merrill, 1974) is the standard source. Hutton, a flamboyant figure, received sensationalistic treatment from James W. Montgomery in *Liberated Woman* (Spokane: Ginko Publishers, 1974).

6. Four of the women (Owens-Adair, Victor, Landes, and Strong) are included in Edward T. James, ed., *Notable American Women*, 3 vols. (Cambridge, Mass: Harvard University Press, 1971), which gives good citations to their personal papers and biographical materials.

7. Ronald W. Taber, "Sacajawea and the Suffragettes," *Pacific Northwest Quarterly* 58, 1 (January 1967): 7–13. See also David Remley, "Sacagawea of Myth and History," in Helen Stauffer and Susan Rosowski, eds., *Women and Western American Literature* (Troy, N.Y.: Whitson, 1982), pp. 70–89.

8. T. A. Larson, "Dolls, Vassals and Drudges: Pioneer Women in the West," *Western Historical Quarterly* 3 (1972): 5–16, and numerous other detailed state studies; Richard Roeder, "Crossing the Gender Line: Ella Knowles, Montana's First Woman Lawyer," *Montana* 32 (1982): 64–75, and G. Thomas Edwards, "Dr. Ada M. Weed: Northwest Reformer," *Oregon Historical Quarterly* 78 (1977): 5–40. For recent eastern work on suffrage, see especially Ellen Dubois, *Feminism and Suffrage* (Ithaca: Cornell University Press, 1978).

9. Johnny Faragher and Christine Stansell, "Women and Their Families on the Overland Trail to California and Oregon, 1842–1867," *Feminist Studies* 2 (1975): 150–66.

10. Lillian Schlissel, "Women's Diaries on the Western Frontier," *American Studies* 18 (Spring 1977): 87–100.

11. Sandra Myres, "The Westering Woman," *Huntington Spectator* (Huntington Library, San Marino, Calif.), Winter 1980. She continues this attack in her more recent *Westering Women and the Frontier Experience, 1800–1915* (Albuquerque: University of New Mexico Press, 1982).

12. John Faragher, *Women and Men on the Oregon Trail* (New Haven: Yale University Press, 1979), and Lillian Schlissel, *Women's Diaries of the Westward Journey* (New York: Schocken Books, 1982).

13. Faragher, *Women and Men*, p. 178.

14. David Potter, "American Women and the American Character," in Don Fehrenbacher, ed., *History and American Society: Essays of David M. Potter* (New York: Oxford University Press, 1973), pp. 277–303.

15. Julie Roy Jeffery, *Frontier Women* (New York: Hill and Wang, 1979).

16. Richard A. Bartlett says that the masculinity of the frontier society "is as obvious as the sun in the daytime," *The New Country: A Social History of the American Frontier, 1776–1890* (New York: Oxford University Press, 1974), p. 343. See also William A. Bowen, *The Williamette Valley: Migration and Settlement on the Oregon Frontier* (Seattle: University of Washington Press, 1978).

17. T. A. Larson, "Women's Role in the American West," *Montana* 24 (Summer 1974): 2–11.

18. Abe Laufe, ed., *An Army Doctor's Wife on the Frontier: The Letters of Emily McCorkle Fitzgerald from Alaska and the Far West, 1874–78* (Lincoln: University of Nebraska Press, 1962).

19. Gerda Lerner posed this direct question in her 1981 American History Association pamphlet, *Teaching Women's History,* in a section entitled "Teaching Questions Designed to Bring Women into View." The most dramatic example for our region has been the discovery of the vital role of Native American women in the North American fur trade. There are at least five recent doctoral dissertations in the United States and Canada on this topic. See William Swagerty, "Marriage and Settlement Patterns of Rocky Mountain Trappers and Traders," *Western Historical Quarterly* 11 (April 1980): 159–80, and an excellent paper by Mary C. Wright (Rutgers University), "Women and Family in Indian-White Relations in the Oregon Country, 1810–1840," unpublished paper presented at the Conference on the History of Women, St. Paul, Minnesota, 1977.

20. I owe this phrase to anthropologist Bea Medicine, who used it to describe how she pieced together an account of women's activities in the early reservation years from scattered documents that mainly had to do with men. See her "Native American Women as Change Agents: Reaction to External Forces," abstracted in *Frontiers: A Journal of Women Studies* 5 (Spring 1980): 25–26.

21. Georgina Blankenship, *Early History of Thurston County, Washington* (Olympia, Wash., 1914), pp. 322–23.

22. Maureen Beecher, "'Washed Forenoon, Plowed Afternoon': Women's Work on the Mormon Frontier," unpublished paper presented at the Fourth Berkshire Conference on the History of Women, Mount Holyoke College, August 1978; Sue Armitage, "Household Work and Childrearing on the Frontier: The Oral History Record," *Sociology and Social Research* 63 (April 1979): 467–74; Glenda Riley, "'Not Gainfully Employed': Women on the Iowa Frontier 1833–1870," *Pacific Historical Review* 49 (May 1980): 237–64.

23. Mary Beth Norton, *Liberty's Daughters* (Boston: Little, Brown, 1980).

24. Karen Anderson, *Wartime Women* (Westport, Conn.: Greenwood Press, 1981) and Karen Skold, "The Job He Left Behind: American Women in Shipyards During World War II," in Carol R. Berkin and Clara M. Lovett, eds., *Women, War, and Revolution* (New York: Holmes and Meier, 1980), reprinted in this volume.

25. This was a main theme of the exhibit, "Washington Women's Heritage: Working and Caring," funded by the National Endowment for the

Humanities (1980–82) and coordinated by the Women Studies Program at Western Washington University.

26. The best national work is Mary Ryan's Bancroft Award–winning study *Cradle of the Middle Class* (New York: Cambridge University Press, 1981).

27. Boulder Women's Oral History Project interviews, Boulder Public Library; Sue Armitage, Theresa Banfield, and Sarah Jacobus, "Black Women and Their Communities in Colorado," *Frontiers* 11 (Fall 1977): 45–51.

28. June Underwood, "Civilizing Kansas: Women's Organizations, 1880–1920," *Kansas History* (Winter–Spring 1985): 291–306.

29. In Washington, an important finding guide to existing oral history collections is Margot Knight, *Directory of Oral History in Washington State,* Oral History Office, Washington State University, Pullman. However, many interviews with women are unsatisfactory because the women talk about their fathers, brothers, husbands, and sons, but not about their own lives. Because they were not asked about their own activities, the invisibility of women was perpetuated.

30. Drury, *First White Women Over the Rockies,* vols. 2 and 3; Narcissa Whitman's letters, 1838–1846, printed in *Transactions of the Oregon Pioneer Association* (nineteenth reunion, Portland: A. Anderson, 1892, 91–178; and twenty-first reunion, Portland: George Hines, 1894, 56–93).

31. The first women's college, Mount Holyoke College in South Hadley, Massachusetts, opened its doors in 1837. For a description of its founder and her mission, see Kathryn Sklar, "The Founding of Mount Holyoke College," in Carol R. Berkin and Mary B. Norton, eds., *Women of America: A History* (Boston: Houghton Mifflin, 1979), pp. 177–201. For the teachers who came west, see Polly Kaufmann, "A Wider Field of Usefulness: Pioneer Women Teachers in the West, 1848–1854," *Journal of the West* 21 (April 1982): 16–25.

32. Nancy Cott, *The Bonds of Womanhood* (New Haven: Yale University Press, 1977).

33. Ruth Moynihan's social biography of Duniway, *Rebel for Rights: Abigail Scott Duniway* (New Haven: Yale University Press, 1983), modeled on Kathryn Sklar's acclaimed *Catharine Beecher* (New Haven: Yale University Press, 1973), links the development of Oregon as a state with the intellectual and political development of a complex and interesting woman.

34. A particularly striking example is explored by Jacqueline Hall in *Revolt Against Chivalry: Jessie Daniel Ames and the Women's Campaign Against Lynching* (New York: Columbia University Press, 1979).

35. Karen Blair has explored some of these questions for eastern women in *The Clubwoman as Feminist* (New York: Holmes and Meier, 1980).

36. Recent offending examples include James Thore, ed., *A Governor's Wife on the Mining Frontier: The Letters of Mary Edgerton from Montana* (Salt Lake City: University of Utah Library, 1976) critically reviewed by Gloria Lothrop in the *Pacific Historical Review* 48 (May 1979): 300–301, and Sandra Myres, *Ho for California! Women's Overland Diaries From the Huntington Library,* reviewed by the author in *Frontiers* 5 (Fall 1980): 71–

73. A model of sensitive reading is provided by Elizabeth Hampsten, *Read This Only to Yourself* (Bloomington: Indiana University Press, 1982).

37. At the very least, such an approach would add gender to the list of basic categories of historical analysis. However, as the Organization of American Historians sponsored national project "Integrating Women's Materials into History Surveys" discovered in 1980–81, the inclusion of information about women moves the surveys strongly in the direction of social history. This means a loss of the narrative power and clarity that distinguishes the traditional survey. The problem of how to teach social history is a challenge for us all, feminist and nonfeminist historians alike.

Suggestions for Further Reading

SUFFRAGE

Ault, Nelson A. "The Earnest Ladies: The Walla Walla Women's Club and the Equal Suffrage League of 1886–1889." *Pacific Northwest Quarterly* 42 (April 1951): 123–37.

Bearce, Stella E. "Suffrage in the Pacific Northwest: Old Oregon and Washington." *Washington Historical Quarterly* 3 (1908): 106–14.

Duniway, Abigail Scott. *Path Breaking: An Autobiographical History of the Equal Suffrage Movement in Pacific Coast States*. Portland: James, Kerns and Abbott Company, 1914.

Larson, T. A. "The Woman Suffrage Movement in Washington." *Pacific Northwest Quarterly* 67, no. 2 (April 1976): 49–62.

Montgomery, James W. *Liberated Woman: A Life of May Arkwright Hutton*. Spokane: Gingko Publishers, 1974.

Moynihan, Ruth Barnes. *Rebel for Rights: Abigail Scott Duniway*. New Haven: Yale University Press, 1983.

Sheeran, Marte Jo. "The Woman Suffrage Issue in Washington." Master's thesis, University of Washington, 1977.

Smith, Helen Krebs. *Presumptuous Dreamers*. Lake Oswego, Ore.: Smith, Smith, and Smith Publishing Company, 1974.

WORK

Additon, Lucia H. Faxon. *Twenty Eventful Years of the Oregon Women's Christian Temperance Union, 1880–1900*. Portland: Gottshall Printing Company, 1904.

Anderson, Karen. *Wartime Women: Sex Roles, Family Relations, and the Status of Women During World War II*. Westport, Conn.: Greenwood Press, 1981.

Bagley, Clarence B., ed. *Early Catholic Missions in Old Oregon*. Vol. 2. Seattle: Lowman and Hanford Company, 1932.

Clark, Ella E., and Margot Edmonds. *Sacagawea of the Lewis and Clark Expedition*. Berkeley: University of California Press, 1979.

Daugherty, James. *Marcus and Narcissa Whitman, Pioneers of Oregon*. New York: Viking Press, 1953.

Dembo, Jonathan. *An Historical Bibliography of Washington State Labor and Laboring Classes*. Seattle: Dembo, 1978.

Douthit, Mary Osborn. *The Souvenir of Western Women*. Portland: Anderson and Duniway Company, 1905.

Drury, Clifford M. *Elkanah and Mary Walker, Pioneers Among the Spokanes*. Caldwell, Idaho: Caxton Printers, Ltd., 1940.

Glenn, Evelyn Nakano. "The Dialectics of Wage Work: Japanese-American Women and Domestic Service, 1905–1940." *Feminist Studies* 6 (Fall 1980): 432–71.

Halvorsen, Helen Olson, and Lorraine Fletcher. "Nineteenth Century Midwife: Some Recollections." *Oregon Historical Quarterly* 70 (March 1969): 39–49.

Hazard, Joseph Taylor. *Pioneer Teachers of Washington.* Seattle: Retired Teachers Association, 1955.

Koslosky, Nancy. "A Filipino Nurse in the Thirties: An Interview with Maria Abastilla Beltran." *Backbone* 3 (1981): 28–32.

Miller, Helen Markley. *Woman Doctor of the West.* New York: Julian Messner, Inc., 1960.

Turner, Russel M. *The First Forty-Five Years: A History of Cooperative Extension in Washington State.* Extension Miscellaneous Publication 55. Pullman: Washington State University, Institute of Agricultural Services, 1961.

West, Leoti L. *The Wide Northwest: As Seen By a Pioneer Teacher.* Spokane: Shaw and Borden Company, 1927.

RACE AND ETHNICITY
(see also the bibliography at the end of chapter 7)

Armitage, Susan. "Everyday Encounters: Indians and the White Women in the Palouse." *Pacific Northwest Forum* 7 (Summer–Fall 1982): 27–30.

Barnhart, Edward N. *Japanese-American Evacuation and Resettlement: Catalog of Material in the General Library.* Berkeley, Calif.: University of California General Library, 1958.

Bingham, Robert D. "Swedish-Americans in Washington State: A Bibliography of Publications." *Swedish Pioneer Historical Quarterly* 25 (April 1974): 133–40.

Davidson, Sue. "Aki Kato Kurose: Portrait of an Activist." *Frontiers* 7 (1983): 91–97.

Davis, Lenwood G. *The Black Woman in American Society.* Boston: G. K. Hall and Company, 1975.

Edson, Christopher H. *Chinese in Eastern Oregon, 1860–1890.* San Francisco: R and E Research Association, 1974.

Haeberlin, Hermann, and Erna Gunther. *The Indians of Puget Sound.* Seattle: University of Washington Press, 1930.

Horn, Juana Raquel Royster. "The Academic and Extra Curricular Undergraduate Experiences of Three Black Women at the University of Washington, 1935–1941." Ph.D. dissertation, University of Washington, 1980.

Mumford, Esther Hall. "Group Portrait: My Mother, My Grandmother, and I." *Backbone* 3 (1981): 33–37.

———. *Seven Stars and Orion: Reflections of the Past.* Seattle: Ananse Press, 1986.

Sone, Monica. *Nisei Daughter.* 1953. Paperback ed., Seattle: University of Washington Press, 1979.

Sunoo, Sonia S. "Korean Women Pioneers of the Pacific Northwest." *Oregon Historical Quarterly* 79 (Spring 1978): 51–63.

THE ARTS

Blair, Karen J. "Seattle Ladies Musical Club." In Thomas C. Edwards and Carlos Schwantes, eds., *Experiences in a Promised Land*. Seattle: University of Washington Press, 1986.

Campbell, Esther W. *Bagpipes in the Woodwind Section: A History of the Seattle Symphony and the Women's Association*. Seattle: Symphony Women's Association, 1978.

Cunningham, Imogen. *After Ninety*. Seattle: University of Washington Press, 1977.

DiBiase, Linda Popp. "Culture at 'The End of the Line': The Arts in Seattle, 1914–1983." Master's thesis, California State University at Los Angeles, 1984.

Dodds, Anita Galvan. "Women and Their Role in the Early Art of Seattle." Master's thesis, University of Washington, 1981.

Elberson, Stanley Denton. "The History of the Tacoma Little Theatre, 1918–1932." Master's thesis, University of Utah, 1961.

Fields, Ronald. "Abby Williams Hill: Northwest Frontier Painter." *Landmarks* 3 (Winter 1984): 2–7.

Grant, Howard F. *The Story of Seattle's Early Theatres*. Seattle: University of Washington Bookstore, 1934.

Gunther, Erna. *Art in the Life of the Northwest Coast Indians*. Seattle: Superior Publishing Company, 1966.

Mills, Hazel E., ed. *Who's Who Among Pacific Northwest Authors*. Salem, Ore.: Pacific Northwest Library Association, 1957.

Pollard, Lancaster. "A Checklist of Washington Authors." *Pacific Northwest Review* 3 (January 1940): 3–96.

———. "A Checklist of Washington Authors: Additions and Corrections." *Pacific Northwest Quarterly* 35 (July 1944): 233–66.

Powers, Alfred. *History of Oregon Literature*. Portland: Metropolitan Press, 1935.

Queener-Shaw, Janice. "Fidelity to Nature: Puget Sound Pioneer Artists, 1870–1915." Seattle: Museum of History and Industry, November 1986.

Reynolds, Helen Louise. "Ella Higginson, Northwest Author." Master's thesis, University of Washington, 1941.

Rohrer, Mary Katherine. *A History of Seattle's Stock Companies from Their Beginnings to 1934*. Seattle: University of Washington Press, 1945.

Contributors

LILLIAN A. ACKERMAN received a Ph.D. in anthropology from Washington State University in 1982. She is an associate in research in anthropology at Washington State University, and is employed as a consultant to Alaska native corporations and government agencies. She has conducted research on the social organization of the Nez Perce and Colville Reservation Indians, and done an ethnoarchaeological study of a Yupik Eskimo village with her husband, Robert E. Ackerman. Currently she is conducting research on the kinship organization of the Colville Reservation and on the phenomenon of Yupik Eskimo matrilocality.

SUSAN H. ARMITAGE, director of women studies at Washington State University, holds a Ph.D. in history from the London School of Economics and Political Science. She is the author of a number of articles on western women, and the co-editor (with Elizabeth Jameson) of *The Women's West*, published by the University of Oklahoma Press in 1986. Her essay for this collection grew out of a paper prepared for the First Annual Pettyjohn Symposium "A Changing Historiography for the Pacific Northwest" in 1980 at Washington State University.

KAREN J. BLAIR has a Ph.D. from the State University of New York at Buffalo and is assistant professor of history at Central Washington University in Ellensburg. She is the author of *The Clubwoman as Feminist: True Womanhood Redefined, 1868–1914* and is currently doing research for "The Torchbearers: Women, the Arts, and Feminist Politics, 1890–1930." She has won a Woodrow Wilson Doctoral Dissertation Fellowship and a Rockefeller Foundation Humanities Fellowship.

PATRICIA VOELLER HORNER has an M.A. in American history (1978) from Eastern Washington University. For eight years she has taught courses on contemporary women's issues and women's history at Eastern Washington University in Cheney. She has served as assistant director of the Center for Extended Learning. She recently traveled throughout the state of Washington as a lecturer for the Washington Humanities Commission series, "The Inquiring Mind."

LAUREN KESSLER has a Ph.D. in communications history from the University of Washington (1980). She is currently director of grad-

249

uate studies and associate professor in the School of Journalism at the University of Oregon. She has written *The Dissident Press: Alternative Journalism in American History, Uncovering the News: The Journalist's Search for Information* (with Duncan McDonald), and *When Words Collide: A Journalist's Guide to Grammar and Style* (with Duncan McDonald).

RUTH BARNES MOYNIHAN earned a Ph.D. in American history at Yale University in 1979. Her biography of Abigail Scott Duniway, *Rebel for Rights,* was published by Yale University Press in 1983. She is currently teaching at the University of Connecticut and is a member of the Connecticut Center for Independent Historians. She has been a visiting professor at Lewis and Clark College and Yale University.

GAIL M. NOMURA has a Ph.D. in history from the University of Hawaii. She is director of the Asian–Pacific American Studies Program and is an assistant professor in the Department of Comparative American Cultures and the Department of History at Washington State University.

DORIS H. PIEROTH has a Ph.D. in history from the University of Washington. An independent historian, she is past president of the Pacific Northwest Historians Guild. She recently completed editing a collection of letters from World War I, "A Scholar's Odyssey: Early Letters of Stuart Ramsay Tompkins" (unpublished). She is working on a larger social and political study of Seattle's history between World War I and the Depression, of which her Mayor Landes article is a part. The article won the Washington State Historical Society's Charles M. Gates Memorial Award "for the most scholarly contribution to the *Pacific Northwest Quarterly* in the year 1984."

JANICE L. REIFF, a historian with a Ph.D. from the University of Washington, directs the Computer Program at Northwestern University in Evanston, Illinois, and is a research associate at the Newberry Library in Chicago.

DIANA RYESKY received a Ph.D. in 1977 in anthropology from the New School for Social Research. She has taught costume and textile history at the University of Washington, where she is an affiliate assistant professor in anthropology. She also works as a technical editor at Microsoft Corporation. An earlier version of this essay was presented at the annual meeting of the Costume Society of America, Oakland, 1982.

KAREN BECK SKOLD received a Ph.D. in sociology at the University of Oregon in 1981. Since then, she has been an independent researcher-scholar affiliated with the Center for Research on Women, Stanford University.

DEBORAH GALLACCI WILBERT is a freelance journalist living in Spokane. She holds an M.A. in American history from Washington State University. The recipient of the 1982 Joel E. Ferris History Award from the Eastern Washington Historical Society, she has done extensive research on the history of minority women in the Northwest.

Index

HQ 1438 .A19 W65 1988

Women in Pacific Northwest
  history